Teachers as Collaborative Partners

Working With Diverse Families and Communities

Teachers as Collaborative Partners

Working With Diverse Families and Communities

Sandra Winn Tutwiler
Washburn University

This book was typeset in 10/12 pt. ITC New Baskerville, Bold, Italics
The heads were typeset in ITC New Baskerville Bold

First published by Lawrence Erlbaum Associates, Inc., Publishers
10 Industrial Avenue
Mahwah, New Jersey 07430

Transferred to digital printing 2010 by Routledge

Routledge

270 Madison Avenue
New York, NY 10016

2 Park Square, Milton Park
Abingdon, Oxon OX14 4RN, UK

Family Diversity Project Images courtesy of the Family Diversity Projects, a non-profit organization with four award-winning traveling rental exhibits that tour communities nationwide and internationally. For information visit the Family Diversity Projects website at www.familydiv.org or email: info@familydiv.org.

Library of Congress Cataloging-in-Publication Data

CIP data is available

10 9 8 7 6 5 4 3 2

For Madeleine Grace, who is surrounded by a loving and diverse family.

Brief Contents

Contents

Preface

WHY A BOOK ON TEACHER, FAMILY, AND COMMUNITY COLLABORATION?

The possibility that teachers will interact with families who look, behave, and function in ways different from their personal experiences of family has substantially increased, along with a persistent call for increased parental and community involvement in the formal education of children. Most preservice teachers receive cursory exposure to school–family relations in their teacher-preparation programs, and in the process miss opportunities to develop professional skills in an area now understood to be integral to effective teacher practice. Educational researchers and policy makers recognize that teachers must understand more about students' lives outside of school, as a means for facilitating improved performance inside schools. This knowledge will be incorporated into educational practice in two ways. First, teachers are being called on to integrate what is known about students' everyday living experiences into what is taught and how it is taught to support school learning and performance. Second, teachers will be expected to use what they know about families and communities to develop and sustain relationships that contribute to the educational well-being of children and youth. *Teachers as Collaborative Partners* uses Interstate New Teacher Assessment and

Support Consortium (INTASC)[1] principles as a guide to provide preservice and inservice teachers with foundational knowledge important for understanding families and communities, while exploring conditions that influence family–school–community interactions.

INTENDED USES OF THE BOOK

Given the diversity among families today, it is extremely difficult for a single text to address the intricacies of life among all families. A more realistic goal is to assist future and inservice teachers in developing a research-based framework for understanding the dynamics of school, family, and community relations. This text is not meant to be a guide for working with families and communities, nor does it present a set of prescriptive teacher behaviors that all teachers should adopt to work with all families. Rather, the foundational information included in the text intends to engage the critical reflective capability of teachers that will support their ability to work with diverse families in a variety of teaching contexts.

The goals of the text are supported by pedagogical tools that provide opportunities for future teachers to make connections between information included in each chapter and realistic family–community–school situations. Case studies are embedded in most chapters, and most are abstracted from voices of parents describing their experience of school, family, and community. These cases serve to complement research-based content with authentic and personally articulated experiences of parents. Teachers then have the opportunity to make connections between theory and lived experiences.

Inquiry and Reflection questions are threaded throughout each chapter, and Guided Observations are included at the end of each chapter. These exercises rely on case-study analysis, situated learning exercises, and classroom and community observations and reflections. They are meant to enhance teacher candidates' understanding of ideas and concepts included in each chapter as they are manifested in contemporary family–school–community situations. As a result, the text is most effective when used in a field experience-based course that provides both classroom and community observation opportunities.

As a final pedagogical tool, the text introduces the Family–Community–School Profile (FCSP) as a teacher-generated summary that allows for evaluation of dynamics existing in specific community–school contexts. The

[1]The Interstate New Teacher Assessment and Support Consortium, a group consisting of state education agencies and national education organizations, was created in 1987 with the goal of focusing on teacher education reform. In 1992, the group developed 10 principles that address the knowledge, performances, and dispositions all new teachers should possess.

profile also provides teacher candidates opportunities to engage in self-introspection around school–family–community issues before becoming an interacting member of a school–family community. Inquiry and Reflections and Guided Observations completed throughout the text are used to generate the profile. These exercises have been coded to align with specific profile components. The profile, which is also aligned with INTASC principles and National Board for Professional Teaching Standards (NBPTS)[2] propositions, easily becomes a portfolio section documenting teacher skills and knowledge associated with school, family, and community dynamics. Completion of the profile is described in depth in Chapter 10 of the text.

Finally, although the text aligns with standards and field experiences that are a part of preservice teacher education programs, it is also appropriate for inservice teachers desiring to improve their skills and knowledge in the area of school–family–community relations. The text content and exercises will be helpful for teachers wanting to document skills and knowledge in this area as required for national board certification.

ORGANIZATION OF THE BOOK

Part I, *Exploring Family and Community Contexts: Social and Cultural Perspectives,* focuses first on the social, cultural, and historical roots of the family, with specific attention given to the evolution of public schools and the family as interdependent social institutions. The discussion then moves to the multiple attributes that constitute family and community diversity. Emphasized are the multiple ways families conceive of and conduct family life, as well as the impact of community attributes on the work of families and schools.

Understanding School–Family Interactions: Social, Political, Legal, and Educational Issues is the subject of Part II. Social and political issues that influence family–community–school dynamics are reviewed, as well as educationally based initiatives designed to address them. Included in this section of the text are various meanings attributed to parental involvement, expectations parents and schools have of each other, and expectations that society at large has of both.

The benefit of educators connecting with families and communities is well documented. The nature of that interaction has changed, however, and teachers are being called on to rethink their practice in order to

[2]The National Board for Professional Teaching Standards (NBPTS) is an independent, nonprofit organization, organized in 1987 with the goal of setting rigorous standards for accomplished teachers. The organization's Five Core Propositions describe the knowledge, skills, and dispositions accomplished teachers exhibit. NBPTS provides a vehicle through which accomplished teachers may voluntarily become nationally certified.

accommodate new roles families and communities play in the education of children and youth. Part III, *Creating Mutually Respectful and Responsive Family, Community, and School Partnerships* addresses educational practices that respond to authentic partnerships with families and communities. Three skill areas that support anticipated changes in educational practice are addressed: (a) teachers' skill in using the diversity of experiences that students bring to the school setting to support learning; (b) their skill in communicating with parents and community agencies and organizations in ways that suggest mutual, albeit different, roles in the education of children and youth; and (c) their skill in assessing the needs of the context in which they work, as a means for working collaboratively with families and communities to generate solutions to mutually agreed-on needs.

THE MEANING OF RACE, ETHNICITY, AND CULTURE

The terms *ethnicity, culture,* and *race* are used throughout this text. Ethnicity refers to a shared or common ancestry, history, or culture among a group of people. They may share geographic origin, language, values, religion, and family patterns. Ethnicity will be used when family issues are influenced by historical or ancestral connections among a group of people. Culture, in this text, is used to address the *learned* system of beliefs and behaviors that are passed from one generation to the next. Included in the concept of culture are values, customs, and traditions that evolve and change in response to the environment. Hence, the multicultural environment of the United States results in various cultures influencing and being influenced by each other. The term culture is used when family issues and circumstances are influenced by the context in which the family finds itself. In some instances, the combined terms ethnic–cultural are used as a means for discussing family circumstances that are shaped both by historical or ancestral influences and by the living context in which the family currently lives. Finally, race is a social construct that is commonly used to separate individuals and groups based on physical characteristics. As a result, this term is used when discussing social influences on the family that are meant to distinguish among families having certain physical characteristics.

Chapter Alignment With Selected Interstate New Teacher Assessment and Support Consortium (INTASC) Principles

INTASC Principles	*Chapter* 1	2	3	4	5	6	7	8	9	10
Principle 2. Child Development and Learning Theory: The teacher understands how children learn and develop and can provide learning opportunities that support their intellectual, social, and personal development.		•	•			•		•	•	•
Principle 3. Diversity and Learning Styles: The teacher understands how students differ in their approaches to learning and creates instructional opportunities that are adapted to diverse learners.			•						•	•
Principle 5. Motivation and Behavior: The teacher uses an understanding of individual and group motivation and behavior to create a learning environment that encourages positive social interaction, active engagements in learning, and self-motivation.	•	•	•	•	•				•	•
Principle 6. Communication: The teacher uses knowledge of effective verbal, nonverbal, and media communication techniques to foster active inquiry, collaboration, and supportive interaction in the classroom.				•		•		•		•
Principle 7. Planning for Instruction: The teacher plans instruction based on knowledge of subject matter, students, the community, and curriculum goals.	•	•	•	•	•			•	•	•
Principle 8. Assessment: The teacher understands and uses formal and informal assessment strategies to evaluate and ensure the continuous intellectual, social, and physical development of the learner.						•	•	•	•	•
Principle 9. Professional Growth and Reflection: The teacher is a reflective practitioner who continually evaluates the effects of his or her choices and actions on others (students, parents, and other professionals in the learning community) and who actively seeks out opportunities to grow professionally.	•	•	•	•	•	•	•	•	•	•
Principle 10. Interpersonal Relationships: The teacher fosters relationships with school colleagues, parents, and agencies in the larger community to support students' learning and well-being.	•	•	•	•	•	•	•	•	•	•

Chapter Alignment With Selected Components of National Board for Professional Teaching Standards (NBPTS) Five Propositions for Excellent Teaching Standards

	Chapter									
NBPTS Proposition	*1*	*2*	*3*	*4*	*5*	*6*	*7*	*8*	*9*	*10*
Proposition 1. Teachers Are Committed to Students and Their Learning • Teachers recognize individual differences in their students and adjust their practice accordingly • Teachers have an understanding of how students learn and develop • Teachers treat students equitably • Teachers' mission extends beyond developing the cognitive capacity of their students		•	•			•			•	•
Proposition 2. Teachers Know the Subjects They Teach and How to Teach Those Subjects to Students • Teachers command specialized knowledge of how to convey a subject to students • Teachers generate multiple paths to knowledge	•	•	•	•	•				•	•
Proposition 3. Teachers Are Responsible for Managing and Monitoring Student Learning • Teachers call on multiple methods to meet their goals • Teachers orchestrate learning in group settings • Teaches place a premium on student engagement • Teachers regularly assess student progress	•	•	•	•	•				•	•
Proposition 4. Teachers Think Systematically About Their Practice and Learn From Experience • Teachers are continually making difficult choices that test their judgment • Teachers seek the advice of others and draw on education research and scholarship to improve their practice	•	•	•	•	•	•	•	•		•
Proposition 5. Teachers Are Members of Learning Communities • Teachers work collaboratively with parents • Teachers take advantage of community resources	•	•	•	•	•	•	•	•	•	•

Case List

Acknowledgments

This book came to be over the seasons of a family's life. There have been commitment ceremonies, marriages, divorces, births, relocations, illnesses, recoveries, graduations, and career changes, among other important family life events. I thank my family for their patience, knowing that I was not always as attentive as I should have been to family life changes while I worked to complete this project.

There are a number of people whose support, insights, and assistance made completion of this book a doable project. The comments of my reviewers: Gloria Boutte, University of North Carolina, Greensboro, Martha deAcosta, Cleveland State University, Jacque Ensign, Southern Connecticut State University, and Charles Jackson, Augusta State University, were instructive and absolutely necessary in the process of fine tuning the book. Judy Druse, Mabee Library, Washburn University, provided invaluable assistance as I waded through the process of seeking permissions to print images. I also want to acknowledge Martina Thompson, who patiently listened to much of the text before it was written, carefully organized reviewers' comments so that they were more readily accessible to me, and who provided creative ideas for the book's cover.

I want to thank Naomi Silverman for her unwavering support throughout the development and completion of this project. I am also extremely grateful to Kathleen deMarrias whose skill and talent in visualizing texts was invaluable as this project began to take form. Her detailed and careful reading of text drafts, thoughtful suggestions, and constant support were instrumental to making this book come alive.

Teachers as Collaborative Partners

Working With Diverse Families and Communities

Part I

EXPLORING FAMILY AND COMMUNITY CONTEXTS: SOCIAL AND CULTURAL PERSPECTIVES

Despite socially sanctioned and preferred norms, families have historically varied in structural configuration, cultural traditions, and available economic and social resources, all of which influence ways in which they conduct everyday life. Schools, however, reflect societal norms and values that have traditionally relied on a specific family form for socialization of children prior to entry into formal schooling and for general parental support throughout the schooling process. Children living in White middle-class nuclear families—a family form consisting of mother, father, and children living in the same home with sufficient resources to care for most of the children's needs—most often reflect the behaviors, values, language, and approaches to learning that our schools value. In the past, many school and classroom practices and much of the curriculum aligned with experiences of children from these homes. As a result, high levels of continuity existed between White middle-class nuclear family homes and the school. Yet all children were expected to conform to school practices based on nuclear family norms regardless of the homes and communities from which they came. Even today, varying degrees of discontinuity exist between many homes and schools, precipitated by differences in expectations and interactions in the school and those in the home.

Part I explores the social and cultural bases for family and community differences for the purpose of understanding how these differences influence school and family relations. Chapter 1 provides a historical overview of events that have influenced the evolution of school–family relations, using cultural explications of mothering as a framework for the discussion. The guiding premise of this chapter is that school–family relations have been influenced by the interaction among the cultural contexts of mothering, changes in mothering processes over time, and fluctuations in the aims of schooling. Mothering, as a social construct, is synonymous with the care of children. Not surprisingly, persons in mothering positions have evolved as the primary link between schools and the family. A review of the mothering–child connection, the diverse experiences that influenced the nature of this connection, and specific events in the evolution of public education provide an important foundation for understanding school–family relations today.

Chapters 2 and 3 further explore family diversity through discussions of multiple family attributes, such as family structure, ethnicity, and socioeconomic background. Although individual characteristics of the family are important, the true essence of a "diversity" among families can be found in ways that various attributes combine to influence the day-to-day lives of families. Family life is also shaped by conditions and circumstances external to the unit, including the community or neighborhood where the family lives. The final chapter of Part I focuses on the social, cultural, and economic influences that shape different community environments and the impact of community attributes on families.

Chapter 1

Exploring Families Through Mothering Across Time and Cultures

Mothers have traditionally been the family contact or liaison between the school and the family. Educators continue to look primarily to mothers as the individuals most responsible for the quality and adequacy of child and adolescent care as it influences school performance. In many ways, expectations parents and teachers have of each other are influenced by a host of social changes that have historically altered the social role and function of both. This chapter begins with a review of the social and cultural events occurring between 1840 and 1920, 1950 and 1960, and 1960 to the present in terms of the influence of these events on perceptions of the function of families and schools as social institutions and the subsequent interactions between the two.

School–family tension has historically centered around differing perceptions of caretaking and the overall needs of children. Mothers from various backgrounds, however, hold different beliefs of what is necessary to care for, nurture, educate, and protect children. Common behaviors, values, and concerns that guide the work of mothers often obscure unique aspects of **mother practice** that emerge from differences in the social, cultural, and economic contexts in which mothering takes place. Mother practice, the day-to-day actions taken and decisions made on behalf of children, is undoubtedly influenced by resources (cultural, educational, financial, social, etc.) brought to the act of mothering.

The focus on mothering in this chapter is not meant to negate or minimize the role of fathers in the lives of children and youth. Mothering, as discussed in this context, is a social rather than biological construct. In this way, **"mothering"** can be defined as a relationship characterized by the nurture and care one extends to another (Nakano Glenn, 1994), deemed necessary in the case of children and adolescents to ensure their safety, growth, and development. Whereas *families* adhering to **dominant culture norms** in the United States are the basic unit responsible for nurturing and taking care of children and youth, women in the family have been the primary caregivers since the 19th-century emergence of the modern or **nuclear family.** Still, given the diversity among families in the United States, it is reasonable to assume that mothering would be perceived, defined, and expressed in many ways and even carried out by various individuals in a child's family or community. Diversity in family structure, to include families in which men are single parents, those in which grandparents are taking care of children, and those that have stay-at-home dads, suggests the likelihood that schools will interact with a variety of individuals who present themselves to schools on behalf of children to address issues traditionally viewed within the realm of mother's work. The focus on the perception and practice of mothering is meant to establish the multiple ways children are cared for, as well as the ways schools have interacted with families around issues of caring, nurturing, and educating children and youth.

19th-CENTURY FAMILY CHANGE

As social institutions, education and the family continue to be influenced by the social, historical, and cultural contexts in which they exist. Berger and Luckmann (1966) defined social institutions as outcomes of routinized interactions among humans that occur over time. Institutions are human constructs that function differently among different societies at different points in history. The numerous institutions of a given society are not necessarily interdependent. The institutions of the family and mass public education, for example, did not originate at the same time or as logically or functionally integrated. In fact, there are numerous historical examples in which the process of educating and caring for children were nonintegrated, separate spheres of activity. For example, in the Greek city-state of Sparta, male children were removed from the home at age 8 to be educated by the state. The option to send children away from home to be educated has been a mainstay for centuries in the U.S., particularly among wealthy families. In other instances, children were taken from their homes with the overt goal of ensuring that families would have little influence on their education, as was the case for children attending Native American boarding schools. That the family and public education are viewed as functionally integrated today is based first on the fact that they have traditionally shared "relevant areas of conduct" (i.e., responsibility to children—at least for families with children). Second, and perhaps more important, the tendency to view the family and education as logically integrated institutions reflects the human desire for integration and consistency in their social world. Hence, there is no a priori basis for integration among specific institutions—integration originates with human needs.

In the contemporary United States, education and families are integrated social institutions responsible for the education and social development of youth. Although the bond formed between the two institutions is expected to be a cooperative one, its functional capability has historically been tempered by fluctuating perceptions of responsibilities, not only as perceived by each institution, but as perceived by the wider society as well. The pattern of interaction established between families and schools as the latter emerged as the major educating entity in the late 1800s continues to influence the current relationship between the two institutions.

The institutionalization of education, part of an "institutional explosion" in the early 19th-century (Katz, 1986, p. 11), paralleled the emergence of the modern or nuclear family. Social and economic changes occurring within the wider society during this period precipitated long-standing changes in both the function and the conceptualization of the family. As its economic, protective, recreational, religious, and educational activities increasingly were transferred to agencies outside the home, the family became a unit of companionship, rather than the cooperative, self-sufficient economic unit that had previously characterized it (Burgess & Locke, 1945; Mintz & Kellogg, 1988).

The roles and responsibilities of all family members were altered by early-19th-century changes in the family. Before this period, families were patriarchal, with male members of households having complete authority to rule over wives and children. This authority came with responsibility for the education and training of all members of the household. For example, laws enacted as early as 1642, principally in Virginia and Massachusetts, held men legally responsible for the education of household members. In Massachusetts, this responsibility included ensuring that household members knew how to read, that they understood laws of the commonwealth, and that they understood the codes of Puritanism.

In addition to obligations for the educational training of family members, 17th- and 18th-century men figured prominently in all aspects of child rearing. Fathers provided both physical and emotional care for children and made decisions, such as what they would eat, wear, and learn, as well as when they should begin work, leave home, and whom they should marry (Berry, 1993). In some instances, fathers' work with respect to children was a shared endeavor with mothers. Still, until the late 1700s, parenting was viewed as a male endeavor, with motherhood generally devalued. A unique mothering role was further obscured by the tendency of households to include other adults (e.g., adolescent servants) who took part in child-rearing activities (Bloch, 1978).

Mothering in the Modern, Nuclear Family

With the advent of industrialization, men's activities became less family centered as the nature of their work took them away from the home. At the same time, expectations of shared economic roles among family members gave way to men being the sole financial resource for the family. In fact, a woman in the labor force reflected poorly on her husband, who would be judged unable to provide for his family, and thus unable to fulfill this new head-of-household role (Thornton Dill, 1988). By the late 1800s, women no longer had an economic role within the family unit. Instead, they were charged with child rearing and home maintenance.

Social support for this role began early in the 19th century. According to Mintz and Kellogg (1988), a "cult of true womanhood" emerged that

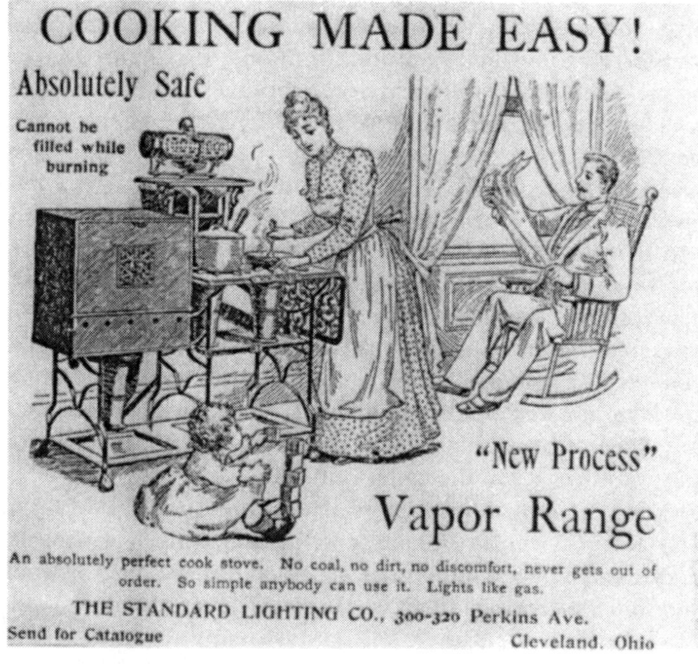

From: *Ladies Home Journal,* March 1893
Fathers' activities were less home centered after industrialization. In upper- and middle-class families, women were charged with child rearing and home maintenance, and fathers were the sole financial resource for the family.

glorified the American wife and mother as the "personification of... piety, submissiveness, purity, and domesticity," and that defined American women as "purer than man, more given to sacrifice and service to others, and untainted by the competitive struggle for wealth and power" (p. 55). This view of women was evident through literature, the media, the church, and the nature of work and types of education available to women at the time. Earlier notions of characteristics essential for child rearing included theological understanding, self-discipline, rationality, and control of one's emotions—attributes that were more associated with men (Bloch, 1978). Changes in the conceptualization of childhood that focused on the importance of growth and development during the early years, however, demanded different parental attributes—those more associated with "true womanhood."

Inquiry and Reflection 1A: The media have historically played a major role in projecting family images. What is the image of family projected in the media (e.g., magazines, newspaper articles, movies, television) today? What is the image of mothering? Are multiple ethnic/cultural family images included?

Like the mother, the child was no longer important to the economic activity of the family. Indeed, the years between 1870 and 1930 have been characterized as the period of the economically "worthless" but emotionally "priceless" child (Katz, 1986). Childhood emerged during these years as a distinct, important, and valuable period of life. Children were in need of nurturance and protection, given that vulnerability and innocence were a part of their nature. This perception of childhood directly contrasted earlier views of children as innately sinful and possible to restrain only through parental authority. Transformation from a patriarchal to democratic family form coincided with parents instilling independence in children so that they would be self-reliant and self-directed adults (Mintz & Kellogg, 1988).

It is important to note that even as this socially constructed model of the family became accepted as the preferred norm, it more commonly reflected familial patterns of middle- and upper-class families. The same social and economic changes that resulted in the nuclear family form for middle- and upper-class families brought about different family patterns for poor and working-class families who made up the majority of the population until World War I (Mintz & Kellogg, 1988). Unlike their middle- to upper-class counterparts, unstable work conditions, periods of unemployment, and a transient lifestyle plagued poor and working-class families as they moved frequently in search of work. In fact, the inability of men to find stable work often led to their desertion of the family.

Still, many poor women attempted to carry out socially sanctioned roles of wife and mother, even though their husbands' earnings did not afford

Many women produced goods from their homes, often with the assistance of their children, to help support their families.
Family of Mrs. Mott Making Artificial Flowers. Lewis W. Hines, Photographer, 1911. *Library of Congress, Prints and Photographs Division, National Labor Collection. [Reproduction number LC-USZ62-999382]*

them the financial security experienced by middle- and upper-class women. In an effort to remain wives and mothers in the home, many women produced goods for pay and extended services (e.g., taking in boarders) that could contribute to the household income. In other poor and working-class families, women and children entered the labor force as a means for family survival, experiences contrary to that of their middle- and upper-class counterparts. Furthermore, the view of children as economically worthless did not apply to poor children. In fact, the economic worth of poor children increased; they provided cheap labor for a booming factory-based economy while contributing to the household income (Katz, 1986).

Despite overt differences in living conditions between middle-class and poor families, poor families were evaluated using the new conception of the family and criticized for activities used for survival. Women in the labor force, for example, were criticized for not having time to care and cook for their families. Working families in general were charged with exploiting their children by requiring that they work to help support the family.

Children living in poverty worked in agriculture, mills, and factories to help support the family, even though child labor laws existed as early as 1830. Boy Sweeper Alongside a Carding Machine. Lewis W. Hines, Photographer, 1908. *Library of Congress, Prints and Photographs Division, National Labor Collection. [Reproduction number LC-USZ62-91451]*

Mothering in African American Enslaved Families

Social and economic class differences influenced the extent to which White women were able to carry out expectations for mothers in the modern family. Life circumstances of African American and Mexican American women, however, engendered practices for child and family care that were even further removed from the American family ideal. Social, political, and economic policies tended to work against these women as members of the "cult of true womanhood" and were not supportive of their establishing environments supportive of priceless and precious children.

Under the dehumanizing system of slavery, neither Black men nor Black women were expected to fulfill the newly constructed roles for women and men in the family unit. In fact, in direct contradiction to men as heads of a closely knit nuclear family, many slave men preferred to marry women not living on their plantation, primarily because they did not want to witness the mistreatment of their wives (Franklin, 1997). Still, in acts of defiance to a system in which human worth was defined primarily in terms of economic value, slave women and men structured a family life that has played a historically key role in the struggle to combat the effects of oppression. Within this structure, Black women engaged mother practices that addressed the needs of children whose general well-being outside the home was of concern only to the extent that it affected the wealth, power, and social status of those who owned the slave family.

As dominant-culture families moved toward the nuclear family ideal, slave families relied on a kinship system of extended family that included both blood and **community kin.** Kinship networks on and across plantations continued a tradition used by Africans before enslavement in the United States. The involvement of extended kin was the means by which enslaved women handled child rearing and other domestic responsibilities. Given the dual role of slave women as laborers and caretakers of home and children, **communal care** of children was essential for women to accomplish the various types of work expected of them. Although slave men and women had similar work roles and responsibilities as field laborers, their roles were more clearly delineated within the family, with women's responsibilities aligning those of dominant-culture women (Thornton Dill, 1988).

Among many Whites, the multiple roles of slave women figured strongly in a perception that social roles appropriate for Black women were profoundly different from those appropriate for White women. For example, many Whites were highly critical of postslavery Black women when freedom allowed some families to adopt, in more overt ways, socially sanctioned division of labor between men and women. Black women able to work solely in the home were acting in ways inappropriate for them, according to some White observers (Berry, 1993; Thornton Dill, 1988). Still, for most Black women, the dual roles as laborers and caretakers continued after slaves were freed. As Berry pointed out, "Though no longer slaves, Black women were required to balance husbands, housework, and jobs, including the care of their own, and other's children" (p. 70).

Mexicano Mothering in a Climate of Change

Like African Americans, Mexican Americans were involuntarily incorporated into the United States. The first group of Mexican Americans did not immigrate to this country but lived on the land that is today California, Texas, Arizona, Nevada, and Colorado. Following the Mexican–American War, this land was ceded to the United States by the 1848 Treaty of Guadalupe Hildago. Mexicans living on the newly conquered land were granted American citizenship, but like African Americans, were not invited to take part in the 19th-century American way of life. Nevertheless, economic, social, and political systems alien to their way of life had an impact on them. Baca Zinn and Eitzen (1996) described life among Mexicans before and after being conquered:

> Mexicanos ... were largely peasants, whose lives had been defined by a feudal economy and daily struggle on the land for economic survival. This pastoral life was disrupted. With the coming of the railroads and the damming of rivers for irrigation, the Southwest became an area of economic growth, but the advantages accrued mainly to Anglos. Mexicans no longer owned the land; now they were the source of cheap labor, an exploited group at the bottom of the social and economic ladder. (p. 58)

Both the structure and function of the Mexicano family were profoundly affected by these changes. Prior to the Mexican American War, men in Mexicano families were in charge of sustaining the family through work in the fields, and women were in charge of maintaining the home and taking care of husbands and children. Although motherhood was revered, children benefitted from an extensive network of relatives that made for a close-knit family of cousins, aunts, and uncles. A *compadrazo* system of godparents extended ties between families, resulting in several adults having responsibility for the social and economic well-being of children (Baca Zinn & Eitzen, 1996). With the economic growth of the region, men became laborers with railroad gangs and in mining camps, work that took them away from the fields, but also away from their families. Women were often left to raise children alone, and many eventually entered the labor force, along with their children in some cases. In this way, the new social and economic order brought about disruption in the traditional Mexicano way of life.

Chinese Mothering in Separated Families

Unlike African Americans and Mexican Americans who did not initially choose America as their home, Asian Americans were among the many groups to immigrate to the United States, with Chinese Americans being the first group of Asian descent to arrive on American soil in the 1850s. Through interaction of legislation and a series of social and economic policies, family development among Chinese Americans was severely hindered in the United States. Restrictive immigration polices for Chinese women figured prominently in the structure and function of Chinese families in the West. When Chinese women were able to emigrate, they left behind roles in extended families that placed them in subordinate positions to their husband's mother. In China, wives were not only expected to submit to their husbands, but to serve the needs of all members of the extended family.

Once in the United States, families became more nuclear in structure, and unlike their position in traditional Chinese families in China, women became the primary female in their households, no longer subordinate to their husband's mother.

Still, families in China adapted cultural obligations of women (and men) to economic necessity (Peffer, 1992). In these instances, both husbands and wives were allowed to emigrate to the United States, and as a result, Chinese husband-and-wife working couples were fairly common before the 1870s. For example, the work of fishermen required the labor of both husbands and wives. Chinese women in urban areas worked outside the home with their husbands in laundries, restaurants, groceries, and in the garment and other businesses (Ling, 2000).

Even so, negative evaluations of the Chinese surfaced, based on knowledge of the extended family structure in China and dominant culture views of appropriate roles for men and women in the modern American family. Immigration among Chinese was influenced by American policy makers of the period who believed that respectable Chinese women remained in their homeland to fulfill their roles in the extended family. Chinese men too were viewed as temporary emigrants, arriving in the States alone to earn money to support their families in China and making routine sojourns to their wives and children in the homeland.

Given beliefs of cultural restrictions on the mobility of Chinese women and the view of Chinese men as "sojourners," Chinese women in the United States were routinely labeled concubines or prostitutes. In actuality, the Chinese family was not so unlike the pre–Industrial Revolution White colonial family in which the family was the basic economic unit, with all members contributing to the economic well-being of the family. Yet the lives of Chinese immigrants were judged through dominant culture views of appropriate male and female roles in the family that did not allow for differentiation among the purposes of emigration among Chinese women. The perception that large numbers of Chinese women in the States were prostitutes led to passage of the *Page Law of 1875* that prohibited the importation of women for the purpose of prostitution. The effect of the legislation was to restrict the immigration of all female Chinese to the United States. This law, followed by the *Chinese Exclusion Act of 1882*, restricted immigration of all Chinese, but further reduced the number of women immigrating.

Family development among Chinese living in the United States was negatively influenced by the shortage of Chinese women in the States and the prohibition of intermarriage between Chinese men and non-Chinese women. It was common for Chinese families to be separated for decades. Wives often remained in China raising their children and carrying out the role of traditional Chinese women in the homeland. Husbands and fathers remained in the States, with sojourns to their homeland separated by many years. Middle-aged and even elderly men were often fathers of young children. The age differences and physical separation between father and child resulted in formal and distant father–child relationships, whereas a stronger emotional bond characterized mother–child relationships (Ishii-Kuntz, 2000).

Native American Mothering Amid Deculturalization

Mothering in separated families was a common occurrence for women of color in the United States, brought about by 19th-century social and economic policies. Ex-slave mothers and fathers attempted to consolidate their families after years of being sold away from each other. In some instances, they faced resistance from former slave owners who had claimed the children as apprentices (Berry, 1993). Separation of Chinese mothers from the fathers of their children was imposed by immigration laws. The separation of children from families was also a predominant theme for Native Americans, who unlike other people of color were targets for assimilation rather than exclusion in the 19th-century American way of life.

The estimated number of Native Americans in North America before the arrival of Columbus ranged from 25 to 75 million. Although the exact population remains a topic of debate, estimates of approximately 350,000 Native Americans in the United States at the beginning of the 20th century are presented with more certainty. Death due to diseases transmitted by Europeans and war as tribes attempted to retain their land and way of life were initially the major causes for decreased numbers of Native Americans living on land that subsequently became the United States. The *Indian Removal Act of 1830* further reduced the number of Native Americans. Over a 10-year period, members of the Five Civilized Tribes (Cherokee, Choctaw, Chickasaw, Creek, and Seminole) were relocated from their homes to areas selected for them to live. Thousands of Cherokee, for example, died of famine, disease, and from the inability to survive the harsh conditions on the Trail of Tears.

Although initially viewed as unworthy of an invitation to join the American way of life, concerted efforts to assimilate Native Americans emerged by the late 1800s. **Assimilation** required a process of **deculturalization** (Spring, 1994), in which Native Americans would be expected no longer to speak their native language or practice native customs. Recognizing the importance of the family in maintaining native customs, reformers and missionaries first believed it necessary to convert the Native American family so that it would more closely emulate processes and practices characteristic of the modern American or nuclear family.

The roles and responsibilities of mothers emerged as a major point of intervention in the deculturalization of Native Americans, given dominant-culture views of the role of mothers in the growth and development of children. Instilling the young with certain customs and values would ensure

Apache woman hoeing rows of corn while carrying an infant typifies the multiple responsibilities of Native American women. *Library of Congress, Prints and Photographs Division, Curtis S. Edwards Collection. [reproduction number LC-USZ62-46945]*

sustained change in a way of life over time. The roles of Native American women in the family differed significantly from those of 19th-century White women, however. Gender roles in Native American tribes were flexible, fluid, and democratic. Women were in charge of nurturing and taking care of children and were also responsible for gathering and processing food, cooking, and making tools and clothing. Some tribes were matrilineal, which meant that women played powerful roles in kinship relations and exercised considerable power in tribal governance and economic matters—spheres deemed inappropriate for women in traditional dominant-culture families.

Missionaries and reformers were unable to eradicate successfully Native American culture among adults. Their activities with Native American children proved to be a more effective, albeit harsh, means for assimilating Native Americans into an American way of life. During the latter part of the 19th century, Native American children were removed from their families and tribes at an early age and placed in nonreservation boarding schools.

These schools were designed to destroy Native languages and customs and build allegiance among Native American children to the United States. Native American children were forbidden to use their native language and Indian ways and were inculcated with American culture and values.

Inquiry and Reflection 1B: At times, social, political, and economic policies historically resulted in the separation of children from their mothers, fathers, or both. What modern-day social policies lead to the separation of children from parents?

19th-Century School–Family Relations

Changes in dominant-culture families paralleled changes in mass public education. Schools emerged as one of a number of agencies assuming responsibilities previously believed to be that of the family. Beliefs about the nature of women and children profoundly influenced perceptions of the type of teacher required to address the needs of children and youth. The period between 1840 and 1920 has been noted as the period of transformation in the teaching profession from one dominated by men to the realm of women. A successive group of powerful child-centered educators and psychologists, including Horace Mann, Edward Austin Sheldon, Francis W. Parker, G. Stanley Hall, and William Kilpatrick, were the major architects of the feminization of the teaching profession. Although each had somewhat different views of the aims of education, all believed female attributes would more readily serve the developmental needs of children and youth (Suggs, 1978).

Before the feminization of the teaching profession, characteristics such as theological knowledge, self-discipline, and rationality were valued in schoolmasters, just as they were in fathers in the patriarchal family. As a result, male schoolmasters commonly used authority and force, figuratively with a rod in one hand and a Bible in the other, to accomplish desired behaviors among their students. In a similar way, parallels may be drawn between 19th-century dominant-culture mothers and female teachers. Force and authority gave way to nurture and support, as mothers and teachers were encouraged to structure home and school environments to aid natural developmental transitions of childhood.

According to Suggs (1978), the **"motherteacher"** emerged, whose character was not so unlike mothers in the home. At the same time, an alignment between home and school evolved, ostensibly to provide a seamless environment for children to grow and develop. This connection is particularly important to note, because it establishes a historical marker for the

Male schoolmasters commonly used authority and force to accomplish desired behaviors among their students. Thomas Fogarty, Artist, Library of Congress, Prints and Photographs Division.

interdependence between public schools and a specific type of home environment (i.e., White, Protestant, middle- and upper-class, mother focused on the developmental needs of children). Moreover, the similarity in roles of women in the home and school was instituted as a mainstay in the growth, education, and development of children.

By 1890, two out of every three teachers were women (Sexton, 1976). More important, however, what it meant to be a teacher had been modified to such an extent that it no longer mattered whether the teachers were male or female. Suggs (1978) described the transformation of the personhood of a teacher and the act of teaching by suggesting that the "the element of compassionate, supportive mothering in her approach was described increasingly not as a biological feminine characteristic, but as a professional aspect of teaching, regardless of the sex of the teacher" (p. 139). Furthermore, according to Suggs, although the feminization of teaching was initially more prominent with younger students, the motherteacher was just as common in secondary schools by the close of the Civil War.

Inquiry and Reflection 1C: How would you describe the characteristics and needs of children and youth today? What teacher characteristics best align with their needs?

Changes in the appropriate and related roles of mothers and teachers coincided with one additional social change that continues to influence the way schools and families interact today. Between 1882 and 1920, more than 22 million immigrants were admitted to the United States. Italians, Poles, Irish, Russians, Croatians, and other southern and eastern Europeans dominated this period of mass immigration. Unlike the experiences of their northern and western immigrant predecessors, the new immigrants were not well received. In fact, evaluations of the new immigrant families were especially derogatory. Children of these immigrants were believed to be inferior, incapable, and less intelligent than native-born White children. Even child-centered proponent G. Stanley Hall suggested that children of the "new" immigrants were "an army of incapables for whom any form of advanced schooling was a waste of time" (Hunt, 1976, p. 42).

Similarities in home and school environments did not exist for new immigrant children. Indeed, the cultural practices of the new immigrants, large numbers of whom were poor and illiterate, were extremely foreign and troubling to social reformers, policy makers, and educators. Concern revolved around the impact of social and economic differences on child rearing among these groups, as well as the effect of cultural differences on the child's upbringing. As has been the practice in the past, public schools were to be the vehicle through which immigrant children were to be Americanized. In ways similar to the deculturalization of Native American children, educators and social reformers of the late 19th and early 20th centuries sought to remove children from the negative influences of their families and to place them under the "benign influence of the state and school" (Lasch, 1977, p. 13). Although children of the new immigrants were not physically separated from their families, the process of deculturalization served as an instrument of cultural separation between family and child (Hunt, 1976).

The interest of educators and social reformers in the education and well-being of children was not limited to new immigrant families, however. Near the close of the 19th century, concern over the stability of middle-class families emerged as well. Reformers were disturbed by rising divorce rates, increased participation of women in the workforce, low marriage rates among educated women, and falling birth rates among educated native-born Whites (Katz, 1986). In fact, these events represent an early indication that some women were not satisfied with their roles as primary caretakers for children and the home. Increased levels of education, sexual abstinence that led to smaller family sizes, and work outside the home allowed some women to create a life for themselves that was not solely tied to the home.

Social reformers and educators were convinced that families could no longer provide for their own needs and for the special needs of children without expert intervention. Subsequently, educators felt schools were compelled to take the place of the family because the family seemed incapable of carrying out its function. Instead of being responsible for teaching the "elements of knowledge" the school must also be responsible for the "physical, mental, and social training of the child as well" (Lasch, 1977, p. 12). Housewives, Lasch contended, were persuaded that they could not function independent of expert advice. The experts, he argued, "monopolized knowledge and doled it out in the form of parent education" (p. 18). For poor and immigrant families, state and professionals' intervention went beyond giving advice. Compulsory school attendance and child labor laws were directed at these groups as a means for minimizing the effects of these families on their children. Required school attendance would ensure that children learned the language, values, and customs of dominant-culture America, thereby increasing the possibility of successful assimilation.

Between 1890 and 1920, the role of schools as a mediating influence between the family and the social order was solidified (Kliebard, 1995). Schools were to be the instruments of cultural conformity—the vehicle through which all youth, despite differences upon entering public schooling, would be socialized through the process of education to fit into an adult world dominated by European American and Protestant values and mores. School personnel emerged in a position of experts on issues of education and development of children both inside and outside of schools. White middle-class families where mothers were principally in charge of the day-to-day care and nurture of children most often reflected the image school personnel believed to support the appropriate development of children. At the same time, a contemptuous yet **paternalistic** attitude toward the poor and members of certain ethnic groups was incorporated within the system of public schooling, supporting the belief that certain families were ill suited to be in charge of the education and development of their children. This belief presaged a mandate for educators to determine appropriate home environments and parental behaviors supportive of the work of schools. The reverse, the extent to which parents were able to determine appropriate education for their children in public school settings, was substantially minimized as school personnel clearly held a position of power with respect to the public education of children and youth.

RESURGENCE OF THE NUCLEAR FAMILY—MOTHERING IN THE 1950S

Stephanie Coontz (1997), referring to results of a 1996 Knight-Ridder poll, reported that more Americans pointed to the 1950s as the best decade for children to grow up over any other decade since that time. In fact, the 1950s are often referred to as the "golden age of the American family" (Mintz & Kellogg, 1988, p. 178). A number of social and economic supports existed that elevated the status of raising a family during that period to levels akin to patriotism and loyalty to a nation focused on distancing itself from the hardships of war and fighting the ever present threat of Communism. On the heels of the return of men to their families following World War II, a 1950s resurgence of the modern nuclear family as the preferred family form resulted in many women working in the home. Women were expected to release wartime jobs and return to the home in roles of nurturers and guardians of culture (Kaledin, 1984). Furthermore, Kaledin suggested that unchecked discrimination against women in the workplace rendered work in the home a more desirable option for women who chose not to challenge a work world that openly discriminated against them. Labels meant to shame, frighten, or ostracize were attributed to those who did not marry and have children. Fear of being labeled neurotic or otherwise emotionally unstable, irresponsible, immature, or homosexual motivated many women to conform to a preferred role. Finally, the position of women as stay-at-home moms was supported by media that glorified this image of women, first through print and later through television advertisement and sitcoms.

Inquiry and Reflection 1D: Women who mothered young children in the 1950s are likely between 70 and 80 years old today. Talk with an elderly member of your family who mothered during the 1950s. How does she compare mothering today with mothering in the past?

The years between 1945 and 1960 were characterized by a period of economic boom in the United States, and as such, economic improvements and social support allowed substantial numbers of working-class families to move into middle-class status. Government-supported mortgages lead to an explosion of home ownership on the outskirts of cities and served as an additional support for the nuclear family. The development of the highway system and increased automobile ownership made life outside cities a desirable and attainable option, and as a result, the country experienced a tremendous growth in suburbs. Life in suburbia exemplified the nuclear family ideal—family units that included mother, father, and children. Home ownership, stay-at-home moms, and fathers as the heads of households and breadwinners were symbolic of the nuclear family and symbolic of middle-class status as well, even though not all suburbs reflected middle-class status economically.

The child centeredness of the nuclear family was reemphasized during this period, spurred by the advice of child experts such as Benjamin Spock and Arnold Gessell. Child-rearing practices associated primarily with middle-class families called for an air of permissiveness for children. Children were encouraged to take the lead in activities, freed of adherence to strict schedules, and encouraged to discover appropriate behavior on their own. At the same time, children were to receive an appropriate amount of physical affection from parents as they experimented with independence and self-regulation (Selander, 1991).

As established earlier in this chapter, differences in social, cultural, and economic circumstances among American families resulted in differences in the ways in which they were able to carry out preferred patterns and behaviors for families. Just as families in the past were criticized for their inability to structure family life reflective of middle-class nuclear family norms, families unable to measure up to these norms in the 1950s received the same evaluations and in some instances were ridiculed in a very public way. For example, Mintz and Kellogg (1988) described the differences in the ways middle- and working-class women were portrayed on television, a medium believed to mirror reality of family life:

> The working-class wife was a flighty scatterbrain, whose life is confined to a separate sphere but who longs to play a role outside of the home. Lucille Ball epitomized this character.... When television portrayed middle-class family life in "Leave it to Beaver," "Father Knows Best," or "The Donna Reed Show," a sharply contrasting image appeared.... Unlike the working-class wives... suburban wives do not spend their time talking to neighbors. Their lives are spent as full-time mothers, looking after their children, straightening the house and baking cookies. (pp. 192–193)

Mothers were believed to be central figures in the emotional, physical, and psychological well-being of their children. **Mother blaming,** the practice of holding mothers solely responsible for actions and physical and psychosocial conditions of their children, mushroomed during the 1950s and took a form unlike that evident at the turn of the century. Armed with scientific justification principally from the field of psychology, experts felt able to declare that the home environment and practices and personality of the mother could lead to psychological distress and other maladjustments in children. Mothers who were overattentive or rejecting, or overprotective or too domineering, risked raising children to be delinquent, alcoholic, or susceptible to engagement in criminal activity. The work of highly respected psychologists such as Erik Erickson emphasized the importance of nurturing early in the child's life. In his now classic 1950 publication *Childhood and Society*, Erickson outlined the "eight stages of man," which suggested that with appropriate nurturing early in life, children would develop into trusting, autonomous, industrious young people, able to show initiative in many situations. Children lacking appropriate nurturing would have a tendency to be mistrustful, exhibit shame and doubt, and operate out of a sense of inferiority and guilt.

The importance of women staying in the home was further substantiated by 1950s studies that addressed issues such as the child's attachment to the mother and the impact of mother absence on the child's development (Ladd-Taylor & Umansky, 1998). Remaining in the home was not enough, however. Women were warned by experts that their aspirations could have a negative effect on the development of their children, suggesting, for example, that the mother who "displaced her own frustrations and needs for independence and achievement onto her children" could be the cause of a severely emotionally damaged child (Mintz & Kellogg, 1988, p. 189). Psychological justifications for the nuclear family were corroborated by sociological views that the small nuclear family with a stay-at-home mom was particularly suitable for raising children in an industrial society.

The lives of many women in the postwar United States did not reflect that of the ideal American woman. For example, African American women, for the most part, remained in the workforce beyond the war, and many were able to expand their earning power. President Truman's postwar edict to end discrimination in federal hiring provided opportunities for some African American women to move beyond domestic and unskilled blue-collar labor into the growth sectors of jobs for women, such as clerical work. African American women continued to participate in professional positions such as teaching and nursing that had traditionally been open to them (Hines, 1989; Shaw, 1986). Entry into positions that did not require as much professional education and training as teaching and nursing, however, improved the ability of African American women to secure better paying jobs—many with career and promotion possibilities. As a result, the 1950s is often viewed as a decade of progress for African American women (Kaledin, 1984).

Progress among African American women was in direct contradiction to expected roles and responsibilities for women of the time. Marriage for African American women did not automatically lead to work solely as a housewife and mother. In fact, working outside the home was viewed as part of a woman's role for substantial numbers of African American women regardless of socioeconomic class. For many African Americans, the concern was not necessarily whether women worked or not, because the historical and cultural precedent of men and women working side by side continued to be valued. Rather, the focus was on the nature of the work in which women engaged; the progress of women to well-paid and more professional work was a symbol of progress and source of pride for all African Americans (Jones, 1985).

Even so, 66% of African American children in any familial configuration lived in poverty during the 1950s, as did 50% of African American two-parent families. The employment of many African American wives and mothers allowed these women an opportunity to improve the economic plights of their families. Although dominant-culture women were encouraged by a number of social pressures to remain in the home, fully 40% of African American women with small children worked outside the home to support their families (Coontz, 1992).

COMPLEX AIMS OF SCHOOLING: IMPACT ON SCHOOL–FAMILY RELATIONS

Belief in the necessity of women as stay-at-home moms concurred with a considerably complex decade for U.S. public schools. The aims and roles for schools received extensive scrutiny between 1950 and 1960 and were challenged for appropriateness given the roles schools needed to play in the lives of children and youth. Public schools had historically exceeded a role focused solely on academic endeavors and traditionally functioned as an agency for socialization as well (Spring, 1985). This function aligned with aims of schooling proposed in *Education for All American Youth,* a National Education Association report published in 1945. Outlined in this document were 10 imperative needs of all children and youth to ensure that they developed into responsible adults. Their education, as suggested in the document, should develop skills and attitudes that led to wise consumer behavior, good health and physical development, wise use of leisure time, respect for ethical values, understanding of the responsibilities of democratic citizenship, and an understanding of conditions necessary for successful family life, among others.

The goals of life adjustment education were in keeping with the ideas outlined in *Education for All American Youth.* Although difficult to define, Kliebard (1995), quoting Harl Douglas, a vocal supporter of the movement, described life adjustment education as "an adequate program of secondary education for fairly complete preparation for all the areas of living in which life adjustment must be made, particularly home living, vocational life, civic life, leisure life, and physical and mental health" (p. 214). Life adjustment education proponent Charles Prosser was convinced that education of this nature would serve the needs of the 60% of high school students who would not be among the 20% attending college nor the 20% entering vocational fields upon completion of high school (Kliebard, 1995; Spring, 1985). Dropout rates that had reached one third to one fourth of high school populations in some cities were a major concern of educators and policy makers during this period. A strong cadre of educators believed vocational training with general education that addressed skills appropriate for life adjustment would stem the tendency of students to drop out of high school because of disinterest, while ensuring that young people were prepared to live in the world (Kliebard, 1995).

Life adjustment educators enjoyed support from many in the education community as well as from society at large. Some educators, however, saw the movement as antiintellectual and a waste of time for most students. Arthur Bestor was among critics of life adjustment education in the early 1950s. He suggested it was not the responsibility of schools to take the place of other social institutions (e.g., the family) unable to carry out their roles in the life of a child. For Bestor, the distinctive function of schools to develop the intellectual potential of young people should not be compromised (Kliebard, 1995).

Bestor, in essence, articulated a role that had not historically been the only function of public schools—that of developing the intellect of students (Spring, 1985). Even so, criticism for life adjustment education continued in a social, political, and economic climate that focused on competition with the Soviet Union. The country's effort to win the Cold War and the position as the most powerful country in the world was threatened when the Soviet Union successfully launched *Sputnik* in 1957. A decade of life adjustment education, in the view of educators and legislators alike, played a major role in the United States' position of inferiority in mathematics, science, and technology, compared with the Soviet Union. The status of U.S. schools was perceived as a national emergency that was to be ameliorated by passing the *National Defense Act of 1958*. Federal funds were provided to revise the school curriculum to one that focused more specifically on math, science, and foreign language.

Elimination of a perceived watered-down curriculum was not the only change needed to improve the position of the United States in the Cold War. Policy makers were increasingly concerned over the image projected to the world of a nation where racial segregation and other forms of discrimination existed juxtaposed to proclaimed beliefs in the freedom and rights of the individual. The perception that the eyes of the world were watching the ways in which prejudice and discrimination played out in the United States influenced legislation from the 1940s through the 1960s. The National Association for the Advancement of Colored People likely recognized this period as a prime time for pursuing litigation to overturn the "separate but equal" doctrine that had existed since the Supreme Court ruling in *Plessy v. Ferguson* in 1895 (Spring, 1989). In *Brown v. Board of Education of Topeka*, the Supreme Court ruled that segregation violated the 14th Amendment of the Constitution. Schools, and subsequently other areas of public life, were ordered to desegregate.

Clearly these events had a profound impact on the nation as a whole, but they also signaled important changes in school–family relations. Kliebard (1995) proposed that even during the period of industrialization and urbanization, the bond between schools and communities was beginning to disintegrate. Public schools more and more became vehicles through which social agendas could be carried out, the nature of which were not necessarily supportive of the family. Although the elimination of life adjustment education and related curricula did not necessarily signal an end to the seamless bond between schools and some families, the nature of the bond certainly shifted. Recall the 19th-century notion of mother and motherteacher structuring compatible environments supportive of the growth and development of the child. Even in the 1920s, similarities in the home and school were evident, as both exhibited practices proposed by behaviorist psychologists. In this instance, strict schedules, discipline, denial, and other forms of rigidity and control in the child's life replaced the permissiveness suggested for schools and home life of children at the turn of the century.

The 1950s focus on the centrality of mothers in the child's life paralleled a more pronounced manifestation of the home and the school having *separate* spheres of responsibility. Schools would focus on the academic and social development of the child that went beyond expectations of the family. Families were responsible for creating home environments to support the healthy emotional and physical development of the child. A woman's presence in the home was believed to be imperative for home environments needed to support children's school achievement.

Schools as centers of academic achievement not only rendered life adjustment and related curricula at the elementary level untenable, but also influenced school policies that altered school–home relations. **School consolidation,** the process of collapsing schools from smaller school districts into larger, comprehensive educational centers, resulted in children traveling farther from home to attend schools. In many school districts, the increased physical distance between school and home resulted in parents, even stay-at-home moms, no longer being personally involved with the schools their children attended. Furthermore, although school desegregation is often viewed as a step forward in equality of educational opportunity for all children, many African American schools were closed as African American children integrated into White schools, more so than the reverse. As Siddle-Walker (1993) argued, the tendency to describe the negative influences of segregation often overshadows the extremely positive impact all-Black schools had on African American children. In many instances, strong connections existed between these schools and the homes from which students came, particularly in terms of a mutual understanding of the pivotal role of education in advancing the success and achievement of African Americans. Thus, schools, broadly construed as centers of academic achievement, resulted in increased social and physical distance between schools and African American parents as well.

As the belief that children needed a certain type of home environment to perform well academically was emphasized, the extent to which families differed from the traditional nuclear family raised concern over the negative consequences for the social development and subsequent educational achievement and attainment of the nonnuclear family child. The familial configuration, social and economic status, and cultural content of nuclear families were linked with home environments that led to development of the motivation, learning skills (e.g., cognitive and language), attitudes, and behaviors that facilitated academic achievement in school settings. Generally, educators favored traditional or nuclear family norms, believing them to be requisite for children's academic success.

THE FAMILY IN DECLINE OR TRANSFORMATION?: MOTHERING IN THE 1960S AND BEYOND

A number of social, political, and cultural events occurred in the 1960s that profoundly disrupted the notion of a common American way of life, as multiple levels of dissatisfaction challenged the status quo. The Civil Rights movement, led primarily by African Americans, contested inequality through "nonviolent" practices, while the more radical Black Power movement confronted the legal, cultural, and political status quo through more militant activism. Influenced by a climate of change, the Chicano movement gained momentum and in the process challenged racism that had relegated them to marginal social, political, and economic positions. Both Chicanos and African Americans confronted self-disparaging perspectives among their respective groups by promoting cultural pride. Slogans such as "black is beautiful" and "brown is beautiful" advocated reclamation of ethnic identities that had been ignored or denigrated by society at large. Native Americans, faced with the threat of a termination policy that would eliminate the trust status between Native American tribes and the federal government, fought throughout the 1960s for self-determination that would allow for self-government and preservation of tribal cultures and societies. Unpopular among many segments of society, the Vietnam War was the focus of antiwar demonstrations protesting U.S. involvement in the war. The tumultuous decade between 1960 and 1970 also bore witness to the assassination of national figures including Malcolm X, President John F. Kennedy, Robert Kennedy, and Martin Luther King Jr.

These events occurred along with a tendency for many middle-class youth to reject the values and lifestyles their parents had worked so hard to attain. The nuclear family that had gained strength in the 1950s was also challenged by the feminist movement of the 1960s. Led predominantly by White, educated women, this movement confronted the existing social and economic positions accorded women with a demand for equal rights and opportunities. The 1960s have also been noted for the sexual revolution, which challenged the generally accepted belief that sex was most appropriate between married men and women. Social attitudes and behaviors around sexuality shifted, and the view that sexuality was attached to personal freedoms increased among various sectors of society. Reproductive choice among women, the emergence of a gay and lesbian rights movement, increased commercialization of sexuality by mass media, and freedom in sexual expression were among the outcomes of the sexual revolution of the 1960s.

Inquiry and Reflection 1E: Search for a journal or newspaper article published in the 1960s that focuses on the family. To what extent are social challenges occurring during that period reflected in the article? What position regarding the status of the family is projected?

Popenoe (1993) pointed to the 1960s as the beginning of the decline of child centeredness in American culture and a diminished value of **"familism."** Since that time, he suggested, the family as an institution has been in the throes of decline, evidenced by the fact that families have:

> lost functions, social power, and authority over their members. They have grown smaller in size, less stable, and shorter in life span. People have become less willing to invest time, money, and energy in family life, turning instead to investments in themselves. (p. 528)

In Popenoe's view, the diminished willingness or capacity of domestic units to carry out family functions such as reproduction and socialization of children; the care, affection, and companionship of family members; economic cooperation; and sexual regulation contributes to the family in decline. In fact, the number of individuals living in traditional family arrangements make up a smaller percentage of households, and the number of people living without children has steadily increased. The number of U.S. households with children declined from approximately 49% to 35% between 1960 and 1990. This family form continues to decline; the latest census places family-with-children households at 25%.

The cultural ideal of the stay-at-home mother and father as the primary provider and ultimate family authority also declined. As their numbers increased in the labor market, women were less dependent on men economically and men were more willing to leave the family unit. Divorce became more acceptable socially, whether there were children in the family or not, further contributing to the decline of the family. According to Popenoe, ties between parent and parent and parent and children weakened, and children became more influenced by peers and the mass media. The family as an institution, in Popenoe's view, also lost power to other social institutions. Mandatory school attendance and the ability of agencies to investigate families for child abuse or neglect are among the ways families lost power to schools and state agencies.

Although the conditions of family life outlined by Popenoe cannot be disputed, Coontz (1997) argued that engaging a discourse of decline to characterize family change diverts attention away from support needed by families in a period of transition. The problem, in Coontz's view, was not that the family as a social institution was changing, but that the rate and nature of change was not sufficient to align with changes in other social institutions. Furthermore, outdated perceptions of the way families work hindered the support other social institutions could extend to aid the family as a social institution in transition. According to Coontz, the appearance of the nuclear family was met with resistance and "a syndrome of distress, denial, and scapegoating" (p. 111) not unlike contemporary reactions to family change. She pointed out that:

> The male breadwinner nuclear family system that was put together in the mid-nineteenth century to resolve that particular crisis of transformation no longer meets the needs of today's families. Now, as then, clinging to old values and behaviors merely prolongs the period of transition and stress, preventing us from making needed adjustments in our lives and institutions. (p. 114)

Coontz's arguments rest within **"cultural lag"** explanations for family change that suggest social transformations disrupt understandings and practices associated with social institutions long before new practices that address institutional change are firmly established, routinely implemented, and collectively accepted.

The idea of the family in transition is also advanced by those who believe technological development precipitates changes in all social institutions. Shifts from horticultural to advanced agricultural systems and agricultural to industrial systems are examples of transitions in technological development that had profound influences on all social institutions, including the family (Kain, 1990). For example, Carnoy (1999) speculated that the shift from a national to a global economy is having a powerful influence on family change. Unlike the economic transition from an agricultural to industrial economy, however, women are more vociferously, and in larger numbers, rejecting the role of primary caretaker of children and the home. They are less amenable to devoting their lives to raising children, with many seeking careers. During the 1970s, increased numbers of women entered the workforce, many as part-time and temporary workers. According Carnoy, women's labor participation precipitated change not only in the family, but also in the community and the workplace. Chief among these changes was a shift in the relationship between worker and workplace that continues to affect the family.

Carnoy stated that economic competition is leading employers to "reorganize work around decentralized management, customized products, and work differentiation, such that work tasks become individualized and workers differentiated" (p. 411). As a result, workers' identities will be based on skills and knowledge they possess, rather than the "place" of their employment. "Disaggregated workers of the globalized age" will tend to be more mobile and shift jobs more frequently. Yet employment mobility often means loss of the social and community networks common among workers in the past who developed lifelong associations with a company and coworkers. More transient work situations result in loss of connections such as friends at work and long-term social connections, as well as commitment to the community in which one lives.

Families, Carnoy suggested, are under stress because social cohesion responsibilities of the family increase in times of economic transition. Thus, the nuclear family is particularly strained, owing to the destabilizing effect of change in the nature of work. The family structure with two-career oriented, often highly educated adults has steadily increased. Carnoy agreed with Popenoe that over the past 30 years, child rearing has become less central to the lives of adults. Even stay-at-home moms are averaging 14 years caring for children as their primary work, and because families consist of fewer children, men who are the sole financial resource of families spend fewer years financially and emotionally supporting children in the home.

Carnoy, however, articulated a need to redefine the traditional family as a social form, suggesting that stability of the traditional nuclear family structure was lost once women ceased to focus their activities on the home. He believed a family form centered around knowledge-based production and reproduction activity would emerge. This family form, with two highly educated adults and their children, will need to temper stress associated with an individualized economic and social life that will be a by-product of disaggregated labor. Demands on their time will include not only their work, but also time needed to acquire new skills and education often required with shifts in employment. The number of young adults postponing marriage or having children (or both) will likely increase as they realize the stress work and career place on the family. The decision of whether or when to form a family will be influenced by the status of their careers, as well as by their ability to access skills and knowledge needed for their work.

Although the status of the family as an institution is explained from different perspectives, clearly mothers play a pivotal role in these deliberations. Any discussion of family welfare eventually centers on questions of who will care for children. A preference for mother care has existed in the United States since the appearance of the modern nuclear family. Evidence suggests however, that some women have historically resisted this role, with the greatest challenge occurring in the 1960s and 1970s as the number of women in the workforce increased. Even media support for women working in the home as wives and mothers declined during these decades, as women with jobs and careers were more commonly celebrated.

Many sectors of society pushed strongly during this period for federally supported child care. Although Title VII of the *Civil Rights Act of 1964* prohibited sex and race discrimination in employment, federal support of child care for working women was elusive despite protests that inadequate child care hindered employment opportunities for women. Justification for the opposition on the federal government's part came in the form of the 1963 report of the Commission on the Status of Women, which reported that women could work and perform traditional roles of women in the home. Thus, federal child-care discussions in the 1960s focused primarily on women on welfare. The goal of providing child care to women receiving **Aid for Dependent Children (AFDC)** was to free them to work and eventually no longer need federal aid (Berry, 1993).

The popular regard accorded those arguing against mother care primacy was squashed by the call for a return to traditional American family values and gender roles in the 1980s. Middle-class women were expected to put family first, despite work or career demands and aspirations. Many Americans today, however, are skeptical of the idealized vision of a modern nuclear family with a mother at the center. Still, children are clearly in need of adult supervision and guidance, as well as a need to know that they are valued by their parents and by society. Even though nuclear families of the past were characterized by child centeredness, psychologist David Elkind concludes that we are in need of a family form that meets the needs of both children and adults (Scherer, 1996).

Inquiry and Reflection 1F: Is the institution of the family in decline or transition? What indicators have you observed or experienced to support your view?

THE FAMILY IN TRANSITION: IMPACT ON SCHOOL–FAMILY RELATIONS

As the social institution most closely aligned with the family in the care and education of children, schools have experienced "tremors" as the family moves through a period of change. The combination of societal response to family change and shifting social and political agendas have resulted in fluctuating educational policies and practices as well.

Historically, educational policy and practice perceived social, economic, and cultural differences as elements that could be mitigated through conforming school experiences. The social, political, and legal activities of the 1960s and 1970s that were geared toward equal rights and equality in the broader society influenced school practices as well. A host of legislation mandated that school personnel pay closer attention to issues of differences among students with respect to gender, disability, socioeconomic status, and cultural background. Title IX of the *Education Amendments Act of 1978* barred discrimination based on gender in any federally funded education program or activity. Hence, educational institutions were required to pay attention to programs that might discriminate against girls. Attention to students with disabilities was fostered by the *Education for All Handicapped Children Act* (Pub. L. No. 94-142) in 1975, which mandated free and appropriate education for all handicapped children and youth. Public Law 94-142 had a strong "parental involvement" component, in that parents were to be informed of and involved in the identification, evaluation, and placement activities of handicapped children. Later amendments included parent training to increase parents' effectiveness in working with educators at the child's school. In a sense, federal intervention mandated teachers and parents working together for the child's education. However, more often than not, parent involvement and training efforts focused on mothers, who continued to be the liaison between family and schools.

In many ways, President Lyndon Johnson's **War on Poverty** was intended to minimize the impact of economic differences through direct federal intervention into lives of families living in poverty. His strategies led to increased numbers of women on AFDC, to the establishment of Medicaid and the Food Stamp Program, and to subsidized rent and low-income housing. One could argue that the federal government took on the "father provider" role, allowing increased numbers of single mothers in poverty to remain in the home with children while having their basic needs met. Yet companion War on Poverty strategies suggested a lack of confidence in poor, stay-at-home moms' ability to provide home environments supportive of the linguistic, social, and motivational skills necessary for school success. The *Elementary and Secondary Education Act of 1965*, legislation accompanying War on Poverty efforts, included a strong **compensatory education** component. Compensatory education was based on the notion that a changed school environment could compensate for the "disadvantaged" background of certain students, thus mitigating poor or negative experiences provided in the home.

The limited success of compensatory education programs as a single strategy for educational improvement led educators to seek additional answers to the disparity between educational achievement and attainment of White and middle-class youth and that of poor children and children of color. Many educators concluded that multicultural education, which shifts explanations of performance differences from those based on "cultural deprivation" or "cultural disadvantage" to those based on "cultural difference," could respond to educational disparity among students from different socioeconomic and ethnic and cultural backgrounds. They proposed that structuring learning environments that recognized and incorporated language and communication styles, behavioral styles, and values and experiences representative of the multiple cultures existing in the United States could improve the educational achievement and experiences of increased numbers of students.

As a result of an emphasis on multicultural education, more educators view children and youth from diverse backgrounds in a different light. Concomitant attitudinal changes in views of families and communities, however, lag behind. Multicultural education most often focuses on adult–child or teacher–child interactions in the educational process with less attention to the impact cultural differences have on adult–adult interactions. A lack of understanding of family diversity at best leads many teachers to believe they must parent poor children and children of color; worse is the tension that emerges between educators and parents, as misunderstanding between adults interferes with the mutuality necessary to attend to the education and well-being of children and youth.

Recent increases in stress-related illnesses, suicide, alcoholism, and other substance-abuse-related illnesses among children and youth from middle-class families leave teachers feeling more responsibility to parent middle-class children as well. Elkind (Scherer, 1996) attributed some of the duress among children to two working parents—in effect the lack of solutions to family functioning when the mother is no longer in the home as the primary caretaker. He further suggested that although teachers have a tendency to address the emotional needs of these children, they must recognize limits to their role as providers of the kind of attention these children may need. In this sense, schools clearly feel repercussions of families in the midst of change.

CONCLUDING COMMENTS

The modern or nuclear family was established during the 19th century; however, many families were inhibited or prohibited from joining this way of life because of social, economic, and, in some cases, legal restrictions. Sudarkasa's (1997) notion of the family as an adaptive institution was clearly evident among poor and **ethnic minority** families, as they derived strategies and practices for day-to-day existence and survival, many of which differed from dominant-culture nuclear family norms for behavior and attitudes.

The role of mothers as primary caretakers of children and the home environments in which they develop emerged as central to nuclear families, and subsequently to school–family interactions as public schools became the major educating agency. Yet mother practice has been tied to the socioeconomic and ethnic–cultural background of the family. As a result, multiple mother practices have coexisted in this country over its history. An outcome of diversity in mother practice is that children arrive at school with a variety of behaviors, values, and communication and cognitive styles. Despite progress toward embracing multicultural perspectives, schools continue to represent dominant-culture values and norms. School personnel have historically been concerned about their ability to educate children from homes not aligning with expected dominant-culture, nuclear family norms. This concern has been exacerbated over time as even nuclear family mothers began to engage in activities (principally work outside the home) that disrupted traditional ways in which mothering takes place.

Because schools and families will continue to be influenced by social and economic changes, it is more helpful to view school–family interactions as fluid and changeable. Growing diversity in the United States portends additional challenges to school–family relations because the rules applied to White middle-class families may not work as well with families from backgrounds different from this structure. Key to the ability to enter into effective school–parent relations is an understanding of how the family characterizes and achieves the care of children.

GUIDED OBSERVATIONS

1G. Attend a parent night, parent conference, PTA-PTO meeting, student program, or other event where parents are expected to connect with schools on behalf of their children. Who are the primary attendees (mother, father, both parents)? Are their differences in attendance among parents from different socioeconomic and ethnic–cultural backgrounds? Write a reflection that includes your views of the reasons for parental attendance or lack of attendance to these events.

1H. Use the guide questions that follow to interview two adults who are in the "mothering" role for children at your observation school site. Make sure one adult has a socioeconomic or ethnic–cultural background different from your own. Write a summary of your findings making sure to compare and contrast views expressed by your interviewees.

1. What are the most important roles and responsibilities of mothers today?
2. How are the ways in which you are raising your children different from or the same as the ways in which you were raised?
3. What are the biggest challenges to mothering today?
4. How has this school been supportive of goals you have for your children? In what ways has the school been nonsupportive of those goals?

Chapter **2**

Family Structure and Membership: Multiple Meanings of Family

Family structure addresses the multiple arrangements members of a household might exhibit. Families are distinguished by the combination of adults and children who are members of the family unit. As a result, a variety of family structures exist, including single-parent families, traditional nuclear families, gay and lesbian families, blended families, adoptive families, and mulitgenerational families. In 2000, 69% of households were defined as "family households" by the U.S. Census Bureau (2001). Family households consist of two or more members related by blood, marriage, or adoption. Nonfamily households are defined by the Bureau as including persons living alone or householders who share a home with nonrelatives only. A number "nonfamily households" refer to themselves as "families," however.

Families with children live in a number of configurations, with two legally married adults living with children being the most common. According to the 2000 census, 69% of U.S. children lived with two parents, 26% lived with single mothers, and 5% lived with single fathers. These figures do not include children living in unmarried partner households (41% of these households have children), children living with grandparents, and may not include children living with gay and lesbian parents. Given the possibility of social or legal ramifications, gay and lesbian parents may have been more reluctant to classify themselves as partners during census interviews. The purpose of this chapter is to discuss characteristics that are generally attributable to various family structures, although exceptions will always exist.

> Inquiry and Reflection 2A: What was the makeup of your family as you were growing up? How were you advantaged or disadvantaged educationally by this family structure?

MARRIED-COUPLE FAMILIES

Diversity exists in married-couple families, and these families conduct everyday life in a number of ways. Day-to-day living experiences among married-couple families are influenced to some extent by the interaction of socioeconomic status and ethnic–cultural backgrounds, and to some extent by choices made by adults in terms of how they wish to conduct family life. One way to describe differences among married-couple families is to examine the manner in which they care for children. Hertz (1999) identified three approaches to child care: mothers caring for children in the home, parents hiring someone to care for children, and what she refers to as the "new parenting" approach that includes full participation of both parents in child-rearing activities.

Families in which mothers care for children in the home while fathers work outside the home most closely resemble the traditional nuclear family that emerged in the 19th century and resurfaced in the 1950s, and again in the 1980s, as the preferred family form. This family type reflects the living situations for only 19% of two-parent households, however. Decreasing numbers of this family form represent the decline of the "American family" for many religious leaders, sociologists, policy makers, and others concerned with the welfare of the family.

Many two-parent families today are described as dual-earner families because both adults have jobs outside the home. Some women seek work outside the home to complement their roles of wife and mother and as a means for self-expression and fulfillment. Other women seek work outside the home to contribute to the household income when it becomes evident that the family cannot survive on the man's salary alone. More than two thirds of women with children under age 18 work either full- or part-time jobs. The largest number of working women live in suburban counties in close proximity to major metropolitan areas, locations that offer short commutes to work with good neighborhoods and schools for children. Women working in urban counties represent the second highest group of working mothers, with the lowest numbers of mothers working outside the home to be found in rural areas (Fetto, 2000). Interestingly enough, although husband and wife dual earners have and continue to be viewed as contributing to the decline of the traditional family, dual-earner families are a return to earlier norms in which men and women both worked to contribute to the economic well-being of the family (Coontz, 1997).

Child care in dual-earner families may take many forms. Families who seek child care may choose among large child care centers, providers offering care in private homes, and providers working inside the family's home. An increasing number of children are spending substantial amounts of time with child-care providers. The need for child care is not limited to families with preschool children. Many families are concerned about the care of school-age children and must make arrangements for children arriving home before an adult is present to supervise their activities. In some instances, an older sibling may be responsible for a child after school, or an extended family member such as a grandparent may supervise the child after school. Even with these strategies, an estimated 8 million children in urban, suburban, and rural communities are believed to be "latchkey" children—that is, children who go unsupervised after the regular school day has ended (U.S. Government, 2001). Federally funded after-school programs have recently been organized as one strategy to ameliorate this concern.

Some dual-earner families are seeking creative ways to care for children without using child-care providers. Depending on the level of cooperation from their employers, some parents are able to arrange for more flexible work schedules or fewer work days, which allows for more time with children. Family-friendly employers may offer other benefits, such as parental leave and on-site day care that support the desire of some employees to increase the time they have with children. Still other parents may take on a "tag-team" approach, with both parents taking on the responsibility of caring for children. These parents may work opposite shifts, for example, so that one parent is always available for the children (Hertz, 1999).

Fathers are taking on the role of primary caretaker in a growing number of married-couple families. Although this phenomenon is not without historical precedent, it is often viewed as creative because it differs from the expected contemporary role of men. Coontz (1997) reminded us that American fathers were displaced from the center of the family as a result of the 19th-century changes in the role of men in the family. Over time, their parenting skills were disparaged, and they lost direct emotional access to their children that colonial fathers had possessed. The return of men to the role of primary caretakers is the most workable and sensible choice for some families. It benefits the entire family unit and often provides a more nurturing and sensitive man in the life of the child (Hertz, 1999).

Case 2A: Stay-at-Home Dad

Our family has been fortunate in that we've been able to have a parent stay at home with our kids. We have two children, a 3½-year-old son and 1½-year-old daughter. When our first child was born, we felt strongly that one of us should stay home, but neither my wife nor I felt particularly drawn to do so. We decided that I should leave my full-time position to care for our son. A number of factors affected our decision. My wife was on a more definite career path, and I was less directed. Also, I was able to work part time as a handyman in the evenings and on weekends. It was easier for me to work around my family's schedule.

One drawback to our arrangement was that my wife and I tag-teamed with the children and didn't have a lot of full-family time. We tried to remedy this by reserving Sundays as our family day, but this wasn't always possible to maintain because of our erratic work schedules. It often felt like I was swimming upstream while staying home with the kids, and this manifested itself in the strangest ways. Most noticeably, I found it difficult to gain purchase in a culture where women don't always welcome the presence of a man in their playgroups. This often led to feelings of isolation. I should add, however, that since some of the mothers have gotten to know my wife, we have been included more often.

I love my kids in ways other working fathers may never experience. Instead of always running to mom when something happens, the kids sometimes come to me. I love it. I've shared nearly 4 years with my son and almost 2 with my daughter. I beam when his preschool teachers say what a joy he is to have in class. Even so, my wife and I are currently in the process of switching roles. I am returning to work and eventually to school to complete my bachelor's degree. She wants to spend more time with our kids and is willing to put her career on hold for a few years to facilitate these changes. (Dan Spurgeon, 2003)

Inquiry and Reflection 2B: Fathers are increasingly taking on a family role that was held by mothers for more than a century (see Case 2A). What are your thoughts on the impact of this phenomenon for the age or grade level you are teaching or intend to teach?

BLENDED FAMILIES

It estimated that for every two marriages in 1999, there was one divorce. At least 75% of divorced people remarry within 5 years of their divorce, and many of these remarried couples bring children from previous marriages to the union to form a new blended family. It is also possible that a child may live with a stepparent in a blended family while being coparented by a biological parent. Another possibility is the binuclear family in which the child spends time living with both biological parents, who themselves have remarried someone with children (Crosbie-Burnett & Lewis, 1993).

Although the blended family is often a married-couple family, this family form brings additional challenges to the family unit. Pasley, Dollahite, and Tallman (1993) proposed that the success of second marriages has more to do with the quality and nature of stepparent–child relations than with the relationship of the two married adults. Issues of jealousy and favoritism appear to be a major source of tension in these families. As is possible with all families, tensions at home may well spill over into the school.

Children in newly established blended families need time to adjust to new family dynamics. Similarly, parents may experience confusion over their roles and responsibilities with children in the newly formed family unit. Schools working with these families need to be prepared to work with multiple sets, as well as a variety of configurations of adults who will be intimately involved with the well-being of a child or children. A "parent conference," for example, might involve a mother and stepmother, both interested in developing strategies to support a child.

SINGLE-PARENT FAMILIES

Women most often head single-parent families, although growing numbers of these families are headed by men. Single-parent families include children and an adult who is divorced, never married, or one who has experienced the death of a spouse. Between 1970 and the late 1990s, the number of women raising children alone increased from 3.4 million to approximately 10 million. By 1998, more than half of first children were born to or conceived by an unmarried woman, a milestone influenced by both divorce rates and the more recent phenomenon of increasing numbers of "30-something," never-married women deciding to have children (Eckel, 1999). An increase in single-male-headed households concurred with the legal system's slow retreat from a view that it is almost always in the best interest of the children to award custody to the biological mother in the case of divorce. The growing numbers of single-father-headed households is influenced by the more frequent occurrence of men being awarded custody of their children in divorce cases, as well as more social acceptance of single men as adoptive fathers.

Children living in single-parent households are less likely to live with a college-educated parent compared with children living in a two-parent household, and this tends hold true for both male and female single-parent households, although men in such families tend to have higher educational attainment (Amata, 2000). Divorced women who are single parents tend to be more educated, however, and have higher incomes than women who never married and are single parents.

In the past, children from single-parent families were described as coming from "broken homes." Single parents continue to be evaluated as less

Single-parent families include children and an adult who is divorced, never married, or one who has experienced the death of a spouse.

capable or less interested in meeting the needs of their children compared with two-parent homes. In fact, living in a single-parent home is regularly listed as a characteristic of children at risk for failure in school settings. A growing body of research, however, suggests that much of what is viewed as incapability on the part of single mothers in particular, is actually the impact of structural influences on the ability of single mothers to run a household and raise their children.

Nearly half of female-headed families live below the poverty line, making them disadvantaged in terms of housing, health, and other family support resources many two-parent families are able to purchase. Many single mothers who are divorced will often receive less than 60% of the child support awarded to them (Kissman, 1991). Further, Polakow (1993) maintained that the number of women and children living in poverty is sustained not only by the lack of paternal financial support, but also by the disadvantaged status of women in the labor market. Conversely, fathers raising children alone tend to have almost twice the personal income of single mothers, with substantially fewer single-father-headed families living in poverty than single-mother families (Garasky & Meyer, 1996).

Being a single parent can be stressful, particularly for those single parents with limited financial and emotional support. The lack of financial resources results in a tendency of single parents to rent as opposed to own their homes. In some instances, they pay larger proportions of their income for housing that is often substandard, overpriced, and inadequate for their family's needs. Amata (2000) pointed out that single-parent families tend to be more transient compared with their two-parent counterparts, as they seek appropriate and affordable housing for themselves and their children. White single parents tend to be more mobile than African American and Latino single-parent families.

The ability to purchase health insurance becomes an issue for women in minimum-wage jobs. Relatedly, many single mothers have jobs that lack flexibility during the workday or jobs that have limited sick or personal leave days that would allow time to attend to the needs of their children. For some women who are single parents, handling the day-to-day issues associated with the care of children alone becomes a challenge. The pressure of ensuring that adequate child care, food, clothing, and transportation exist can be overwhelming, particularly in absence of familial or other types of support.

The lack of both a mother and father in the home is often viewed as having a particularly negative impact on children's social, emotional, and educational well-being among educators and by society at large. Along these lines, it has been generally accepted that children are advantaged in a number of ways by having both a male and female in the home. Without identification of specific factors that advantage one family structure over the other, we have a somewhat narrow perspective that the mere presence of a mother and father in the home makes for a more advantaged home situation. Downey, Ainsworth-Darnell, and Dufur (1998), however, reported that only 27% of children in mother–father families experience high father involvement, compared with 46% of children in father-only families. Relatedly, 56% of children in mother–father families experience high mother involvement compared with 49% of children in single-mother families. Thus, the presence of two adults in the family does not necessarily result in two highly involved individuals in the child's life and therefore does not guarantee that a child experiences the benefits believed to exist in mother–father families. Florsheim, Tolan, and Gorman-Smith (1998) warned of limitations in attempting to distinguish between mother–father and single-mother homes based on isolated or single factors, such as the structure of the family alone.

Clearly two engaged adults provide for the needs of children in ways that differ from strategies a single adult might construct. Still, when attempting to understand a single-parent-headed family, a combination of family characteristics should be considered, including the age, ethnicity, and educational level of the parent, as well as the network of support, both kin and nonkin, available to the family. In this way, teachers and other school personnel are better able to make connections that build on the strengths and assist, where appropriate, the challenges faced by the single-parent family.

GAY AND LESBIAN FAMILIES

Other family configurations of adults living with children exist that span all ethnic, cultural, and social class groups. Some children live in families headed by two unmarried adults. About 3% of children are living in families with biological mothers and fathers who are not married. Children also live in families headed by gay or lesbian parents. Gay- and lesbian-headed families may take the form of two adults in a committed relationship or a single adult raising a child or children. It is estimated that approximately 10% of the total population is lesbian or gay, and that 4 million gays and lesbians are raising approximately 10 million children. Yet single parents who are lesbian or gay and same-sex partners do not have the protection of the law, and in many states, the relationship between gay and lesbian parents and their children is not legally protected.

Inquiry and Reflection 2C: Choose two family structures you believe are least likely to provide for the needs of children and discuss your perceptions regarding the lack of capacity for these families. Find three research-based sources that support your beliefs and three that contradict them. What impact do these resources have on your perceptions?

Children in gay and lesbian families may be adopted or children born to a heterosexual union before a divorce. In some cases, lesbians may choose to become pregnant through artificial insemination with an unknown or known donor. In the latter case, a lesbian and a gay male may choose to have a child or children together and may choose to be coparents. It is also common for gay and lesbian parents to structure extended-family arrangements in which a child may have a number of nonconsanguine adults responsible for the well-being of the child.

Although acceptance of gay and lesbian lifestyles has increased, prejudice and discrimination persist. Same-sex couples continue to be stigmatized and often face legal and moral challenges to their desire to become parents. Beliefs that children raised in lesbian and gay households are negatively affected emotionally and socially are common among adults, both inside and outside of schools. Numerous studies conclude that children having heterosexual parents and those having gay or lesbian parents do not differ significantly in the areas of gender identity, gender role behavior, sexual orientation, peer relations, cognitive functioning, or other personal development areas (Bailey, Bobrow, Wolfe, & Mikach, 1995; Flaks, Fischer, Masterpasqua, & Joseph, 1995; Green, 1982; Green, Mandel, Hotvedt, Gray, & Smith, 1986; Patterson, 2000).

It is estimated that approximately 10% of the total population is lesbian or gay and that 4 million gays and lesbians are raising approximately 10 million children. Photo of Jang/Otto family © Gigi Kaeser from the book and traveling photo-text exhibit, *Love Makes a Family: Portraits of Lesbian, Gay, Bisexual, and Transgender People and Their Families* produced by the Family Diversity Projects.

Many gay and lesbian parents are concerned about the reaction of school personnel to them and their children. Teachers and other school staff members need to be aware of their personal beliefs about gay and lesbian adults. Homophobic views may hinder the ability of teachers and administrators to establish positive working relationships with gay and lesbian parents and their children. Wickens (1993) suggested that schools be responsible for professional development that assists teachers working with gay- and lesbian-headed families by helping them to see that acknowledging a student's home life does not necessarily mean that one agrees with it. Relatedly, Lamme and Lamme (2003) noted that schools must provide safe, supportive, and inviting environments for all children and their families, including families headed by sexual minorities.

INTERGENERATIONAL AND MULTIGENERATIONAL FAMILIES

Grandparents are raising increased numbers of children in their homes. This family structure may take the "skipped generation" or intergenerational form in which the family consists of grandparents and grandchildren, or the family may be multigenerational and include grandparents, adult children, and grandchildren. Even in the latter case, grandparents in the household may take on the major responsibility for raising the child. In

1997, approximately 4 million children lived in homes where grandparents were the primary caretakers, which represented a 44% increase over the previous decade (Fuller-Thomson, Minkler, & Driver, 1997; Roe & Minkler, 1998–1999).

Grandparents may become primary caretakers for a number of reasons. Traditionally, grandparents served as a safety net for children in instances of the death of a parent, divorce, or when children were abandoned. A number of factors currently contribute to parents being unable or unwilling to care for their children. Grandparents are assuming the role of parents for children born to young or teenage parents, as well as for children born to parents who are substance abusers, who engage in child neglect or abuse, or who are incarcerated. Finally, a number of grandparents are caregivers to children whose parents are living with AIDS.

Rather than the "love them and leave them" role played by many noncustodial grandparents, grandparents heading households with children are said to be "offtime" in the life cycle, given their custodial roles with their children's children (Fuller-Thomson et al., 1997; Pinson-Milburn, Fabian, Scholssberg, & Pyle, 1996). Grandparents raising children range in age from 40 to 80, with the median age being 57. In situations when their children had children in the teen years, a grandparent may be in his or her 30s. The typical grandparent raising a child is married, White, and living above the poverty line. A disproportionate number of African American grandparents are primary caretakers for their grandchildren. Multigenerational households are not a new phenomenon among African American families, however, and this living situation was actually quite common before programs such as Aid to Families with Dependent Children (AFDC) encouraged and enabled young mothers to live alone with their children (Sudarkasa, 1997).

Custodial grandparents of any ethnic–racial background are 60% more likely to live below the poverty line than their counterparts who are not primary caretakers. In most instances, women are the primary caretakers, although some grandfathers take on this role as well. The length of time grandparents are taking care of grandchildren ranges from as little as 6 months to 10 years or more. The ages of children living with grandparents also varies, although about three fourths of children come as infants and preschoolers (Roe & Minkler, 1998–1999).

Although many grandparents are willing to take on this new responsibility, the onset is often sudden and unexpected. Many grandparents do not have the financial resources to take care of a child because many are on fixed incomes and others may have to reduce work hours to care for the child. Some grandparents are able to receive federal foster care benefits even though they are related to the child (Roe & Minkler, 1998–1999). Still others attempt to raise a child feeling they have little support not only from welfare agencies but from the legal, educational, and health systems as well. Roe and

Minkler also cited stress, high rates of depression, poor health, decreased socialization with family and friends, and higher poverty rates as additional social concerns grandparents who become primary caretakers experience.

Clearly becoming a child's primary caregiver is a life-changing event for grandparents. It is also challenging for children in these situations. Many are leaving behind traumatic and unfavorable home circumstances, and it is common for psychological and developmental issues to emerge that reflect the absence of a parent being due to more socially unacceptable behaviors, rather than reasons such as death (Pinson-Milburn et al., 1996). Teachers will want to be attuned to the vulnerability exhibited by these children, both at home and at school. At the same time, they will want to be aware of the types of support available for custodial grandparents, such as local support groups, after-school care, and agencies that will provide resources for financial, health, and other types of assistance.

Many intergenerational and multigenerational families do not experience the stressors discussed here and simply exist as an alternative to the nuclear family. Still, social, economic, and legal issues, as well as social expectations of the role and position of the elderly in dominant-culture America, add to challenges faced by the intergenerational and multigenerational family. Although this family structure may be viewed negatively, Fuller-Thomson et al. (1997) suggested that the continued existence of intergenerational bonds is actually positive for family life in the United States.

ADOLESCENT-PARENT FAMILIES

Like grandparents who raise children, adolescent parents are also viewed as offtime in the life cycle, given their premature responsibility for the care of children. A cycle of having children as adolescents exists in some families; adolescent mothers tend to have had mothers who gave birth while adolescents. Additionally, approximately 30% to 50% of all adolescent mothers have a second pregnancy, with 25% having a second birth within 2 years of the first (Williams & Sadler, 2001). Even so, the rate of adolescent pregnancy appears to be declining. According to the National Center for Health Statistics (2001), there was a 19% decline in the rate of pregnancies among adolescents between 1991 and 1997. This decline is attributed to increased use of condoms and other contraceptives and a leveling of teenage sexual activity.

Adolescents who have children face a host of health, developmental, and socioeconomic issues that contribute to the stress of being an adolescent parent. Adolescent mothers are more likely to have premature and low-birth-weight babies, often because of poor prenatal care. As a result, higher incidences of birth defects and other health problems exist in children of adolescent mothers compared with children born to mothers in their 20s. From a developmental perspective, many teenagers have reached neither the psychosocial nor cognitive developmental levels needed to handle responsibilities and issues associated with being a parent. According to Hulbert, Culp, and Jambunathan (1997), adolescents who become parents have not had ample time to deal with developmental dilemmas associated with role identity and intimacy before they are absorbed by the needs of a child. Furthermore, many adolescents have not reached a level of formal thinking that supports their ability to make decisions required of most parents (Harris, 1998). In fact, in her study of African American adolescent parents, Harris found that illogical thinking about sex and becoming a parent played a prominent role in unintended pregnancies.

From a socioeconomic perspective, adolescent parents, both mothers and fathers, tend to live in poverty and be unemployed or employed in low-wage positions. They often have lower levels of educational attainment and higher dropout rates than their nonparent adolescent counterparts. Although most attention is given to adolescent mothers, adolescent fathers experience the same psychosocial, developmental, and socioeconomic issues that teenage mothers face. Adolescent fathers often expect to be blamed for fathering the child and for shirking responsibilities that, in reality, they are ill prepared to handle. In many instances, adolescent fathers abandon the family as a means to relieve stress, leaving the adolescent mother a single parent (Lowenthal & Lowenthal, 1997).

As parents, adolescents generally have limited understanding of child development and thus have unrealistic expectations of infants and young children that can lead to child maltreatment. Young children in adolescent-parent families frequently live in home environments with a young parent who is depressed about her or his circumstances and less positive about being a parent. Children of adolescent parents are at risk because their parents tend to smile, vocalize, and touch them less as infants than would an older parent and are apt to use verbal and physical punishments more than their older-parent counterparts (Williams & Sadler, 2001). School-age children of adolescent parents as a group do not perform as well as children born to more mature parents. Sommer, Whitman, and Borkowski (2000) found cognitive developmental delays in children of low socioeconomic adolescent parents at 8 months, 4 years, and 7 years. Based on their review of literature related to the social and emotional development of children of adolescent parents, they concluded that characteristics such as aggressiveness, hostility, and distractability are often observed in children of adolescent parents. Furthermore, children from adolescent-parent homes may be uncommunicative, overly conforming, and exhibit insecure attachments. These characteristics, when combined with cognitive developmental delays, portend children who will experience difficulty in the early school years.

It is difficult to generalize such characteristics to all children of adolescent parents. Differences in socioeconomic status and the level of support received from adolescent parents' families will influence experiences of children born to adolescents. Even support received by young parents outside of the family unit appears to make a tremendous difference in their life course and their ability to parent. For example, Williams and Sadler (2001) found that school-based child-care programs that included counseling, health care, and child development education had a profoundly positive impact on the grades and rate of school completion among participating adolescent mothers. There were also fewer repeat pregnancies among those who were a part of the program. Although adolescent parents are engaged in an adult activity (i.e., raising children), Williams and Sadler believed it to be important for programs to focus on the developmental characteristics of adolescent parents, while providing needed child care and social support.

ADOPTIVE AND FOSTER FAMILIES

Some couples and single adults choose adoption or foster care as a means to form families with children. Adoptive and foster families exist in a number of structures, ranging from single female- or male-headed families to those headed by a legally married or gay or lesbian couple. Mulcare and Aquinis (1999) pointed to the impact of medical advances on adoptive families, suggesting that some children are semiadopted, having been born as a result of artificial insemination by donor sperm. In this case, the child is genetically related to the mother but not to the social father—who may then adopt the child. There are also instances in which artificial insemination with a surrogate mother takes place, with the social mother in a position to later adopt the child.

According to Miller, Xitao, Mathew, Grotevant, and van Dulmen (2000), disagreement exists over whether adopted children have more psychological, school, and behavioral problems than nonadopted children. In a careful review of literature related to the emotional health of adopted children, they concluded that adopted children tend to be more involved in mental health services than nonadopted children. They proposed, however, that adopted children may have more problems than nonadopted children, that adoptive parents may tend to seek treatment for their children more often than nonadoptive parents, or both. Borders, Black, and Pasley (1998) suggested that most studies of adoptive parents and their children emanate from deficiency models that focus on presumed negative and problematic differences between adoptive and nonadoptive families. In a study of nationally based matched groups of adoptive and biological parents, they found

Foreign adoptions remain a viable choice for many families. A majority of children adopted are Russian or Chinese, although many are South American, Asian, or Eastern European.

no significant differences between perceptions among adoptive and biological parents in areas such as parental well-being, attitudes toward family life, discipline practices among parents, and the at-risk status of their children.

Families continue to adopt, and a great deal of diversity exists among adoptive and foster families. A number of White families choose to adopt children of ethnic–racial backgrounds different from their own. Transracial adoption became popular in this country as families began adopting children orphaned by wars (i.e., World War II, Korean War, Vietnam War). The acceptance of American-born children of color by White families increased, as transracial adoptive families with children of color from other countries became more common in White communities. When the numbers of healthy American-born White children available for adoption declined in the 1960s, White families turned to transracial adoption of American-born children of color to complete their families (Hollingsworth, 1998).

Foreign adoptions remain a viable choice for many families, with the number of these adoptions increasing from 7,093 in 1990 to 15,774 in 1998. The majority of children adopted were Russian and Chinese, although many were South American, Asian, or Eastern European. Many families who adopt children from other countries seek support in "culture camps" or other support groups that provide a means for foreign-born adoptees to interact with children like themselves, as well as to help both children and parents learn about the culture from which the child originates (Pan & Keene-Osborn, 1999).

It is common for parents who adopt foreign-born children of color to seek resources that will help their children develop skills needed to be a minority in a country where racism persists. Still, the tenacity of racism in the United States persuades some people of color to oppose transracial adoptions and foster care for American-born children of color. They believe children of color should be placed with families of color, so that they develop a healthy sense of self and attain the skills needed to survive in a racist society. Proponents of transracial adoptions argue that many children of color available for adoption remain in foster care, owing to limited numbers of individuals of color willing or able to adopt them. Hollingsworth (1998) concluded that transracial adoption should not be the only strategy to address the perceived overrepresentation of children of color in the child welfare system. The inclusion of culturally sensitive family recruitment activities, as well as attention from policy makers to social and economic issues that contribute to larger numbers of children of color in the child welfare system, could reduce the number of children of color in need of child welfare services.

Adoption is generally viewed as a more permanent and preferable living situation over foster care. The exception may be kinship foster placements in which dependent children are placed in the homes of relatives who have been approved as foster parents. This type of family form is common among children of color and describes many intergenerational family bonds as well. Foster parents in these situations intend to care for the child as long as needed or as long as they are able, many without the intention of formally adopting the child. For example, cultural notions of family, particularly the value of extended family, lead many African American kinship foster caregivers not to seek formal adoption (Hollingsworth, 1998). The grandparent, uncle, aunt, or cousin providing care perceives himself or herself as already "in family" with the child and thus sees no need to adopt. Furthermore, in the view of some kinship foster parents, legal adoption would be confusing for the child and could result in conflict with the child's biological parents.

Some foster children are labeled hard to place, with diminished possibilities of being adopted. Agencies find it difficult to find adoptive homes for minority children, severely disabled children, those over 12 years old, and those in foster care for 4 or more years. Foster caregivers often encounter children who exhibit the effects of being neglected, abused, or exposed to other unhealthy living situations. Frequent placements and separation from biological parents are traumatic experiences for foster children. As a result, the "high needs" status of some foster children are more often situationally rather than genetically rooted. Either way, both the home and school must develop strategies to assist the adjustment of these children. Foster children may exhibit behavior problems such as academic failure, failure to turn in homework, cheating, school phobia, or truancy that are common to many school-age children. Teachers, however, must be sensitive to the possibility that the causes for these behaviors differ between foster children and those living in biological or adoptive families (Noble, 1997).

School-age foster children may have experienced repeated school transfers. They are challenged to adjust to different learning environments at the precise time that they are concerned about survival needs. Frequent school transitions prevent foster children from making strong connections with the school, other students, and their teachers, thereby adding to the lack of stability in their lives. It is helpful for schools to have a plan for enrolling and integrating foster children into school on short notice. As they generate strategies to respond to the needs of foster children, school personnel will also have to become accustomed to working with both the foster parent and the child's caseworker. Because the attention of some foster parents may be divided among several unrelated foster children living in the home, school personnel may have to take a more active role in ensuring that parents understand how to assist school-age children who may be below grade level or in need of special services.

An increasing number of families intend to adopt children placed in their homes as foster children. "Fost adoption" programs (Barth, Courtney, Berrick, & Albert, 1994) were designed to remove the temporary nature of foster placements with the expectation that adoption would take place if child welfare agencies were unable to reunite children with their biological parents. Children are exposed to care that is a vast improvement over past foster care situations in which foster parents were encouraged not to become emotionally attached to foster children. Although most fost care arrangements conclude with legal adoption, the possibility of reunification between child and biological parents exists until adoption is finalized. Such instances can be emotionally devastating to foster parents, but call for readjustments on the child's part as well.

BIRACIAL AND MULTIRACIAL FAMILIES

Families may include individuals from more than one race. Multiracial families may result from parents of one race adopting a child from another. Interracial marriages or other unions also result in multiracial families, with many producing biracial and multiracial children. During the 1960s, fewer than

Social emphasis on race places biracial children under considerable pressure. In some cases, they are at risk for prejudicial treatment from both sides of their heritage. Photo of Akamatsu Family © Gigi Kaeser from the book and traveling photo-text exhibit: *Of Many Colors: Portraits of Multiracial Families*. Produced by the Family Diversity Projects.

2% of the population was biracial, the most common resulting from African American and White unions. Currently, approximately 9% of the population is biracial, and it is estimated that the numbers will climb to 21% by the year 2050. Differences exist in the rate of intermarriage among members of various ethnic–racial backgrounds. African Americans tend to have within-group marriages, with 10% choosing partners who are not African American. In contrast, 54% of Asian American women marry outside their race, and 57% of Hispanics choose non-Hispanic mates. Although first-generation immigrants tend to marry within race, succeeding generations are more likely to intermarry.

Inquiry and Reflection 2D: The number of multiracial families is increasing. What social conditions contribute to this phenomenon? What are your views of multiracial families?

Race remains an important and distinguishing attribute in the United States, and it is often central to many social, legal, and political activities in the country. For example, race is at issue as groups establish political clout and is often a consideration in allocation of federal funds. Measuring the status of individuals in various race categories enables the federal government to monitor progress toward removing disparities along quality-of-life measures (e.g., education, health care, income) existing among various racial

Case 2B: Family Dynamics in a Multiracial Home

I am a half breed, and my children are quarter breeds. My mother... is a Haida/Tlingit Indian from Southeast Alaska. My father was a German.... I want to tell you about the outrageous attitudes that I have experienced with my daughter, who is extremely White looking. From her infancy I have had to tolerate attitudes that I wasn't good enough for my daughter or that I in fact was her babysitter or nanny.... I find this subtle or outright attack on my relationship with my child very destructive. It has even at times in her early childhood caused her to deny that I was her mother to her classmates. She told them I was her babysitter. I love my only daughter dearly and hardly think of her in terms of color, as you can understand if you are a mother. My daughter is my flesh. I even had my son... ask me if the reason I always wanted my daughter to go shopping with me was because she was so White looking, thereby allegedly raising my acceptability or perhaps allaying racial fears by bringing along a safe White person. That hurt—that the question of race should enter my household, between family members. I never even conceived that such a thing could happen. You know, being an Alaskan native woman, or at least half, means that we are a matriarchal people. The women rule the family. So naturally my daughter is my right-hand man, or woman as it were. Will my sons think that my daughter sits in a position of authority in the house just because she is White? I have even had to change her name.... I feel her former name carried too much power with it. (Anonymous)

groups (Grotto, 2001). Before the Census of 2000, biracial individuals were made to choose one side of their heritage over the other. In this way, they were made to deny a part or parts of their racial makeup because the right to self-identification was disregarded. Beginning with Census 2000, biracial and multiracial individuals were able to self-identify by selecting more than one race category if they chose to do so.

Racism has historically been the basis for both the social and legal rationale against mixed marriages. Laws against **miscegenation** (i.e., laws that prohibited individuals of different races to marry) existed as early as 1661; however miscegenation was still against the law in 17 states when the Supreme Court ruled against its constitutionality in the 1967 *Loving v. Virginia* decision (Funderburg, 1994). Although no longer illegal, elements of social disapproval of mixed marriages and the children born to those unions remain and take many forms. The equivocal status of mixed-race or biracial children born to an interracial couple is observable, for example, by the limited representation of this family form in the media and on television sitcoms.

Societal emphasis on race differences places biracial children under considerable pressure. In some cases, they are at risk for prejudicial treatment from both sides of their heritage. They are often faced with many hurdles, including resolving ambivalence related to their ethnic identity, coping with labels imposed on them by others, and articulating a racial description of who they are in their own words. Internal family dynamics around issues of identity in mixed-race families are sometimes influenced by racist reactions of outsiders to family members. Although the mother of biracial children in Case 2B felt able to meld the two heritages of her children within the home, differential treatment associated with race outside the home caused her to rethink her mother practice.

Inquiry and Reflection 2E: Children or youth may be sensitive about the structure of their families (see Case 2B), in many instances as a result of a social stigma or negative evaluation of a family characteristic. What should be the teacher's role when children or youth are defensive, embarrassed, or ashamed of some aspect of their family structure?

Ultimately, support of biracial children must begin with the educator's personal evaluation of prejudice against interracial bonds and biracial and multiracial individuals. Inside schools, biracial children need to feel their unique background is accepted by their peers and by school personnel. Teachers able to create environments that celebrate diversity support the development of a positive sense of self among these children.

CONCLUDING COMMENTS

Regardless of structure and membership, families with children have in common the legal and moral responsibility to care for children and youth in the family. Caring for children is multifaceted and includes the day-to-day physical care of the children, as well as attention to their social, emotional, and educational well-being until they reach adulthood. Teachers determined to enter into collaborative relationships with families must be aware of their beliefs about the relationship between family capacity and family structure. Using family structure as a primary indicator of families' capacity to attend to the needs of children could lead teachers to misread signals of family capability. As a result, they may not pay attention to contributions certain families (e.g., single-mother-headed family) could bring to the educational arena and miss the opportunity to support other families in need (e.g., distressed two-parent nuclear family). Given the multiple structures of families today, it is increasingly necessary for teachers to approach the development of relationships with parents being fully aware of their biases regarding family structure. This is the first step in developing professional dispositions that lean toward a willingness to come to know the strengths and challenges of individual families within the context of a given family structure.

GUIDED OBSERVATIONS

2F. Conduct a scan of your observation classroom and construct a chart of the various family structures existing among your students (many students' families have more than one family structure characteristic, for example, single father, multiracial family). What aspects of the classroom climate are affected (either negatively or positively) by this family structure makeup?

2G. Are there federally funded after-school programs in the district of your observation site? What other types of after-school programs (e.g., church-run programs, YWCA/YMCA programs, community agency programs) are available to students? Who do these programs serve?

2H. How are teachers at your observation site working with representatives from agencies outside of the school (e.g., caseworkers) to support the needs of school children and families?

Chapter 3

Social and Cultural Contexts of Family Life

A family's social class or socioeconomic status presents a complex interaction among income, social status, and everyday living contexts. Income, educational level, and occupation are commonly used to classify families at poverty, low-income, middle-income, and high-income levels. Resources available for housing, the extent to which a family is food secure, its access to health care, and its material wealth and overall economic well-being are all influenced by socioeconomic status.

Everyday life is also influenced by the extent to which families follow values and customs that are a part of the multiple and diverse ethnic, cultural, and religious traditions existing in the United States. According to the U.S. Census Bureau, there were 70.2 million children in the United States in 1999. The rate of growth in the number of children began to increase in 1990, with much of the current growth attributed to increases in the numbers of children of color. Non-Hispanic White children actually decreased from 74% of the population to 65% of the population between 1980 and 1999. During this same period, the percentages of African American and American Indian/Alaska Native children remained fairly stable, representing 15% and 1%, respectively, of American children. Latino children represent the fastest growing segment in the population, increasing from 9% to 16% between 1980 and 1999. Based on this rate of growth, it is expected that one in five children in the United States will be of Hispanic origin by 2020. Asian/Pacific Islander children doubled in population between 1980 and 1999, increasing from 2% to 4% of all children in the United States (America's Children 2000a, 2000b). Broad ethnic–racial categories, however, do not fully represent the extent of diversity existing in the United States. Intergroup diversity provides additional insight into the multiple traditions and values families hold, alongside those that families adopting dominant-culture norms hold.

Religion also plays a major role in the lives of many families, with religious affiliation crossing ethnic and racial lines. In many instances, families choose the extent to which religious doctrine influences the day-to-day functions of the family. For some groups, however, religious beliefs serve as the major framework for structuring family life. The social, economic, ethnic–cultural, and religious backgrounds of families, when combined with family configuration, embody the true essence of diversity among families. Through exploration of family characteristics separately, teachers are in a better position to understand the complexity of family life as it is influenced by attributes that combine to define unique family situations.

SOCIOECONOMIC STATUS

The U.S. Department of Agriculture estimates that it will cost families $160,140 ($237,000 when adjusted for inflation) to raise a child born in 1999 from birth to age 17. Imagine the cost of raising three or more children. Many families will not have incomes that allow them to contribute this amount to raising their children, whereas others can contribute much more. The percentage of families living at various income levels with respective annual incomes are summarized in Figure 3.1. Although more children lived in medium-income families than any other group, the percentage of children

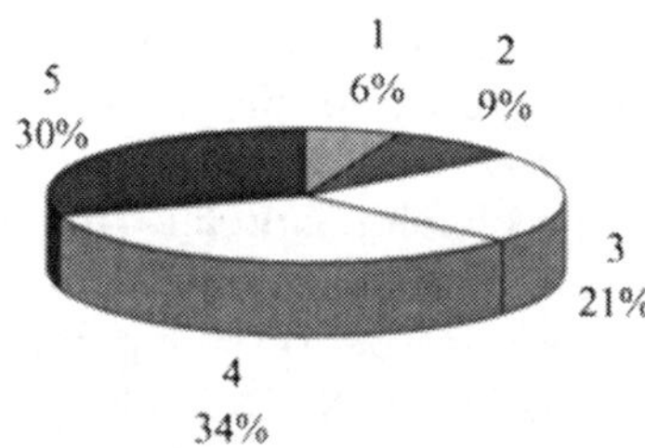

Figure 3.1 Proportion of children living in families at different income levels.
Source: America's Children 2004. Estimates based on family of four with children 18 years old or younger in 2001. Annual Incomes: 1. extreme poverty—$9052; 2. poverty $9052–18,103; 3. low income—$18,104–36,207; 4. medium income—$36,208–72,415; 5. high income $72,416 and above.

living in these families dropped from 41% in 1980 to 34% in 2000. Children living in high-income families increased from 17% to 30% during this period, and there was a slight decrease in children living in extreme poverty situations (decline from 7% to 6%).

Cultural and Structural Explanations for Social Class

Baca Zinn and Eitzen (1996) described two approaches to conceptualizing social class that are closely tied to families' participation in society. Cultural explanations focus on each economic group having distinct sets of attitudes, values, and behaviors that constitute a "culture" shared by those falling into specific income and occupational levels. The notion of a "culture of poverty" that depicts a deficit explanation for families living in poverty emanates from this perspective. The poor are generally viewed as having attitudes, values, and behaviors that sustain their position at the bottom of the social and economic ladder. In addition, they are believed to pass on these traits to children, thus cultivating a status of poverty from one generation to the next.

Structural explanations for social class focus on the impact of differences in resources accessible to families that in turn influence everyday living situations. In this case, it is suggested that social class shapes the nature of relationships between and among families, individuals, and institutions, providing resources for some and withholding resources from others. Baca Zinn and Eitzen (1996) explained that "different connections with society's opportunity structure produce and require unique family adaptations and . . . that structural power and control produce advantages for some and disadvantages for others" (p. 135). Class privilege, the unearned advantages, prerogatives, and options available to certain status groups, emerges as a fundamental factor that sustains the power and social position of certain status groups (i.e., middle- and upper-income groups) over others (i.e., low-income and poverty groups).

Individuals benefitting from class privilege may be unaware of or unwilling to accept advantages granted as a result of their class status. Furthermore, they may be unwilling to acknowledge the implications of their advantaged status for the disadvantaged, in this way concluding that the two status positions exist in isolation of each other. According to Marks (2000), studies of family diversity with respect to social class tend to focus on the problems of poverty, in absence of close scrutiny of the problems of advantaged class status and its associated class privilege. Aspects of poverty and privilege have implications for understanding family dynamics, and both affect teacher–student and school–family interactions and relations. The reflections of Marks as an upper-middle-class child and Gloria as a child living in poverty (Case 3A) indicate how family resources affect the extent to which

Case 3A: Marks and Gloria: Divergent Childhood Experiences

Marks

From a very young age, I was primed for success. I was given to the belief that any difficulties I encountered should yield quickly to my efforts to surmount them and that life was an opportunity to express myself. At times when I might have faltered, my father's money and the resources and skills he could buy for me—speech therapist . . . prep school, tutors when I needed them, college tuition and all my living expenses at a small private liberal arts college—these were like a steady wind at my back blowing me forward, fueling the illusion that I was an individual creating my own destiny. My father's money, my family's Whiteness, and my maleness were a triumvirate of capital I could rely on without becoming aware of how they were subsidizing me. (Marks, 2000, p. 616)

Gloria

I don't want them [her children] to be like when I was little, when I went to school. . . . They [teachers] didn't care if I knew how to read or not. All they did was kept passing me, passing me, passing me. . . . Til I went to Smith High, then that's when . . . them teachers, they noticed that I didn't know how to read. And they started putting me in special classes for that . . . by that time I dropped out. I dropped out of school . . . I didn't go back anymore. (Gloria, single mother of five living in poverty)

each child, and indeed the family, must rely on schools as the primary support for academic success.

Inquiry and Reflection 3A: Write an opinion of the merits and deficiencies of cultural and structural explanations of social class, using the perspectives presented in Case 3A. What do you believe is the basis for poverty?

Inequality in social power is one aspect of social stratification, but particularly damaging in school situations are the evaluative components of class status that support beliefs of one group as more competent, valued, and deserving than another. These beliefs are shared within a society, telling us how to treat and interact with individuals from certain social class categories. Ridgeway and Erickson (2000) offered **status construction theory** as a means for understanding how structural inequalities in the distribution of resources transform into beliefs that favor members of one group over another. Through a series of interactive social processes, evaluative beliefs about differences among people are created, shared, and maintained. These processes are so powerful that even individuals having a disadvantaged status come to share the same negative beliefs (i.e., that they are less competent, of less value) that are diffused throughout society. When these beliefs enter the classroom, they perpetuate a cultural hegemony for families like that of Marks and further marginalize families like Gloria's.

Influences on Social Class Instability

While Marks' and Gloria's social statuses appear relatively stable, the social and economic positions of some families have a fluctuating quality, altered by events such as divorce, loss of employment, remarriage, or change in the number of children in the household (Rank, 2000). Thus, a medium-income family may have an annual income that places them at the poverty level for a period of time, only to have their economic position restored after employment is found. The overall pattern of families' economic position provides more insightful information about their well-being than their status in any given year. Some families have "poverty spells" where they temporarily fall below the poverty line. Economic positions of other families remain more stable over time. Rank discussed families, for example, who experience chronic poverty and are sometimes referred to as the underclass. Family structure, skill or educational level, ethnic background, and gender of the employable members of the family may contribute to their disadvantaged status in the labor market, and thus to the family's status as chronically poor (Polakow, 1993; Rank, 2000). Although many chronically poor families live in inner cities, the highest concentration of poverty exists in the rural areas of the Appalachian Mountain region, from the Carolinas to Arkansas and on the Louisiana deltas; in the Rio Grande Valley and Texas Gulf Coast; and on American Indian reservations in the Southwest (Flynt, 1996). Many rural families living in poverty have at least one, and in some instances two, working adults. Even so, these families are chronically poor because they are most often working in low-wage, low-skill jobs.

Both parents also work in many high-income families, sometimes putting in as much as 50- to 70-hour weeks in well-paid and demanding jobs. These families are likely headed by Carnoy's notion of "disaggregated workers of the globalized age" discussed in Chapter 1. You will recall these workers tend to change and retrain for work over the life of their careers to keep up with changes in the labor market and to maintain their social and economic positions. Knowledge among parents that they are susceptible to the disappearance of well-paying professional or managerial jobs creates stressful home environments for many of these families. Despite high incomes, many such parents experience financial stress in addition to work-related stress. It is common for high-income families to be cash poor, owing to high mortgage payments, child-care costs, college loan repayments, and in some instances costs for private schools (Spiers, 1993). Some high-income families experience anxiety because of limited time with children. Relatedly, children often "act out" in reaction to a lack of attention from their parents.

The socioeconomic status of a family figures largely in the type of educational experience children of the family will receive. Social class, when coupled with family characteristics such as ethnic–cultural background and family structure, unfortunately provides an imprint that allows us to predict a child's success or failure in schools, as schools currently function. Although teachers cannot change this fact in isolation of other social institutions, awareness of the role schooling plays in maintaining the social stratification status quo is a first step in generating strategies to ensure that all children experience the type of education that broadens, rather than constrains, choices that they will have as adults.

The Poorest of the Poor: Homeless Families

By the close of the 20th century, more than 600,000 families and 1 million children were without permanent homes, living in shelters, cars, on the streets, or in campgrounds. Millions of other families were at risk for homelessness (Institute for Children and Poverty, 2001). The typical homeless family is headed by a single mother in her late 20s or early 30s who has two to three children under age 5. Although homeless families exist in all ethnic groups, over half are African American (Nunez & Fox, 1999). Many homeless families experience residential instability before becoming homeless, and for many of these families, homelessness is not a one-time event. At least a third of the women heading homeless families did not finish high school, and although many are unemployed, homelessness does not necessarily preclude employment. Many parents of homeless families experience barriers to employment such as problems with child-care, lack of education and skills, and lack of a permanent address or transportation, and many are substance abusers. Both children and parents suffer poor health and often have chronic illnesses (e.g., asthma, infections, stomach ailments), some of which can be attributed to their homeless status.

Homeless families have been on the rise since 1993 and make up 36% of all who are homeless. Personal issues, such as the desire to escape spousal or child abuse combine with structural issues to increase the number of families without permanent homes. The lack of affordable housing, shifts in the labor market, welfare reform, and the decline in federal assistance have been identified as major structural reasons for the increased numbers of homeless families. Low-income families in some cities are required to pay up to 80% of their income for housing. Unable to pay this amount, families end up leaving their homes, many to double up with other families to save costs, before ending up without a home at all. The shift in the labor market from manufacturing jobs that pay a livable wage to lower wage service jobs has resulted in many parents being unable to make enough money to take care of their families. While the number of families receiving welfare declined as a result of welfare reform, the average annual wages of these families ranged between $8,000 and $10,800, still placing them at the extreme poverty to poverty levels. Finally, the decline in federal assistance for subsidized housing meant longer waiting lists for **Section 8** and public housing (Institute for Children and Poverty, 2001).

Even though the typical child living in a homeless situation is under age 5, the impact of homeless episodes has a lasting effect on the social, physical, and academic development of homeless children. The emotional stress of homelessness results in high incidences of mental illnesses and developmental delays. Furthermore, situations common to homelessness (e.g., constant mobility) contribute to poor academic performance of children who experience homelessness. Intervention and support such as quality relationships with teachers, after-school tutoring and academic support, and, in general, relationships with caring and competent adults appear to have a positive affect on the schooling experiences of homeless children (Hart-Shegos, 1999).

CULTURAL AND ETHNIC DIVERSITY AMONG FAMILIES

The extent of cultural–ethnic diversity in the United States becomes clearer when intergroup diversity within broad ethnic categories is considered. For example, there are currently 500 distinct Native American tribal groups and villages in the United States (Joe & Malach, 1998). Asian/Pacific Islanders include individuals who are Chinese, Japanese, Cambodian, Hmong, Hawaiian, Laotian, Korean, Filipino, Vietnamese, or South Asian Indian, among others. Latinos could be Puerto Rican, Mexican American, Cuban American, or have familial roots in Central or South America or the Caribbean. Black Americans may be African American, meaning individuals having ancestral roots dating 400 years in the United States, or they may be more recent immigrants from Africa, Haiti, or Jamaica, who would not necessarily call themselves African Americans. Individuals who are collectively referred to as European American or White represent numerous ethnic backgrounds, the customs and traditions of which they may attend to in varying degrees. Finally, there are a growing number of biracial individuals who claim all aspects of their ethnic background and wish to be recognized not as either–or but both. In fact, individuals from various cultural or ethnic groups may prefer to be addressed by specific cultural–ethnic group titles. In the United States cultural self-identification is expressed through customs, values, and attitudes and is often tied to a land of origin (Figure 3.2).

It is projected that no ethnic–cultural group will account for a majority by 2050 (Pollard & O'Hare, 1999). No one can predict the exact effect of this demographic on interactions between and among various ethnic–cultural groups, nor the influence that changes in the population will have on preferred cultural and social prescriptions. Currently, mainstream or

Awareness of the origin and meaning of titles applied to groups aids our understanding of why individual preferences exist in terms of how people want to be addressed. Although often used interchangeably, note the differences in origin and meaning of titles applied to Latinos:

Latino—families with Latin American origin but also acceptable for all populations from Spanish-speaking origins

Hispanic—U.S. Census Bureau–derived term for populations of Spanish-speaking origin, sometimes disparaged because it minimizes the diversity among Latinos.

Chicano—ethnically mixed families having Spanish, Mexican, and Native American heritage; also a political identifier for social activism

Mexican American—families having roots in Mexico who want to retain this ethnic identification

Spanish American—families who have immigrated from Spain

Figure 3.2 Cultural self-identification.

dominant-cultural norms exist, and cultural–ethnic groups having minority representation in the population are expected to adhere to these norms. As Greenfield and Cocking (1994) stated:

> In the United States, Europe, and many other parts of the world, a dominant culture is officially sanctioned. The distinctions between minority and majority also implies that the majority group controls most resources and provides the context of acculturation for the minority groups. (p. xiii)

Even though dominant-cultural norms exist, differences persist among various cultural–ethnic groups with respect to processes, customs, and traditions while caring for children. According to Parke (2000), a lack of synchronization exists between our awareness of family diversity and a comprehensive understanding of the processes that contribute to the cultural variation among families. Even so, a number of scholars are contributing to our understanding of the fundamental basis for family diversity, as well as general characteristics of families from various backgrounds. Greenfield (1994), for example, noted the significance of cultural and social history in the ways in which families may choose to rear their children. She suggested that cultural scripts, a by-product of cultural history, serve as the basis for differences in developmental goals and cultural acquisition within different families. Suggested here is the notion that children and young people are inculcated with values and skills that differ on the basis of ethnic group cultural history and the extent to which the individual family identifies with that cultural history. Adults may follow "cultural scripts" in the process of child rearing that are rooted in the family's cultural history.

Inquiry and Reflection 3B: Interview three parents from different ethnic–cultural backgrounds regarding their child-rearing practices. Include questions to determine whether aspects of their practices relate specifically to cultural beliefs.

Although it is important for teachers to understand child-rearing practices generally attributable to an ethnic–cultural group, it is also important to know individual families to understand child-rearing goals embraced by a particular family. Ethnic-minority families differ in the extent to which they adopt traditional ethnic-minority-based family practices. The Assimilation-Enculturation Continuum (Figure 3.3) illustrates the multiple ways ethnic-minority families may choose to conduct their lives. For this reason, it is important to understand both dominant-culture and ethnic-minority traditions as these apply to child care and family life. Some ethnic minority families fully adopt dominant-culture norms, thus incorporating dominant-culture behaviors, beliefs, language patterns, and values into their everyday lives. These families have ***assimilated*** to the dominant culture and transmit these behaviors and beliefs to their children. Other ethnic-minority families may occupy a position of ***acculturation*** with respect to dominant-culture norms. In this instance, families are aware of language patterns, behaviors, and values that constitute dominant-culture norms and use them to interact with dominant-culture social institutions. According Hurtado (1995), although assimilation and acculturation are often use interchangeably, the two differ in an important way. Acculturated families maintain certain aspects of family life that are closely tied to ethnic cultural traditions, which is often not true of fully assimilated families. Other ethnic-minority families engage family practices to ensure that children acquire beliefs, knowledge, and behaviors that allow them to function as a member of the ethnic group

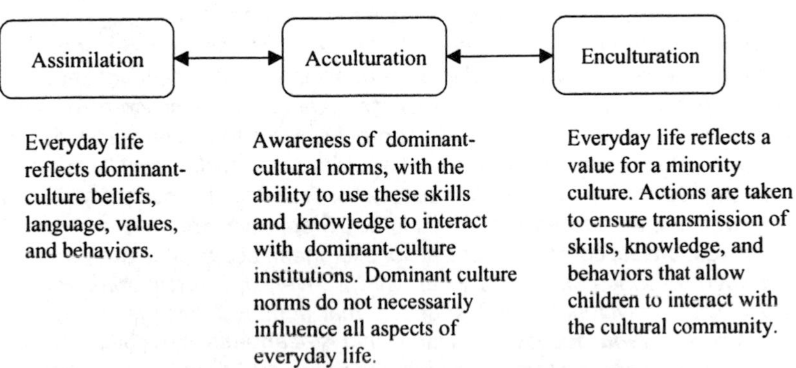

Figure 3.3 Assimilation–Enculturation Continuum.

(Bernal & Knight, 1993). The process of ***enculturation***, if placed on a continuum, would be a direct opposite of assimilation. Even fully assimilated families may wish for their children to understand and appreciate their ethnic–cultural heritage, however, even when these are not necessarily incorporated into the family's everyday life.

Class privilege was discussed earlier as the unearned advantage and prerogatives available to those having a particular social class designation. In a similar way, race privilege serves as a fundamental factor that sustains the power and social position of European Americans over members of ethnic-minority groups (McIntosh, 1989). In the contemporary United States, members of ethnic-minority groups are often less valued and often the target of disparaging and prejudicial treatment. Many families believe enculturation provides children with survival strategies against dangers inherent in a racialized society that may negatively influence the child's emotional and, in some instances, physical well-being. As evidenced in Case 3B, inculcation of strategies to confront racism is an integral component of child-rearing in some families.

Case 3B: Culturally Specific Child-Rearing Practices

Most enlightened African Americans who choose to recognize that racism exists can attest to the almost daily instances where we are treated rudely or in an inferior manner simply because we are black. Sometimes it happens at a store or a restaurant. Other times, it is at our children's school. Sometimes, it is blatant; other times it is subtle. But it is constant. . . . I recall the first time I was aware of my mother being treated in a discriminatory manner. We were shopping for luggage in a local store. . . . The sales clerk, after following us around in a suspicious manner for some time (another common occurrence), asked my mother if she were going to buy the luggage or not. He tried to rush her to buy it and refused to open it for her. She insisted that she would not buy "pork in the pig" (a statement that I came to understand later). Finally, the sales clerk reluctantly opened the luggage. To make a point, my mother did not purchase the luggage. I learned several things from this instance. First, insist on good service. Second, do not buy from businesses that treat blacks disrespectfully. Third, although my mother did not do this, I learned to discuss such instances with your children. My mother was too embarrassed to do this. It is a horrible feeling to be downgraded in front of your children. Fourth, I decided that I would not lose my temper like my mother did. I later learned to complain to a supervisor or write to the company. . . . I have used what I have learned with my daughter, Stephanie. We have even devised typical responses, comments, and actions for these occasions. Many may think that such responses are petty or amount to overkill. I hardly think so. There is a wealth of evidence which suggests that fighting biases is necessary to counteract powerful negative messages that African American children receive. I want her to learn to stand up for what is right and I firmly believe that being treated fairly and with respect is a human right. (Boutte, 1997)

Dominant-Culture Families

The immediate or nuclear family is most often viewed as the family unit in dominant-culture or mainstream United States, when it comes to day-to-day functioning of the family. From a historical perspective, the nuclear family emerged with specific roles and expectations of father, mother, and children in a smaller unit than had existed before this family form. As a result, an extended family was no longer as important in the day-to-day functioning of the family unit. This configuration of the family unit aligns more with an independent or individualistic value orientation, in which responsibility for the well-being of the family resides within the nuclear unit (Greenfield & Cocking, 1994; Lynch & Hanson, 1998). Belief in individualism not only influences patterns of interaction among family members, but also affects interactions with other social institutions, such as schools. Although contemporary roles of members of the nuclear family may have shifted, the notion of the immediate family being primarily responsible for its own welfare persists. In dominant-culture America, the immediate family continues to be valued over an extended one, evidenced by the social, legal, and economic support that exists for this family structure in society at large. Ethnic-minority families tend to exhibit a collectivist or interdependent value orientation toward the family unit (Greenfield & Cocking, 1994; Lynch & Hanson, 1998). An extended family, although defined in different ways, plays an important role in ensuring the well-being of family members.

Latino Families

Familism as a specific family pattern is frequently used to describe Latino families. In this context, familism refers to a strong value for and commitment to the family that is reflected by large extended kin networks, high levels of contact among family members, and reliance on the family as a resource for solving problems. The extended family consists not only of related family members, but also includes unrelated related or **fictive kin.** Many Mexican American families in particular continue to have a *compadrazo* system in which godparents are a second set of parents having socialization and financial responsibilities for children in the family (Chahin, Villarruel, & Viramontez, 1999). These family characteristics are accompanied by geographic closeness, with clusters of extended-kin households located in close proximity to each other (Hurtado, 1995; Vega, 1995).

Disagreement exists over the extent to which the notion of "familism" can be attributed to Latinos of different national origins, with the suggestion that this family pattern is more representative of Mexican Americans (Baca Zinn & Wells, 2000). Hurtado (1995) suggested that dimensions of familism, such as family support and geographic closeness, span Latinos of different national origins as well as families embracing varying levels of acculturation or assimilation. Other aspects, such as the exclusive use of family members as role models or for emotional support, may be in decline.

Approximately 64% of Latino families are Mexican American, followed by Puerto Ricans, Cuban Americans, and Central and South Americans. Large numbers of these families live in poverty, with Cuban American families being the exception (Lynch & Hanson, 1998). Poverty among Latino families has been attributed to higher numbers of female-headed households, young parents, and family size with approximately half of Latino families having four or more children (Soltis, 1995). Poverty persists, even when both adults in two-parent households work. These parents are often disadvantaged in the labor market because of low educational attainment, limited work skills that result in concentration of both men and women in low-wage jobs (e.g., service jobs, food processing, garment industry), and, in some instances, limited English proficiency (Baca Zinn & Wells, 2000; Martinez, 1999; Oritz, 1995; Soltis, 1995). By contrast, Cuban American families, particularly those living in Miami and New Jersey, have experienced more economic success. They tend to have higher levels of education and smaller families. Thus, diversity among Latino family units is influenced not only by national origin, but by social and economic class as well.

African American Families

A collectivist or interdependent orientation in traditional African American families may be evident in a family unit described by Nobles (1997) as a "unique cultural form enjoying its own inherent resources" made up of several households with "channels of authority reaching beyond the household units that compose it" (p. 87). Nobles went on to suggest that a major function of the African American family unit is to promote the well-being of its members by protecting them from racism and by providing resources that are not available from other social institutions. The extended family historically has been a bulwark for African Americans—so much so that it is often viewed as the institution most responsible for their survival, strength, and resilience (Sudarkasa, 1997).

The care of children within an extended-family context has historically characterized the African American family unit. Even today, a child may be cared for by a grandparent, uncle, or aunt, or by an unrelated adult member of the community without the presence of a birth parent. A child raised in this type of family unit is not necessarily viewed among African American as being without "family," owing primarily to the value of extended-family bonds and the view that the child has family beyond the nuclear one of mother, father, and siblings.

The multigenerational family, one that includes several adults and children, is another form of extended family that has historically characterized the African American family unit. These homes might include a mother and her children, the children's grandparents, and perhaps an uncle. Adult members of the family provide emotional and economic assistance to the parent of children in the household, as well as advice and assistance in raising children. Sudarkasa (1997) indicated much was being lost as this structure of the family unit declines among African Americans. One particularly negative consequence is the increase in African American women living at a low socioeconomic level status and raising children alone. Social and economic policies (e.g., welfare policies that required young single mothers to live alone) contributed to the decline of this family form and subsequently to the stress and economic vulnerability experienced by many African American female heads of households.

Quality-of-life measures such as income, housing, and health care for African Americans as a group remain at levels below that of White Americans as a group. In fact, 49% of African American female-headed households live in poverty, as does one third of all African American children. It is for this reason that vestiges of the multigenerational household remain for some African Americans, particularly those living at lower economic levels. African Americans having higher incomes and higher levels of formal education tend to be more assimilated, exhibiting dominant-culture sociocultural attributes and family organizational patterns (Sudarkasa, 1997).

Inquiry and Reflection 3C: Choose a magazine or journal directed toward an ethnic-minority group. What can you cull from magazine articles, advertisements, or journal article content that is culturally specific (i.e., different from a dominant-culture discourse)?

Native American Families

An extended-family system is even more evident among some Native American tribes, where the family unit may be designated by immediate family, clan, and tribe. Traditionally, responsibility for child rearing extends beyond the immediate family, and biological parents often do not have primary responsibility for the child's care. Within the clan, all adults carry responsibility to guide, counsel, and teach children. Furthermore, there is traditionally a strong bond between the grandparent and grandchild. In fact, the primary time for child rearing within some tribes does not occur when one's own children are young, but when one has grandchildren. In the larger family network, the elderly are highly revered and respected for their age and life experiences and will frequently be called on for assistance and advice in raising children. Observers may be confused by titles given various members in Native American families. For example, all cousins are treated as siblings, or a child may refer to the person in dominant-culture families who is the grandmother as mother, and their uncle as father (Joe & Malach, 1998; Sipes, 1993).

Many Native American families exhibit the dynamic between acculturation and enculturation, with some members holding on to traditional tribal customs and others adopting non-Indian ways for some aspects of their lives. Harjo (1999) and Silvey (1999) stated that many Native Americans are seeking to reestablish an Indian way of life and, in the process, recover from U.S. policies toward Indians that have had an exceedingly negative affect on Native American family life. The removal of children from their homes for the purposes of deculturalization and assimilation is viewed as an especially devastating project, one that Silvey maintained had residual effects that transcended generations. According to Silvey, the "Bureau of Indian Affairs (BIA) agents would arrive at the homes of American Indian families unannounced and, by force, remove the children from their families of origin and place them in boarding schools located hundreds of miles from their homes" (p. 76). The experience is close enough historically so that many middle-aged parents today had parents and grandparents who attended boarding schools. Children were severely punished if they did not give up Indian ways, thus resulting in generations of Indians not knowing much about their native culture and often being afraid to share what they did know with their offsprings. Where the U.S. assimilationist policies were effective, the end result was Native Americans growing up to become parents who knew little of how to raise Native American children in traditional Indian ways.

Today Native Americans have the highest birth and mortality rates in the United States. According to Harjo (1999), U.S. polices such as the "taking of land, forced relocation, an institutionally racist educational system . . . U.S. government paternalism, obstacles to self-governance, stripping of tribal recognition, and denial of religions freedom" (p. 71) continue to negatively affect Native American family life. She proposed that unemployment rates (running as high as 65% to 95% among some tribes) and drug and alcohol abuse reflect needs among Native Americans that differ from other ethnic minorities in the United States. Whereas other groups see their struggle as one to be an accepted part of dominant culture, many Native Americans, who make up inherently sovereign nations, seek to maintain control over their land, water, traditions and unique legal rights. They believe that a return to Indian practices and beliefs is needed to preserve Indian ways and Indian families.

The removal of Native American children from their homes for the purposes of deculturalization and assimilation was a devastating event with residual effects that transcended generations.

Asian American Families

As with other ethnic-minority groups, it is difficult to describe a single family unit to represent completely the structure and content of all Asian American families. Such an endeavor ignores intergroup diversity resulting from differences in language, religion, income, education, and immigration experiences of groups having a common geographic origin. Even so, several family-unit characteristics tend to exist across Asian American families who conduct family life along the acculturation and enculturation components of the Assimilation-Enculturation Continuum.

Asian American families tend to be multigenerational, which is in keeping with a collectivist or interdependent value orientation toward the family unit. The family unit may consist of husband and wife, their unmarried children, and a married son and his family. The immediate family may also consist of an extended family of close relatives sharing the same family name and ancestors. For some Asian American families (e.g., Hmong), the extended family is the clan living in the same community (Chan, 1998). Asian American families are traditionally patriarchal vertical units, meaning that males tend to have authority over and serve as the representative for the family (Chan, 1998; Ishii-Kuntz, 2000). Whereas fathers may be viewed as strict, dignified, and aloof, mothers are traditionally more nurturing and are responsible for attending to the emotional well-being of children and caring for the elderly. Given the roles of mothers in the family, children form closer relationships with mothers than fathers, a relationship that extends into adulthood, as husbands are likely to have close relationships with their mothers (Ishii-Kuntz, 2000).

Similar to the familism characteristic of Mexican American families, some Asian American families may choose to live in close proximity to family members, interact frequently, and provide financial support within the family. The well-being, harmony, and reputation of the family are the responsibility of all family members, and individual actions are expected to reflect this duty. In this context, the notion of "family" includes not only its living members, but also the family of ancestors from the past as well (Chan, 1998). Children are expected to comply to family and parental authority, even if this means denying personal ambitions. Thus, many Asian American children learn to exhibit behavior likely to gain approval rather than disfavor of authority figures. In some cases, the family may choose friends, clothing, and the educational direction of children (Ishii-Kuntz, 2000).

Asian Americans routinely are viewed as "foreigners," regardless of the length of time living in the United States, whether they are natural-born citizens, or regardless of the way they conduct their everyday lives. Like other ethnic minority groups, family patterns among assimilated Asian Americans reflect dominant-culture family patterns. In general, mulitgenerational households with traditional gender roles may be less observable among assimilated Asian Americans (Ishii-Kuntz, 2000).

In some instances, gender roles and family structure may be influenced by economic goals of the family. For example, Gold (1999) reported that there are increased instances among Vietnamese families of reduced family size, women working outside the home, and use of child-care facilities as a means to aid the economic well-being of the family. Ishii-Kuntz (2000) pointed out that divorce rates and interracial marriage increase with the length of time Asian Americans are residents in the United States. Multiracial families may choose a range of family processes, depending on the extent to which the family incorporates values, behaviors, and customs of the ethnic backgrounds represented in the household.

Asian Americans are also viewed as the "model minority," an image that is based on lower divorce rates, higher academic achievement rates, and higher levels of economic and occupational success compared with other ethnic-minority groups. Although these attributes tend to be generalized to all Asian American groups, differences in economic success exist, influenced by recency of immigration, levels of education, and levels of occupational skills gained while in the United States or those possessed at the time of immigration. For example, between 3% and 11% of Japanese, Filipino, and

Chinese families lived in poverty according to the 1990 census. For the same period, the percentages of Vietnamese, Cambodian, Laotian, and Hmong families living in poverty were 28, 42, 32, and 61, respectively. A large number of Asian Americans have low educational attainment and occupational skills that relegate them to low-wage jobs (e.g., waiters, cooks, assembly-line workers, work in food processing plants), and many are unable to speak English or have poor English-speaking skills. Ishii-Kuntz (2000) suggested that Southeast Asians, who are more likely to be refugees turned immigrants, often experience welfare dependency, high rates of joblessness, or are employed in minimum-wage jobs. At the same time, an informal economy exists to help some groups of recent immigrants. Vietnamese, for example, provide new immigrant families with financial, social, and emotional support needed to adjust to life in the United States. Resources ranging from job referrals to investment capital to start small businesses are available within the Vietnamese community. Family-based income pooling, which may include merging capital, labor, and skills, contributes substantially to the economic achievement of Vietnamese (Gold, 1999).

More than half of the Chinese, Filipino, Korean, and Vietnamese in the United States are foreign born. The cultural, social, and occupational transitions that routinely accompany immigration can be disruptive to the harmony of any family unit. Given the importance of parental authority in the Asian American family structure, however, the point of immigration potentially alters traditional child–parent interactions. Parents may feel less confident in guiding children, and children may see their parents as less credible in the new living environment and feel more emboldened to challenge formerly unquestioned parental authority (Ishii-Kuntz, 2000). Often, English is not the primary language in the home, and children become translators for the family. This contributes to a shift in child–parent relations. Finally, interference in Asian American family life may occur when parents invoke parental practices viewed as injurious to the well-being of children or that are in some cases illegal (e.g., whipping or other forms of physical punishment in the United States).

Inquiry and Reflection 3D: Do you have family practices that are similar to those that are linked traditionally to ethnic groups different from your own? Describe these practices.

RELIGION AND FAMILY LIFE

Religious affiliation in the United States crosses ethnic and racial lines. For example, Catholics may be African American, Latino, or White. Similarly, families affiliating with various Protestant religions (e.g., Methodist, Baptist,

Presbyterian, Episcopalian) will be found among all ethnic–cultural groups. School personnel often become aware of religious beliefs among families when school practices or curriculum conflict with families'religious beliefs and practices. Church attendance and participation in other religious activities vary among families. Additionally, variation exists in terms of the influence of religious doctrine on the day-to-day functions of the family. In this way, two families may affiliate with the same church, yet vary in the ways in which religious beliefs are incorporated into family life.

For some families, religious beliefs serve as the major framework for structuring family life. For example, ethnic identification and religious beliefs combine to serve as a foundation for American Jewish families. According to Wertheimer (1994), however, increased rates of intermarriage, divorce, and delayed marriages that result in a lower birthrate, along with a decrease in family members living within close physical proximity to each other have combined to reduce the number of families transmitting a Jewish identity among the young. Many Jewish leaders find these circumstances troubling, particularly as the number of American Jews embracing a Jewish identity, and thus conducting family life with strict adherence to Judaism, decline. Other religious groups, such as the Amish and Mormons, exist in enclaves designed to ensure that family members are able to structure family life according to beliefs and teaching of the religion. In this instance, families wanting to maintain their membership as part of the religious community structure family life to adhere to religious beliefs.

Islam, the fastest growing religion in the United States, is practiced by Muslims. As a group, Muslims are diverse and originate from the Middle East, Southeast Asia, Africa, and the United States. Although they differ in terms of specific cultures, Muslim families have in common the fact that they are guided by Islam. African Americans who have converted to Islam make up approximately 40% of Muslims in the United States. Although they are guided by the same religious beliefs, little interaction exists between African American and immigrant Muslims.

Muslims have been targets of prejudice and discrimination, primarily because so little is known about the religion and the customs, values, and behaviors that emerge from its teachings. Mistrust and suspicion of Muslims as a group increased following the September 11, 2001, bombing of the World Trade Center and the Pentagon. Because of the strong sense of family and the desire to adhere to Islamic traditions, Muslims tend to be inwardly focused on community (Sherif, 1999). They would likely fall within the acculturation and enculturation position on the Assimilation-Enculturation Continuum because they attempt to maintain ethnic and religious identity while incorporating sufficient dominant-culture behaviors to allow for interaction with major social institutions.

Muslim families exhibit a collective orientation, with a focus on the extended family and practices that are guided by tenets outlined in the Qur'an

(Koran). The family unit is the foundation of social, economic, and religious activities, with responsibility for family members going beyond the nuclear family (Carolan, 1999; Sherif, 1999). Unlike many families discussed earlier, specific roles and responsibilities for Muslim family members emanate from religious as opposed to social dictates.

Much attention has been given to gender relations in Muslim families, particularly because these differ from dominant-culture ideals of social roles for and interactions between men and women. Muslims believe in innate different yet complementary roles for the sexes. According to the teaching of the Qur'an, gender interactions are to be restricted and controlled. Thus, men and women do not intermingle unless they are related to each other. Men are the major authority figures in the home, and all men have the obligation to provide for women in their families, whether the relationship is that of wife–husband, sister–brother, mother–son, or daughter–father. While male Muslims living in the United States have more flexibility to mix with the dominant-culture way of life, women are more restricted. Much of the control over unmarried women, in particular, is a result of the expectation that they will marry a Muslim man. Marriage for Muslim men and women is not a social choice, but a religious obligation with parents often playing a role in the choice of a mate.

Mothers are idolized in the Muslim community, given their roles to care for and nurture children. The presence of children in Muslim families not only ensures that the family line is continued, but is also believed to strengthen marriages. Children have entitlements under Islamic law, with family obligations associated with their care and protection outlined in the Qur'an in ways not so unlike obligations outlined for husband and wife (Sherif, 1999). As in some traditional Asian American families, Muslim children are expected to not question parental authority, and parents play instrumental roles in major life decisions such as whom their offspring will marry. The elderly are also entitled to care, and it is the legal responsibility of children to care for their elderly parents should the need arise.

Inquiry and Reflection 3E: Keeping in mind the legal separation between church and state, how should schools interact with families for whom religion is the major foundation for day-to-day functioning?

CONCLUDING COMMENTS

Diversity among families in the United States results from the interaction of family characteristics, including family structure, ethnicity, socioeconomic status, and religion, all of which influence the values and behaviors among different families. These differences also affect goals and expectations for children in various families. Teachers may initially feel overwhelmed when faced with a classroom of students having diverse backgrounds. Yet the more teachers and other school personnel understand about all children and the context in which they live, the more they will be able to minimize the effects of **psychosocial distances** between themselves and the children and parents with whom they work. Key to success in working with students and parents from multiple family backgrounds and structures will be the ability of teachers and other school personnel to understand and incorporate family differences into school and classroom policies, procedures, and practices.

GUIDED OBSERVATIONS

3F. Conduct a scan of your observation classroom and construct a chart of the various ethnic–cultural and socioeconomic status backgrounds represented by students in the classroom.

3G. Focus on the behavior and attitudes of ethnic minority students in your class. Where would you would place each of these students on the Assimilation-Enculturation Continuum. Write a brief summary comparing and contrasting intergroup behaviors and attitudes among these students.

Chapter 4

Sources of Comfort, Sources of Distress: Neighborhoods and Communities

The previous chapters have addressed family life as influenced by characteristics of the family unit. It is also important to understand community and neighborhood attributes and the influence of these on the nature and quality of life experienced by different families. Families may choose to live in specific communities for a variety of reasons. Community attributes, including socioeconomic status and the ethnic–cultural makeup of residents in an area, are important to some families. Some may choose more homogeneous communities, whereas others seek diversity in their community or neighborhood. The proximity of a neighborhood to place of employment, social and cultural opportunities, or extended family are a consideration for some families. Some families choose densely populated areas, others may seek pastoral conditions offered by sparsely populated areas. Families with children may emphasize the level of safety and reputation of schools within the community when choosing a place to live. At the same time, some families have limited choice of where to live, restricted by the cost of housing or proximity to public transportation, among other things, even when they consider the neighborhood to be not especially safe or welcoming.

Communities are dynamic entities with multiple interrelated dimensions, all of which influence the lives of families and thus the process of schooling within their boundaries. This chapter explores the social, cultural, and economic influences that shape the multiple meanings of "community," and the impact different community environments have on families.

THE MEANING OF COMMUNITY

In a recent account of a decline in civic life, Putnam (2000) asked the following questions: "Is life in communities as we enter the 21st century really so different after all from the reality of American communities in the 1950s and 1960s?... Do we really know our neighbors less well than our parents did?... Are strangers less trustworthy?... Are [baby] boomers and [generation] X'ers really less engaged in community life?" (p. 26). As a preliminary response to his questions, Putnam suggested that for the first two thirds of the 20th century, Americans were actively involved in the social and political lives of their communities, tended to be more charitable to the less fortunate, and were generally trusting of others. According to Putnam, these dispositions gave way to tendencies to be less giving of time and money to others, less likely to attend church or community meetings for collective deliberation, and less trusting of strangers. In short, Putnam speculated that Americans of the last third of the century became less community focused. The notion of the "community" in decline parallels that of the traditional family in decline—generally in the late 1960s and early 1970s. A number of factors contributed to the changes in community among Americans, some which can be more clearly understood by exploring the complex and dynamic dimensions of "community."

COMMUNITY AS PLACE

Communities may be described by geographic location and population density. For example, the Bureau of Census categorizes continuously built-up places and surrounding densely populated areas that collectively have 50,000 or more people as **urban areas.** They label areas having at least 2,500 people living outside of urban areas **"urban places,"** and areas with fewer than 2,500 people living outside of urban places as **rural.** Although it is common to view places in terms of a rural–urban dichotomy, a rural–urban continuum more accurately describes these living places in contemporary America. To catagorize community places as urban or rural leaves out opportunities to explore places having both urban and rural characteristics in terms of living activity. Furthermore, the notion of rural places as pastoral settings of closely knit traditional families is being disrupted by changes that urbanize these places to some extent. For example, residential developments and shopping malls are routinely built in rural places, influencing the lifestyles of those living in the area (Sharpe, 2001). Both rural and urban areas are often diverse with respect to ethnicity, class, or both making it possible to discuss how social and economic differences affect community in both areas. In fact, social and economic trends have been contributing to changes in both rural and urban areas for a number of years, with new communities being created and old communities being reinvented by new inhabitants and new life activities in specific areas.

Rural and Small-Town Communities

Although most Americans live in urban areas, the out-migration from cities to suburbs that began in the 1950s continues. Suburbanization is associated with greater segregation by race, class, education, and lifestyle. The phrase "White and middle-class flight" refers to the event of middle- to upper-middle-class, well-educated families moving to suburbs with little ethnic and economic diversity. Although most suburbs are inhabited by White and middle- to upper-class families, these living areas exist along the socioeconomic continuum ranging from upper class to working class and may also be predominantly African American, Latino, or Asian American. Despite the fact that some suburbs are segregated by race and class, others are more diverse and remain relatively stable with little out-migration by families of a specific race or class.

A more recent phenomenon is the growth of "exurbs," which are communities located outside of suburbs. It is believed by some policy analysts that these communities are the most recent version of White flight (Achs, 1992). Exurbs allow residents to live greater distances from cities, as they change their commute from suburb to city to exurbs to suburbs. When corporations locate headquarters in suburbs, employees can choose to move beyond suburbs into more rural areas. As a result, exurbs offer proximity to corporate jobs, tend to have low-density population, low crime rates, and excellent schools. Newcomers to rural areas are able to enjoy the slow pace of country life with employment, cultural events, and health care facilities nearby.

Exurbs are often the result of **urban sprawl,** which is the act of housing developments spreading beyond city limits. Critics of urban sprawl maintain that open spaces, wetlands, and farmlands are lost as more development occurs in these places. Furthermore, in many instances, workplace and place of residence are separate, resulting in the growth of **bedroom communities.** According to Putnam (2000), a sense of connection among residents is often lessened when substantial numbers of residents work outside the community in which they live. Community engagement is reduced in bedroom communities wherever they occur, not only among those who commute, but also among noncommuters whose motivation to be more participatory is lowered by poor attendance at community events.

Corporate families seeking a different lifestyle are not the only newcomers attracted to rural and small-town places. It is projected that rural and small-town areas will benefit from a preference among "baby-boomer" retirees to settle in these communities. These retirees, many of whom will be former dual-career couples, tend to be younger than traditional retirees, highly educated, and well-off. They will likely settle in states having relatively small populations, mild climates, and rural spaces with striking landscapes (Fetto, 1999).

The cultural baggage brought to rural and small-town communities by both corporate families and retirees often alters the social, economic, and political landscape of these areas. For example, corporate families with children increase the school population, and well-educated families characteristically demand high-quality schools for their children. Districts may find themselves having to build more schools and become competitive as they seek to attract high-quality educators. Some rural and small-town areas that were formally places of low crime may see increases in criminal activity, particularly among bored upper-middle-class adolescents. In most instances, old-timers and newcomers coexist in rural areas, which means farms, residential developments, and even exclusive estates might be located in the same area. One would expect that clashes might sometimes occur over differences in needs and expectations of land use among residents of transformed living places.

Finally, it is common for socioeconomic characteristics of an area to be affected by the inflow of newcomers. Retirees settling in an area may create new jobs, the majority of which will be low-skill, low-wage service sector jobs. At the same time, businesses in the area benefit from retiree residents who are less mobile and thus more likely to spend money in the community. With the arrival of corporate families, school districts may see a mix of children from affluent to low socioeconomic status families, as middle- and upper-class families relocate to areas previously populated by substantial numbers of adults employed in low-wage jobs.

Rural and farming communities are also attractive to large corporations, and many farming communities have undergone drastic economic transformation as a result of the increase in corporate farming. Farming communities were at one time the "hallmark of American life" (Albrecht, 1998), later to become a cultural icon epitomizing some of the center-most values of U.S. culture (e.g., self-reliance, independent thinking; Purdy, 1999). Between 1940 and 1992, however, the number of farms declined from 6 million to 2 million, and the population of farming communities plummeted by approximately 75% (Albrecht, 1998). An initial decline was due to the increased use of technology that allowed fewer farmers to farm larger acreage. The farm crisis of 1980s further reduced the number of farmers (Purdy, 1999). During the 1990s, corporations contributed to an increase in the expense and production of agriculture, making it difficult for individual farmers to compete. Development of meat processing plants and the use of technology and genetic engineering, for example, rendered the knowledge and skills of the traditional farmer obsolete (Purdy, 1999). Farm communities were transformed by what Albrecht (1998) referred to as the industrialization of agriculture.

As corporate agriculture grew, communities solely reliant on agriculture for employment experienced population decline, while those able to attract manufacturing and service industries were able to sustain, and in some cases increase, their populations. Economic necessity motivated many young people to leave rural communities because of lack of jobs, resulting in fewer young people staying to start families. Population decline in these areas resulted in a domino effect of fewer students, reduction in school funding, and the challenge of school districts to offer educational programs needed for students remaining in the community. In some communities, demographics changed as a result of the tendency of corporations to choose inexpensive immigrant labor for their plants, leaving the community to absorb the new residents and their families (Purdy, 1999). Schools in these areas faced increased numbers of children and families for whom English was not the primary language spoken in the home.

Urban Communities

The community change experienced by many rural and small-town places is also common in many cities. Cities have historically been centers of economic growth and technological advances, and thus attractive to people seeking to improve their economic status. Consider, for example, the huge wave of immigration between 1890 and 1920 that contributed to the urbanization of the United States, or the migration of African Americans from the South to northern cities during the middle of the 20th century. The possibility of employment as well as the availability of cultural and other recreational activities draws many people to city life.

Neighborhoods in many cities have a dynamic quality that results in change of residents over time. Processes such as **gentrification** and urban revitalization displace residents and, in the latter case, can dismantle complete neighborhoods. Gentrification, however, has both positive and negative influences on a community. When higher income households replace lower income households, the neighborhood is not only improved by renovated homes or apartments, but new businesses may be attracted to the area as well. At the same time, improved homes and apartments increase rent, often outpricing and thus displacing many families who previously lived in the community (Kennedy & Leonard, 2001).

Cities tend to have a variety of neighborhoods where members share the same ethnic, racial, socioeconomic, or religious backgrounds. Immigrants have historically been attracted to areas where familiarity with the language and culture offer comfort and security as they transition into a new life. It is often the case that new immigrants find family and other members of their ethnic–cultural group willing to provide temporary housing, job leads, and other supports needed for relocation.

Even though areas such as Chinatown, Little Cuba, Latino barrios, or predominantly African American neighborhoods provide social (and sometimes economic) support for residents having the same ethnic background, these areas often grew out of segregation policies that restricted the movement of ethnic minorities to certain areas of the city. Other areas become predominantly ethnic minority as result of corresponding processes of **"racial tipping"** and White flight. In this instance, previously segregated White neighborhoods become integrated by ethnic minorities. At some point, "too much diversity" occurs, with the result of White flight. A newly homogenous neighborhood is established—now occupied by ethnic minorities.

Ethnic minorities are not the only groups to establish ethnic communities. Alba, Logan, and Crowder (1997) found that a number of White ethnic neighborhoods (i.e., Italian, Irish, German) established early in the 1900s continue to exist, despite the assimilation and subsequent out-migration of many of its members. In these communities, one would likely find residents of "unmixed" ancestry living in segregated communities that are resistant to integration by ethnic minorities, both native born and immigrant. Even so, the decline of White ethnic communities is associated with a combination of White flight and ethnic-minority integration, particularly from new immigrants (Alba et al., 1997). White ethnic communities that continue to exist are hubs of cultural activity where cultural heritage is visible through use of the native language, restaurants, shops, and other establishments that are culturally representative. Indeed, the community plays a vital enculturalization role of its members, ensuring that they understand values, customs, and traditions of the group. It must also be noted that although White ethnic communities are common to cities, they may also exist in suburbs.

People may also collect in one geographic location based on religious beliefs, thus forming ethnoracial enclaves (e.g., communities that are primarily occupied by Jews, Muslims, Hindus, etc.). Ethnoracial enclaves may include institutions of faith, services, and materials such as religiously approved foods that allow individuals to observe their faith. It may be the case that multiple ethnoracial enclaves are located in close physical proximity, but are separated by religiously homogeneous boundaries (Livezey, 2001).

Inquiry and Reflection 4A: Search newspapers and interview longtime teachers at your school to determine whether recent social and economic transformations have taken place in the community. What impact have these changes had on the school and its families?

Poverty and the Urban Ghetto

Social and economic diversity provides yet another distinct characteristic that separates groups into different neighborhoods. Urban neighborhoods range from wealthy, exclusive living areas to those exhibiting extreme poverty. A **ghetto** is a community enclave inhabited by a group sharing the same ethnic, cultural, social, or religious background. Contemporary urban ghettos are identified as sites of crime, poor housing, high unemployment, and lack of access to services (Willis, 1998).

The African American ghetto is an interesting example of the dynamic nature of communities and provides an instructive example of the impact of social and economic trends and policies on community life. The social isolation of African Americans in inner city areas existed throughout the 20th century. Wilson (1990) suggested that joblessness, welfare dependency, serious crime, drug and alcohol addiction, and high mortality rates did not become characteristics of urban ghettos until the mid-1970s. According to Wilson, inner-city communities prior to the period beginning in the 1960s, "exhibited the features of social organization—including a sense of community, positive neighborhood identification, and explicit norms and sanctions against aberrant behavior" (p. 3). In fact, ghettos were relatively safe for community residents and even frequented by Whites looking to take advantage of culturally based social life in the area.

Ghetto life is commonly understood through cultural explanations that suggest people living in ghettos share attitudes, values, and behaviors that result in a propensity toward violence and other criminal activity, hopelessness, and general unwillingness or inability to improve their life situations. Wilson (1990), however, advanced structural explanations for life in ghettos that focus on specific economic and social changes that negatively influenced life circumstances in many of the country's inner cities. For example, economic restructuring resulted in the transformation of many industries from centers of production and distribution to centers of administration, information exchange, and higher order services that normally require higher levels of skill and education. People having low **educational attainment** and narrow job skills, many of whom initially migrated to cities for manufacturing and distribution jobs, were unable to adapt to transformed work settings. At the same time, a number of businesses exited cities and moved to suburbs. Thus, the decrease in jobs requiring lower levels of education and lower skill levels contributed to the high unemployment rate of inner-city residents. The higher the level of educational attainment, the more insulated one tends to be from shifts in the economy. Large numbers of people with low educational attainment are concentrated in inner cities and thus vulnerable to changes in the economy.

Wilson (1990) also pointed to the change in the social class structure of inner-city neighborhoods as contributing to the current status of ghetto life. He points out that between the 1940s and 1960s, ghettos were places of vertical integration with respect to social class. Middle-class, working-class, and poor African Americans all lived in the same neighborhoods. The period of economic transformation coincided with legal and public policy changes that expanded upward mobility opportunities for more educated and skilled African Americans, however. Improved economic situations led to out-migration of middle- and working-class families from ghettos, leaving behind the truly disadvantaged, and thus leading to the growth of areas of extreme poverty.

Other ethnic-minority communities with structural issues similar to the African American ghetto experience similar challenges. Wilson (1990) speculated that Chinatowns, for example, which have traditionally been stable communities, are exhibiting increases in unemployment, gang and criminal activities, and higher incidences of youth dropping out of school. Others argue that demographic and other structural changes influencing African American poor differently affect some neighborhoods populated by Latino poor (Moore & Pinderhughes, 1993). Massey, Zambrana, and Bell (1995) proposed that the experience of Latinos living in poverty differs from that of African Americans in at least five areas: the role of immigration, group coherence, the meaning of race, ways in which discrimination and segregation have influenced residential patterns, and the ways in which language influences well-being.

Researchers studying the impact of immigration on Latino communities suggest that whereas the concentration of poverty in African American ghettos resulted from out-migration of working- and middle-class African American families, the concentration of poverty in Latino communities is maintained through immigration. Latino immigrants, many of whom are poor, relocate to poor Latino communities, thereby ensuring a concentration of people living in poverty even when out-migration of upwardly mobile Latinos occurs. Furthermore, where the social isolation of the ghetto poor is associated with deteriorated social conditions, high concentrations of Latino poor resulting from an increased immigrant population may actually have a stabilizing effect on the community. According to Moore and Pinderhughes (1993), traditional values are regenerated by entry of immigrants into the community, social controls are revived, social networks are strengthened, and new institutions that specifically address the needs of community members are established. Latinos as a group tend to value the Spanish language, and thus Spanish is used quite liberally in many Latino communities and contributes to the sense of cohesion among community members. This community characteristic, however, results in some Latino immigrants having limited English proficiency, which negatively affects their employment possibilities (Massey et al., 1995).

As suggested in previous chapters, Latinos are a highly diverse group with different places of origin and therefore bring different sociocultural and historical experiences to contemporary life situations. Massey et al. (1995) suggested that Latinos are differently discriminated against in the United States often based on skin color. Where housing and employment experiences of African Americans as a group have been influenced by a historic legacy of discrimination (Wilson, 1990), dark-skinned Latinos are likely to experience more residential segregation and to be differently compensated in the labor market than lighter skinned Latinos (Massey et al., 1995). Thus, poverty communities resembling those of the African American ghetto poor are more likely to be occupied by Puerto Ricans more than other Latino groups.

While economic transformation left many ghetto poor unemployed, Latinos, particularly immigrants, were willing to take on low-wage jobs resulting from consumer service needs (e.g., food service, clothing, care of home and children) of highly paid employees of transformed corporations. In some Latino communities, the consumer needs of the working poor stimulated development of businesses in the community to serve the needs of this population (Moore & Pinderhughes, 1993). On the other hand, the willingness of immigrants to accept low wages resulted in a drop of wages for native-born Latinos working in service-related jobs.

A final difference between places occupied by the ghetto poor in general and Latino poor communities can be explained through Gonzales's (1993) notion of "integrative ties." Integrative ties allow individuals and groups to rely on the history and culture of the group to address contemporary issues. Latino cultural characteristics such as familism, historical experiences that have led to inclination toward political activism, and the value placed on owning property (i.e., home ownership) influence the stability and vitality of many poor Latino communities. The existence of integrative ties are so important in Gonzales's view that areas having high concentrations of poverty and few integrative ties may be less stable and have fewer structural resources to support residents. For example, poverty communities with a mix of ethnic-minority groups might have fewer integrative ties and thus less support for survival and less protection against despair for its members.

COMMUNITY AS SOCIAL NETWORKS

Putnam (2000) described **social networks** as connections among people that result in norms of reciprocity and trust among those who are a part of the network. Social networks can aid cooperation and mutual benefit and may take on a "bonding" or "bridging" character. Bonding networks tend to be inwardly focused and reinforce the exclusive identity and homogeneity of the group. Bridging networks are outwardly focused with a goal of including others in the network. An exclusive country club is an example of a bonding social network, whereas an ecumenical religious organization is an example of a bridging network. Putnam pointed out that the two dimensions are not exclusive, and some organizations may exhibit both. Black churches, for example, exhibit the bonding dimension by bringing together people of the same religion and race and the bridging dimension by bringing together people across socioeconomic lines.

It is plausible to think of communities as having bonding and bridging characteristics as well. Teachers, particularly those who are not a part of the community where they teach but who seek to work with parents or agencies within the community, should make sure they understand the norms of reciprocity and trust among community members. Understanding how networking in the community is structured may influence the strategies used to gain access to people and organizations within the community. It is also important not to assume physical proximity as the sole marker for existence of social networks or community support. A sense of community remains intact for some groups even when separated by physical distance. For example, the notion of an African American "community" implies norms of reciprocity and trust among African Americans who consider themselves part of a "community" that is not limited to geographic location.

Ethnic-Minority Network Systems

Network systems among ethnic-minority groups have some aspects in common, given that these groups characteristically have a legacy of collectivism, extended-family networks, and group loyalty (Hyoun & McKenry, 1998). At the same time, these systems exhibit specific cultural characteristics and functions that address group goals or needs reflective of the sociocultural and historic experiences of different groups. When comparing social networks among African Americans, Asian Americans, and Hispanics, Hyoun and McKenry found that social networks among African Americans play an important role in the provision of psychosocial and, in some instances, financial support, whereas network systems among Asian Americans lean more toward facilitating occupational success. Whereas African Americans as a group are more likely to rely on the church and political organizations as social network sites, Asian Americans are more likely to be members of business groups and voluntary ethnic organizations. Extended kin serve the networking function for Latinos, and these are often connected to other institutions such as the school or church.

The Church as a Network System

In general, churches are sites of additional social networking and support for many groups. African American churches of many denominations and

Catholic churches have historically had strong commitments to service and social action, making them pivotal institutions for social networking in the communities they serve. Churches are sites of shared norms where trust is developed and where parishioners expect support. They may function as a local community or as part of a larger institutional network. For example, members of a local Catholic church may share norms with Catholics throughout the nation, or even the world.

Churches may be involved in community activities and thus may have contact with congregant as well as noncongregational individuals living in the same community. They may provide a number of community services such as space for meetings, meal services, food pantries, transitional housing, tutoring, and after-school programs (Greenberg, 2000). Kozol (2000), for example, described the role played by St. Ann's Episcopal Church in Mott Haven, a neighborhood of extreme poverty located in South Bronx. The church serves multiple community needs ranging from an after-school program to a place where the hungry can get food. The church has a finger on the pulse of the community, and as such is able to see and articulate needs that may not be observable to an outsider. Teachers may find churches an excellent initial contact for understanding the intricacies of community networking, as well as an entry point to a network of organizations serving community needs.

In some instances, church-initiated community activities extend beyond the church walls and denominational divisions, as problems or issues faced by the community as a whole are addressed through ecumenical efforts that bring together a number of faith traditions (Greenberg, 2000). Teachers might investigate the existence of ongoing ecumenical councils in communities having a number of churches of different denominations for support on issues affecting the school and community. Indeed, some churches, either individually or collectively as political entities, may be involved in school issues because they may or may not support positions adopted by school boards.

Organizations as Network Systems

Like churches, other organizations may serve as a social network entity within communities, many of which may be national organizations with local chapters. These organizations may address the cultural, political, legal, or social action needs of various groups and often vary in terms of political and ideological beliefs. For example, the Urban League and National Association for the Advancement of Colored People, both national organizations, have a long-standing presence in the African American community, serving both local and broader African American community needs. The League of United Latin Americans and the National Council of La Raza are political and social action groups focused on the needs of Latinos. Ideological differences influence their goals for and actions on behalf of the Latino community, however. Teachers may wish to generate a list of local organizations along with descriptions of the focus of the organization and make sure that the list is continuously updated. In this way, teachers and other school personnel can access the list for support based on the needs and interests of their students. Remember, a number of organizations may provide help in the form of school supplies, food, or even shelter. They also may support teaching through provision of culturally relevant information or guest speakers.

Ethnic Celebrations as Network Systems

A final network system exists in communities: celebrations in the form of parades, festivals, or other events. Celebrations are bonding events in that they provide an excellent vehicle for members of ethnic–cultural groups to honor a common history or tradition. They may be bridging events in that others are often invited to share in the celebratory occasion and are

Cinco de Mayo Festival: Celebrations are bonding events where members of an ethnic-cultural group honor a common history or tradition. They may be bridging events that allow others to learn what is valued by various groups in a multicultural society. *Picture Courtesy of American GI Forum of San Jose, California, Annual Cinco de Mayo Parade and Festival.*

thus provided the opportunity to learn what is valued by various groups in a multicultural society. Juneteenth celebrations, St. Patrick Day Parades, Cinco de Mayo events, Pow Wows, and Chinese New Year celebrations are events that increase a sense of pride and cohesion among groups. Once again, school personnel may wish to participate in these events as a means for understanding more about what is valued in various communities.

Inquiry and Reflection 4B: Develop and implement a plan for determining the types of social networks existing in the community of your observation site. Are these bridging, bonding, or combination network systems?

COMMUNITIES AS SITES OF COMFORT OR SITES OF DISTRESS

Overt indicators of the quality of life in communities include the condition of housing, the number and kinds of services, and the overall appearance of neighborhoods within a community. Streets lined with two-story homes surrounded by neatly manicured lawns project one image of the quality of life in a community, whereas streets lined with abandoned cars and poorly cared for homes, some of which have been boarded up, project another.

Some communities have convenient and multiple choices of grocery stores, banks, restaurants, gas stations, and movie theaters that are not available to other communities. Businesses such as pawn shops, pay-day loan businesses, and furniture rental stores may locate in some communities, but not others. External signs of comfort and distress exist in many communities and provide at least initial indicators of the well-being of the communities' families and children. Because public schools are usually populated by students living within assigned attendance boundaries, school environments are unavoidably influenced by the quality of life existing in specific locations. As a result, schools located in communities having concentrated poverty, for example, encounter issues and conditions associated with poverty. In the same way, schools located in high-income areas with high concentrations of well-educated parents are affected by issues and conditions associated with that particular community.

Some school districts have magnet schools or other school sites where school choice options allow parents to determine the school their children attend. These schools will likely have diverse students from various neighborhoods. Given population shifts in rural areas, some schools located in these communities have diverse student populations, often with respect to socioeconomic status, and others remain more homogeneous. Suffice to say, the work of schools is inevitably affected not only by family characteristics but also by the community in which the school is located. Community conditions contribute to the comfort or distress for children and their families, and, as one might expect, affect the school climate as well.

Educational Conditions

Socioeconomic and ethnic–racial characteristics of neighborhoods or communities can be correlated with the level of success in educating children and youth living in the community (Anyon, 1997). Anyon proposed that a city's level of investment in the education of children corresponds to characteristics of the neighborhood. Generally, when neighborhoods become poorer and less White, schools in the community decline. Using the city of Newark, New Jersey, as an example, she suggested that the city's school system was a model for other cities to emulate when Newark was an industrial leader with a majority of higher-middle-class families. The lack of jobs, inadequate school funding, and White and middle-class flight combined to contribute to deterioration of the city's schools.

Inadequate funding leads to lack of books, supplies, and other equipment that support the education of children, as well as the lack of physical maintenance of school buildings. Poorly funded districts also have higher levels of dropouts, more teachers teaching in fields that do not match their education and backgrounds, and more teacher shortages (Anyon, 1997). School districts receive funds to deliver education from local, state, and federal sources. Local funds are based on property taxes, and funding from this source can constitute up to half of the district's funding. State government contributions provide the bulk of the balance of school funding, as federal contributions hover in the single digits. Communities having expensive homes and substantial numbers of businesses have a larger local tax base potentially to support schools. Some states attempt to provide more state aid to poor districts with less ability to generate funds at the local level than wealthier districts.

Inquiry and Reflection 4C: In some instances, communities may not support their schools (e.g., they may not support a tax levy). Interview a school-board member for the district of your observation site to determine his or her perception of the level of support for education existing in the community. What are the reasons for the lack of support from community members?

The lack of a sufficient local tax base that allows for funds necessary to address the education of high-needs students is a primary source for the overall disparity in education offered in many urban and suburban school districts. Generally, suburban school districts have sufficient funds to purchase appropriate and adequate educational equipment and supplies, as well as resources to build and maintain high-quality school buildings. In some instances, they are able to pay higher salaries than is possible in urban districts, which allows them to attract and retain high-quality teachers. Consequently, they tend to have higher levels of educational achievement (as measured by standardized tests), fewer out-of-field teachers, and fewer teacher shortages compared with urban schools. Disparities in the ability to deliver education can also exist between schools within the same school district. Schools serving large numbers of high-need students may not have sufficient funds to meet students' learning needs, even when the addition of federal funds is considered.

Schools within the same district may differ in terms of the amount and character of community and parental involvement in and support of the school. For example, distressed communities and neighborhoods may have limited human and financial resources to provide the kind or level of support available in a community located in a middle-class neighborhood. A parent living in a distressed neighborhood may struggle to feed and clothe his or her child, with little energy to contribute to school activities and events that support the work of schools. In this instance, school personnel may look to community agencies for support. The situation may differ

Case 4A: Parental and Community Support for Schools

Parents at two Shawnee Mission [Kansas] elementary schools have raised nearly $120,000—enough to save the jobs of five staff members whose jobs were about to be cut. . . . Parents at Prairie donated $45,912 in about a week. They will retain their full-time nurse and reading teacher. . . . At Belinder Elementary, parents raised $72,751. . . . The money was raised in a few weeks. Parents at some schools are afraid that the fund-raising efforts will create inequity in the district, which covers several Johnson County cities. Some schools will lose staff members because their communities will not be able to raise the money . . . At Briarwood, the PTA is pitching in about $20,000 to pay for a classroom aide. A separate group will work over the summer to raise money for its nurse, counselor and Spanish teacher. Parents said they had raised about $15,000 of their $70,000 goal.

From: Johnson County parents raise $120,000 to avoid staff cuts at schools. *The Morning Sun.* Web Posted May 4, 2002. http://www.morningsun.net/stories/050402/kan_0504020016.shtml

substantially in middle-class neighborhoods where parents may support the work of schools directly through their involvement, or indirectly through activities and experiences they are able to purchase outside of school. Music lessons, private tutors, and travel, for example, can contribute to students' academic and social development. Middle-class parents often have skills and resources that lead to financial support of neighborhood schools as well. As noted in case 4A, parents' fundraising abilities, for example, can have a significant impact on school environments.

Lack of adequate funding is an issue for some rural schools as well, making it more difficult for some rural districts to reach educational outcomes achieved by districts located in higher socioeconomic communities. As suggested earlier, the population decline in many rural communities negatively affects the amount of funding available for the delivery of education. Furthermore, rural schools may have difficulty attracting and retaining teachers, particularly younger teachers who have yet to start a family and who determine that a particular community offers few possibilities for finding a mate. Sharpe (2001) pointed out that despite the propensity to see themselves as being in competition, many urban and rural districts may have in common the problem of inadequate resources to serve the needs of their schools environments.

Inquiry and Reflection 4D: Parents and the community in Case 4A were willing and able to support schools their children attended with funds to retain positions. Other parents were concerned about the possibility of inequities in the district. As a teacher, would you welcome this type of financial support from parents and the community?

Health Conditions

A relationship exists between the socioeconomic context of a community and the health of residents living there. Environmental conditions, shared knowledge and beliefs among ethnic or socioeconomic groups regarding health practices, and access to health care result in communities reflecting similar health practices and conditions. Researchers continue to study whether the association is due to the sum health conditions of individuals living within a particular community context, or if characteristics of the community itself contribute to health conditions of community residents (Robert, 1999). Some ethnic groups have higher incidences of certain diseases (e.g., African Americans with hypertension, Native Americans, African Americans, Hispanic Americans, and Asian and Pacific Islanders with type 2 diabetes), and diet, smoking, exercise, substance abuse, and incidence of

HIV and AIDS can be linked to socioeconomic status (Zambrana, Dorrington & Hayes-Bautista, 1995). Thus, the work of schools can be influenced by the overall health of the community in which the school is located.

Clearly environmental conditions affect the health and well-being of children in certain communities. Environmentally unjust practices, for example, have resulted in disadvantaged areas, principally those inhabited by poor and ethnic minority residents, being dumping sites for a disproportionate share of environmentally hazardous materials. These practices can contribute to areas where higher incidences of illnesses, such as childhood asthma, are evident in a particular community or neighborhood (Kozol, 2000). Environmental conditions can interact with other specific community conditions and result in higher incidences of ill health among children. For example, emissions from heavy traffic in close proximity to communities made up of older building where lead-based paint was used results in higher concentrations of children with elevated lead blood levels that affect not only their physical health, but can have damaging cognitive effects as well.

The social and economic health of a community also has an impact on the physical health of children. The declining population of rural areas has resulted in hospital closings and an overall shortage of health care professionals, which creates problems with adequate health services. These areas may also be sites where the poor are uninsured and where high rates of chronic illnesses persist. Flynt (1996), in his review of living conditions among the rural poor, suggested that traditional folkways and religious beliefs negatively influence the health of residents of rural poor communities. Diets that contribute to increases in heart attack, stroke, and cancer are tied to traditional folkways. Also, religious-based beliefs sustain the ill advisability of attempting to prevent disease and death. These beliefs, when combined with lack of health insurance and limited health care facilities, result in the rural poor not receiving needed health services.

Although cities are more likely to have quality facilities, low-income families are less likely to make use of these services, except in emergencies. Distrust, as a by-product of interactions with health care professionals who are insensitive to the needs of the urban poor in general and ethnic minorities in particular, results in families avoiding health care facilities (Barrett et al., 1998; Flores & Vega, 1998; Sharpe, 2001). Parents may resist going to medical establishments where their expectations for kind, caring providers with positive attitudes are quashed by interaction with insensitive medical professionals (Barrett et al., 1998). Relatedly, language barriers lead some parents to not seek health care for their children at medical establishments where English is the only language spoken. Finally, parental beliefs about the cause and treatment of an illness may lead others to use home remedies rather than the health care system (Barrett et al., 1998; Flores & Vega, 1998).

A number of families living in cities have no health insurance or what Flores and Vega (1998) referred to as episodic insurance, meaning that insurance may be discontinued because of loss of employment. Poor families often fill emergency rooms for illnesses that could seemingly be addressed by a visit to the family doctor. In many instances, the lack of insurance will send these families to hospitals where they must be treated, regardless of their health insurance status.

Schools depend on children having adequate health care, as health affects school attendance and performance. Children need access to comprehensive and ongoing health care that includes physical and dental exams, hearing and vision screening, immunizations, and preventive and sick care (America's Children, 2000b). Teachers face children with a range of illnesses, from the common cold to HIV/AIDS or other chronic illnesses. Overall, health conditions of children in the United States are reportedly good to excellent with disparity existing between poor and affluent families. Still, when schools are located in areas with high concentrations of unhealthy children, the level of education teachers are able to deliver is diminished.

Safety and Overall Well-Being

Safety can have multiple meanings, particularly when it is viewed as a state of affairs that affects the well-being of children. All children need and deserve an environment in which to grow and develop that is caring and one that ensures safety from hunger, physical harm, and emotional injury. With the advent of the modern American family, this responsibility was given to individual families in spite of the social, economic, and environmental constraints that challenge the ability of some families to address this responsibility.

Case 4B: Community Conflicts

> *. . . the little ones get into it, then their parents want to get into it . . . you know, instead of saying . . . "stop babies, let's don't fight, let's get along with each other, we got to stay in the same neighborhood . . ." there be the parents out there wanting to fight with the little kids. Yea, so that kind of stuff, that will keep you all upset. So, mostly I keep them [her children] in the house. But I know they get tired of staying in the house. Oh, it's something living out here.* (Ella, a low-income single mother)

Conditions such as community violence and other crimes, as well as high incidences of illness and death, are distressful to children and influence their sense of well-being. Distressful conditions also result from high incidences of family mobility and high levels of anonymity or tension between families in a community. Children and youth in these communities may not sense a consensus of care among adults in the community. Compare, for example, the experience of the mother in Case 4B with the period in history when young people received guidance and discipline from any number of adults in a community. The lack of strong, caring communities negatively affects the well-being of children—so much so that an increasing number of researchers believe growing up in distressed neighborhoods has an impact over and above individual or family background characteristics (America's Children, 2000b).

Families remain in communities with overt signs of distress for a variety of reasons. According to Flynt (1996), the rural poor may live in communities with substandard housing, poorly funded schools, and high concentrations of people with health problems because of a desire to be physically located within close proximity to family and church. Others, he contended, remain for fear that lack of education and skill limits their chances for success in a different environment. Mexican American families are concentrated in barrios, another community commonly viewed as having characteristics typical of distressed communities (Delgado & Barton, 1998). Although these communities are made up of low- and working-class families lacking resources of communities with a higher socioeconomic status, strong social networks are evident. These communities are also sites where traditional Mexican American cultural values and norms are reinforced (Chahin et al., 1999). Hence, communities having characteristics that overtly suggest distress may have community strengths that contribute to the well-being of community residents.

Affluent communities are often viewed as places of comfort, providing high levels of safety for children and other residents. Even though these communities have environmental, economic, or social conditions believed to have a positive influence on community life, some suffer distressing situations brought about by the behavior of both male and female youths. Recreational use of drugs and alcohol exists in these communities, and it is common for youth to be involved with burglary, vandalism, and other crime. Other unsafe behaviors, such as group sex parties, take place among community youth that can create health issues affecting a total community. The outbreak of syphilis in an affluent Atlanta suburb that infected 200 young people is a case in point (Walter, 2001). As another example, the nation as whole was shocked by the rash of school shootings that took place in communities believed to be distant from such crimes. As Wise (2001) pointed out although violence certainly exists in urban schools and communities, recent mass murders have taken place in suburban and rural communities. Community residents' perceptions of high levels of safety for their children

Children are likely to be involved in gangs if they:
- have low school involvement
- live in homes in the midst of family change
- live in homes where parental discord exists
- live in homes of low-level family cohesion/supervision
- live in a high-crime/-violence neighborhood or community
- live in communities in ethnic or economic transition

Figure 4.1 Gang involvement.
From: Evans, Fitzgerald, and Dan Chvilicek (1999).

were shattered by school shootings, as many reacted with confusion, disbelief, and sometimes anger.

Youth living in various communities have an impact on the climate of comfort and distress in their communities, often in reaction to family and community conditions. Gang activity, by both girls and boys, causes distress in communities, whether located in urban, suburban, or rural areas. According to Vigil (1999), gang membership among urban Chicano children involves a process of street socialization in which survival and coping strategies are learned to address dangers and lack of opportunities encountered in the community. He suggested that values and skills learned on the street compete with those available in the home and school, with street learning often the winner. Children, he maintained, find parental, teacher, and law enforcement models embodied in long-term gang members (Figure 4.1).

Gang activity, however, is not limited to urban areas. Evans, Fitzgerald, and Dan Chvilicek (1999) reported that gang activity exists in urban, suburban, and rural areas, although children in different areas experience gang involvement differently. Furthermore, the presence of gangs affects communities differently. Although it has commonly been assumed that the rise of rural gangs was the result of urban gang members relocating to rural areas, it appears more the case that rural gangs are "home grown." Still, a major difference between urban and rural communities where gangs exist is that rural youth feel safer and are not threatened by the presence of gangs in their communities (Evans et al., 1999). Even though their locals are different, Evans et al. (1999) suggested that a common set of variables contribute to gang membership in urban or rural settings (Figure 4.1).

Gang activity and violent and criminal acts can menace a total community. Community residents in some neighborhoods fight back through community action that might include organizing neighborhood watches where community residents call police at the first sign of unusual activity, working with law enforcement agencies to shut down "crack houses" that operate in the neighborhood, or staging marches to make public the resistence to distressing conditions. Symbolic group or individual actions against the tyranny of neighborhood violence is often a statement against helplessness and an attempt to regain ownership of one's living space. Even as the woman in Case 4C expresses the emotional duress she felt about a young man's death, the cleaning away of blood symbolizes a need to return to a sense of normalcy in her community.

Case 4C: Neighborhood Watch

I woke up at 5 this morning to the sound of a motor droning outside my bedroom window and flashing red and white lights reflecting along the wall. I got up and looked out the window and saw a fire truck, an ambulance, and four police cars parked across the street blocking the entrance to the alley. I threw my bathrobe on over my nightgown and went down the stairs.... I stepped out into the morning. It was still dark... and... chilly. Across the street, two newsmen talked in low tones as they pulled their cameras out of their vans. "What happened?" I asked. "There's a dead man in the alley, ma'am," the younger one replied. I was stunned, even though I had guessed already that there'd been a murder. A crowd began to gather, oblivious, it seemed, to the cold air, the early morning blackness and the drizzling rain, as they stared down the alley past the yellow ribbon to the bloody body that lay several feet ahead.

"I need to see his face," I muttered to no one in particular. I was desperate to see if he was someone I knew, perhaps one of the kids for whom my home had been a haven when my children were growing up. I eased my way to the outskirts of the crowd and stood like a statue until I was sure no one was watching me.... I took a deep breath and walked slowly toward the body, constantly looking over my shoulder, hoping to get close enough to get a good look at him before they pulled the sheet up over his face. A deep sadness came over me as I looked at the still figure of a young black man. He couldn't have been more than 19, maybe 20 years old. He was lying face up. His L.A. Raiders cap, soaked in blood, lay inches away from his head. The stiff, dark fingers on his right hand were frozen around a McDonald's paper cup as though he'd been struggling to hold onto it, and cold coffee spilled over his hand and onto the concrete. "Oh, Jesus," I moaned. And I began to weep. I wept for that boy's poor mother and for the mothers of the children who have died in wars they didn't plan. I guess I just mourned for all the mothers in this country, the only place in the world where young black men get blown away every day over a pair of sneakers, the wrong colors, or a cup of cold coffee. I stood watch over the body until the coroner finally pronounced him dead and took him to the County Morgue. Then I went home and filled a pail with water and got myself some rags. I went back out into the alley, got down on my hands and knees and I scrubbed and scrubbed until all the blood that the rain hadn't washed away was gone. (Holbrook-Montgomery, 1992)

CONCLUDING COMMENTS

Communities vary in terms of location, size, social and economic resources, and the makeup of people within their boundaries. They are dynamic entities that are transformed over time in response to social, economic, and cultural influences. Many communities in the contemporary United States appear to lack community cohesiveness, and there appears to be limited collective engagement among too many residents living in the same community. This phenomenon concurs with the call for increased school, family, and community partnerships to address the emotional, social, and educational needs of children and youth. Conditions such as the detachment between schools and communities may well be an extension of the detachment existing among residents in particular communities, however. The lack of collective community goals is reflected in, and perhaps to some degree caused by, community families that have more individual than collective goals for education. These conditions will continue to challenge school, family, and community collaboration.

Inquiry and Reflection 4E: Describe the community of your childhood. How is the community of your observation site similar to or different from conditions familiar to you?

All communities have the potential to contribute to the education of children and youth—even those communities with limited economic resources. Understanding the norms and values of a community, as well as the impact of certain conditions on life in certain communities, provides teachers an excellent starting point for working with families in specific community environments.

GUIDED OBSERVATIONS

4F. Write a detailed description of the community surrounding your observation site that focuses on the "community as place" dimension. Make sure to include recent social and economic transformations that may have influenced the community.

4G. Describe the health and overall safety conditions existing in the community surrounding your observation site. How do health and safety conditions affect the school environment?

4H. Take a tour of the community surrounding your observation site. What are the overt signs of community comfort or community distress? Make sure to take note of businesses and services located within close proximity of the school neighborhood.

4I. Community conflicts similar to those described in Case 4A potentially find ways into the school environment. What evidence have you observed of community conflicts and concerns spilling onto your observation site?

Part II

UNDERSTANDING SCHOOL–FAMILY INTERACTIONS: SOCIAL, POLITICAL, LEGAL, AND EDUCATIONAL ISSUES

Numerous studies suggest that children and youth with parents involved in their education are more likely to perform better academically, have higher attendance and graduation rates, and have higher aspirations than children with parents not involved in their education (U.S. Department of Education, 2001). Still, perceptions persist among school personnel and even society at large that too many parents are not involved in the education of their children and that this circumstance contributes to low school performance. It is for this reason that schools are being challenged to construct policies and practices designed to increase involvement of parents in education both at home and within schools. This project has been assigned to schools based on research proposing that parental involvement is influenced more by school and teacher practices than the structure, ethnic–cultural, or socioeconomic background of families, or even the educational attainment of parents (U.S. Department of Education, 2001).

Chapter 5 begins Part II with a discussion of social, political, and legal events that skyrocketed parental involvement into the limelight as a missing link in strategies to support academic achievement among children and youth from all socioeconomic and ethnic–cultural backgrounds. An important part of this discussion is the effort to define parental involvement and associated practices needed to ensure its fruition. As with any social, political, or legal agenda, parental involvement comes with critics who question the extent to which parental involvement will contribute to more equitable educational outcomes for all children. Even so, a variety of structured parental involvement programs and organizations coexist, with a common goal of supporting parents' involvement in education.

Sociopolitical influences on parental involvement efforts of schools exist alongside attributes parents bring to the school–family nexus that may challenge or support schools' parental involvement practices. Parents are, after all, adults who bring a range of social, psychological, and educational attributes to the act of parenting. Chapter 6 surveys parental attributes that teachers are likely to encounter.

Underlying all parent, teacher, and community collaborations are issues of authority, responsibility, and control among adults in the lives of children. Indeed, much of the parental involvement literature positions school personnel as persons in charge of initiating and sustaining the involvement of parents in the educational lives of their children. Chapter 7 explores the nature of authority and responsibility as they relate to school–family relations, and the tension and discord that often accompanies differing perceptions of the appropriate domain of the school, and that of the home.

Chapter 5

From Political Agenda to Academic Strategy: The Sociopolitical Context of School–Family Relations

Parental involvement as a major influence on the effective education of children and youth has received increased attention over the last 30 years, even as the educational community struggled to give meaning to what is now understood to be a multifaceted and complex act. Nevertheless, the notion of "parental involvement" caught the attention of the media and the political community as a strategy that needed to be emphasized if the educational performance of all children and youth was to increase. Many school personnel were convinced as well that more involvement by parents was needed for children to improve academically. This chapter begins with an examination of the educational, social, and political events that led to a focus on parental involvement as a strategy to improve academic performance. A discussion of meanings attributed to parental involvement follows, with an exploration of the efficacy of these interpretations within social, political, and educational contexts. The chapter concludes with a brief overview of the purposes and goals of representative parental involvement programs that are currently operating in the nations school's and communities.

LEGISLATING PARENTAL INVOLVEMENT

Direct involvement of parents in the education of children has not always been viewed favorably by educators. In the late 1950s, James Conant (1959), a noted spokesperson on issues related to education and a proponent of tracking students according to ability, blamed demanding middle-class parents and nonassertive school managers for the failure on the part of school systems to identify and properly educate truly academically talented youth on one hand and to provide for the vocational education of the less academically talented on the other. Middle-class parents, he proclaimed, advocated college preparatory classes for their children even when they did not have the "aptitude for college work" (p. 47). They demanded an "academic" curriculum be available in schools for college-bound youth and that enrollment in these classes be unrestricted. Conant, however, viewed the identification of "truly" talented youth as a national imperative. The actions of middle-class parents, he surmised, hindered the identification of youth who would ensure the nation's need for sufficient numbers of doctors, engineers, and scientists would be actualized. The notion of parents "interfering" with the work of schools by demanding certain types of curricula, learning environments, school personnel, or otherwise questioning decisions made by educators continues to be one argument among some educators against increased parental involvement.

A second element of Conant's argument, that of the role of schools in preparing children to serve national needs as adults, provides, at least in part, a basis for understanding how parental involvement became a national agenda. For more than a half century before Conant expressed his views, public schools and not the family had become the primary institution charged to prepare children for their adult roles as good citizens and productive workers. Prior to 1954, the federal government honored the notion of state and local control of public education by imposing few policy directives and by providing limited funding to local school districts. In the mid-1950s, however, the federal government targeted several specific educational issues believed to be of interest to the national welfare. The courses of these issues were controlled through legislation and federal funding. School desegregation, vocational education, education for national defense, and the educational experiences of "culturally and economically disadvantaged children and youth" were among issues of interest to the federal government (Bailey & Mosher, 1968).

The Elementary and Secondary Education Act (ESEA) of 1965 was unprecedented because it allowed for direct federal intervention into the work of schools. Federal funds were provided for schools to develop projects directed toward the special educational needs of children believed to be educationally deprived because of their economic and cultural backgrounds. Provisions were also made for the improvement of libraries, the purchase of textbooks, and other instructional resources, the development of educational service centers and state departments of education, and to support educational research (Bailey & Mosher, 1968). Since its inception in 1965, the ESEA has undergone eight revisions and extensions. Nonetheless, absent from the original attempt on the part of the federal government to influence the educational achievement of disadvantaged children was any reference to the role of families in that effort.

ESEA's Mandate for Parental Involvement

Where ESEA of 1965 made no provisions for parental involvement, the Education Amendments Act of 1978, passed to extend and amend the ESEA of 1965, made explicit references to parent participation in programs designed for educationally deprived children. According to the law, federal funds would only be extended to school districts having programs for educationally deprived children in which parents "are permitted to participate in the establishment of such programs and are informed of and permitted to make recommendations with respect to the instructional goals of the program and progress of their children in such programs, and such parents are afforded opportunities to assist their children in achieving such goals" (Pub. L. 95-561, 1978, § 124j). More pointedly with respect to academic success, Section 207, Title II, of the Education Amendments Act provided funds for activities designed to "enlist the assistance of parents and volunteers working with schools to improve the skills of children in reading, mathematics, and oral and written communication." Fund-worthy activities included the "development and dissemination of materials that, with appropriate training, parents may use in the home to improve their children's performance in those skills" (Pub. L. 95-561, 1978, § 207). Consequently, funds were made available to encourage closer contact between parents and teachers to better coordinate school and home-learning experiences.

Although primarily directed at educationally deprived children, Title II, the Basic Skills component of the Education Amendments Act of 1978, stated that a comprehensive basic skills program that addressed the needs of *all* children should be developed by parents, teachers, and school administrators. The Education Amendments Act of 1978 was preceded by Public Law 94-142, the Education for All Handicapped Children Act of 1975, which listed safeguards to parents or guardians of "handicapped children." In this instance, federal law focused on the rights of parents or guardians to review records related to identification, evaluation, and placement activities of handicapped children. The parental involvement language of the Education Amendments Act of 1978 extended well beyond issues of informed consent in that it explicitly and prescriptively stated appropriate relations between the school and the home, while implying parental behaviors needed to support academic improvement among children and youth.

What precipitated the dramatic shift from no mention of parental involvement in ESEA of 1965 to language that emphasized the role of parents in the education of children and youth in 1978? At least part of the answer can be found in the clash between the ways in which low-income parents and parents of color were perceived in the mid-1960s and the burgeoning sense of self-empowerment among people of color in general, but particularly among African Americans, that confronted this view. The conceptualization of poor and minority parents that emerged from a University of Chicago research conference in 1964 reflected views held among many distinguished and respected educators and scholars during this period. Leaders in the fields of psychology, sociology, education, and human development convened to discuss cultural deprivation and its effect on education (Bloom, Davis, & Hess, 1965). The scholars cited social change as having a profound effect on the educational system; this social change included an industrialized society that required more literate individuals, along with demands by and governmental responsiveness to "subgroups" (i.e., minority ethnic groups) for education that would allow for more opportunity to compete in an increasingly affluent society.

They agreed that they must first address the substantial group of students not making "normal" academic progress, a group they described as "students whose early experiences in the home, whose motivation for present school learning, and whose goals for the future are such as to handicap them in schoolwork" (p. 4). This group of students, they determined, was

> culturally disadvantaged or culturally deprived, because we believe the roots of their problems may in large part be traced to their experiences in homes which do not transmit cultural patterns necessary for the types of learning characteristic of the schools and the larger society. (p. 4)

Cultural deprivation, they wrote "should not be equated with race [*even though*].... It is true that a large number of Negro[1] children, especially those from homes with functionally illiterate parents are likely to be culturally deprived" (p. 4). They believed awareness of cultural deprivation among an estimated two thirds of African American children living in large cities was aided by the Civil Rights movement and "the rearrangement of Whites and Negroes in the large cities with regard to place of residence and school attendance" (p. 5). Since the United States, in the judgment of conference attendees, had accomplished the dilemma of *access* to education for most children in the country, in their view, the country now needed "compensatory education which can prevent or overcome early deficiencies in the development of each individual" (p. 6).

The scholars had basically articulated the discontinuity that existed between the values, behaviors, customs, and language existing in African

---

[1] Negro was an acceptable term for African Americans in the mid-1960s.

American homes and the nation's public schools, evaluating the former to be a setting of deprivation. The evidence for their evaluation was based on the belief that middle-class homes engaged child-rearing practices and the type of experiences that supported the educational success of their children—generally articulating the continuity between middle-class homes and public school. They were of the opinion that where low-income and African American parents were unable to support the intellectual development of their children, the school must.

The notion of the culturally deprived child corresponded to "incompetence" among parents of African American children living in poverty. The goal of Head Start and other compensatory education programs was to mitigate shortcomings of these parents. Given this view, parental involvement was not necessary for the education of poor and African American children, presumably because their parents were part of the problem, and not instrumental to the solution.

Inquiry and Reflection 5A: How were your parents' school involvement efforts influenced by the social and economic context in which you were raised? Write a paragraph stating your beliefs of how parents ought to be involved in the education of children.

A number of events contributed to the overt decline of cultural deprivation explanations as the primary cause for disparity between the academic achievement of African American children living in poverty and that of middle-class children. Early evaluation of compensatory education programs indicated that these programs did not have the desired affect of improving achievement among African American children. Limited time between implementation and the potential for positive long-term effects of these programs were among justifications proposed for the initial lack of success of compensatory education.

Others have suggested that the basis for compensatory education was flawed. Wilkerson (1970), for example, questioned whether educational characteristics ascribed to disadvantaged children were associated with and caused by impoverished homes or whether they were the consequence of the kinds of educational experiences in schools attended by these children. Wilkerson suggested that compensatory education programs emerged as an alternative to school desegregation, ostensibly because compensatory education would be easier to implement than school desegregation.

Wilkerson's views corresponded to those held by many African Americans during the mid-1960s. Lightfoot (1978) pointed out that frustrated African Americans perceived schools as the reason for the lack of academic progress among their children and that public school integration could not be relied on as a remedy for improved educational outcomes. They felt that desegregation was not occurring in the nation's cities following the *Brown v. Board of Education* ruling, evidenced by the growing number of predominantly African American schools in inner cities. African American parents were concerned about city schools with high concentrations of African American children and limited resources. Furthermore, the view of African American children as disadvantaged emerged in the midst of a social and political climate in which the Civil Rights and Black Power movements were spawning a growing sense of community and cultural pride among African Americans. Many Black Americans were unwilling to acquiesce to a scholarly discourse that summarily identified their home life as the cause for poor academic achievement among their children. African Americans successfully used school boycotts and other political action to demand changes in the education of their children. It is likely the Education Amendments Act of 1978 reflected this desire of parents to be involved in the education of their children—to in effect be a part of the solution to the educational challenges their children faced.

Parental Involvement as Parental Control and Power

The federal government's role in encouraging parental involvement was not to be limited to parents of color and those living in poverty. Title II of the Education Amendments Act of 1978 alluded to the need for basic skill programs to address the needs of all children and that parents were to be involved in planning basic skills programs. Later, President Ronald Reagan advocated yet another avenue for parents to be involved in the education of their children. As the 1983 Congress addressed education assistance legislation, Reagan (1983) urged the Congress to use funds authorized under Chapter I of the Education Consolidation Improvement Act of 1981 (formerly Title I of ESEA) to establish a voucher program that would allow parents of children eligible for compensatory education to choose any school they felt would best serve the educational needs of their children. Parental choice as a form of parental involvement in the education of children would, in Reagan's view, eliminate feelings of exclusion among parents by providing them more control over their children's education. Reagan also believed that the quality of both public and private schools would improve if these educational units had to compete for students. Although not instituted across the nation as a whole, school voucher programs continue to emerge as legislative issues at both the state and federal levels.

The last two revisions of ESEA combine aspects of parental involvement directives that preceded them. The Improving America's Schools Act of

1994 (Pub. L. 103-382) and No Child Left Behind Act of 2001 (Pub. L. 107-110) included detailed parental involvement components that empower parents to be a part of their children's educational programs, while charging Title I (formerly Chapter I of the Education Consolidation Improvement Act of 1981) funded schools to provide avenues for them to do so. Both laws increase means for parents to monitor and evaluate not only the academic progress of their children, but also the capacity and performance of schools in meeting state-mandated achievement outcomes.

Improving America's Schools directed schools to provide parents with information on how to monitor and work with teachers to improve children's progress. The role of parents as monitors of academic progress was extended in No Child Left Behind to include parents' rights to monitor the extent to which teachers are qualified to teach their children. The "Parents Right-to-Know" section of the law requires funded schools to notify parents that they have the right to request information on the qualifications of their child's teacher. Parents can inquire into whether teachers have met all state licensure requirements for the grades and subjects they are teaching, as well as information on college degrees granted. Both laws note schools' responsibility for ensuring that parents understand state content standards, achievement standards, and assessments as a means for monitoring their child's progress. The last two revisions of ESEA promote the idea of compact agreements that address shared responsibilities of schools, parents, and students for academic achievement.

Inquiry and Reflection 5B: Locate the written parental involvement policy for the state or school district of your observation site. Summarize the rights and responsibilities of teachers and parents. In your opinion, what is the value of having this policy documented?

Multiple references are made in the ESEAs of 1994 and 2001 to involving parents in the planning and evaluation of academic and parental involvement programs and the need for parental participation to constitute "meaningful involvement." Funded states and local school districts are required to have written parental involvement policies that outline how parents will be involved in the planning, review, and improvement of educational programs. To facilitate meaningful involvement, both state and local educational agencies are directed to communicate with parents in language and formats that are understandable to all parents. Finally, in an effort to increase the capacity of school personnel to work with all parents, provisions are made for school districts to educate teachers and other staff on the value of including parents in the education of their children, with the expectation that parents play a role in developing this training.

Both laws build policy based on the assumption that all parents can contribute to the educational success of their children. Schools, therefore, are directed to identify barriers to parental participation (e.g., limited literacy, limited English proficiency, ethnic minority background) and use this information to design, and revise where necessary, strategies to increase parental involvement. Relatedly, both laws recognize the continued disparity in achievement between children from advantaged and disadvantaged homes. It is noted, however, that conditions outside the home may also negatively affect students' academic progress. Addressing problems such as inadequate health care, unsafe neighborhoods, homelessness, or unemployment of a parent through coordinated services (e.g., health and social services) aids the ability of schools to meet national educational goals.

Inquiry and Reflection 5C: Federal parental involvement initiatives have been influenced by the social and political climate of the country at the time the legislation was passed. What social and political circumstances influence parental involvement mandates in No Child Left Behind? In your opinion, how will these mandates influence school–home relations?

Improving America's Schools Act of 1994 and No Child Left Behind Act of 2001 indicate the need to improve the quality of education for all children so that all can reach higher standards. In 1984, Reagan sought to move schools toward quality by shifting decision making about education to parents, students, states, and local districts and limiting the federal role in education. Presumably, more choice and control to parents would lead to improved learning environments. The detailed parental involvement sections in Improving America's School and No Child Left Behind make provisions for parents not only to monitor and control the direction of education for their children, but also to choose schools attended by their children. Children may attend parent-selected charter schools and should they choose to do so, parents can play a role in developing these schools. In opposition to Reagan's wishes, the federal role in education is evident, particularly as it has played an instrumental role in fostering the direction of parental involvement in education for more than 40 years through legislation and associated allocation of federal funds. Although it is possible to use federal funds to hold schools accountable for parental involvement initiatives, there are no mandates to force parents to take part in school initiatives. Attempts are made to influence parental behaviors through use of the media and parental involvement literature that purport the importance of parents being involved in the education of their children. Still, the perception remains that parental involvement has not reached levels desired by schools and society at large.

THE MEANING OF PARENTAL INVOLVEMENT

Perceptions of the need to promote, encourage, and facilitate the involvement of parents in the education of children is a relatively new phenomenon, brought about by shifts in power and responsibility between public schools and families. The concept of "parental involvement programs" is somewhat remarkable, given that the home was once the center of teaching and learning. In mid-twentieth century, Hymes (1953), reacting to tension existing between schools and families, pointed to the need for unity between the two institutions. He described home–school relations as a new field lacking a knowledge base from which to draw. There has been a tremendous increase in school–community–family relations' literature, but consensus on what it means for families and communities to be involved with schools appears to be lacking (Jordan, Orozco, & Averett, 2001). This is problematic for several reasons. First, meanings attributed to parental involvement influence expectations that schools have of parents and that parents have of themselves. Confusion and strained relations come about when clarity in expected responsibilities are lacking. Second, when researchers operationalize or define parental involvement differently, school–family relations as a field of study takes on an arbitrary character, and existing research can no longer be compared, contrasted, or serve as a basis on which additional research can be built. The ability to connect parental involvement to existing theory is hindered, as is the progress toward generating new theoretical models or frameworks from the multitude of research on school–family relations. Third, a field of study lacking agreement on the meaning of its center-most construct (i.e., parental and community involvement) leaves the educational community without a definitive knowledge base to serve as a guide for interactions with parents and communities (Jordon et al., 2001).

Epstein's (1994) work is viewed as a major step toward providing a theoretical framework for understanding parental involvement in education. She outlined six major partnership practices believed to lead to comprehensive school, family, and community partnerships (Figure 5.1). Her framework implies what it means for parents to be involved in the education of their children and lists reciprocal practices to be engaged in by both schools and families. Epstein proposed that parental involvement is too narrow a descriptor to express fully the nature and scope of relationships possible among adults responsible for the education and development of children.

Epstein promotes the benefits of partnerships among schools, communities, and families where shared influence and responsibility for children exist. Clearly, all aspects of parental involvement in the education and development of children are epitomized in families in which children are home schooled. In this educational arena, there is no need to isolate or identify specific roles for parents in their children's education. The study of parental

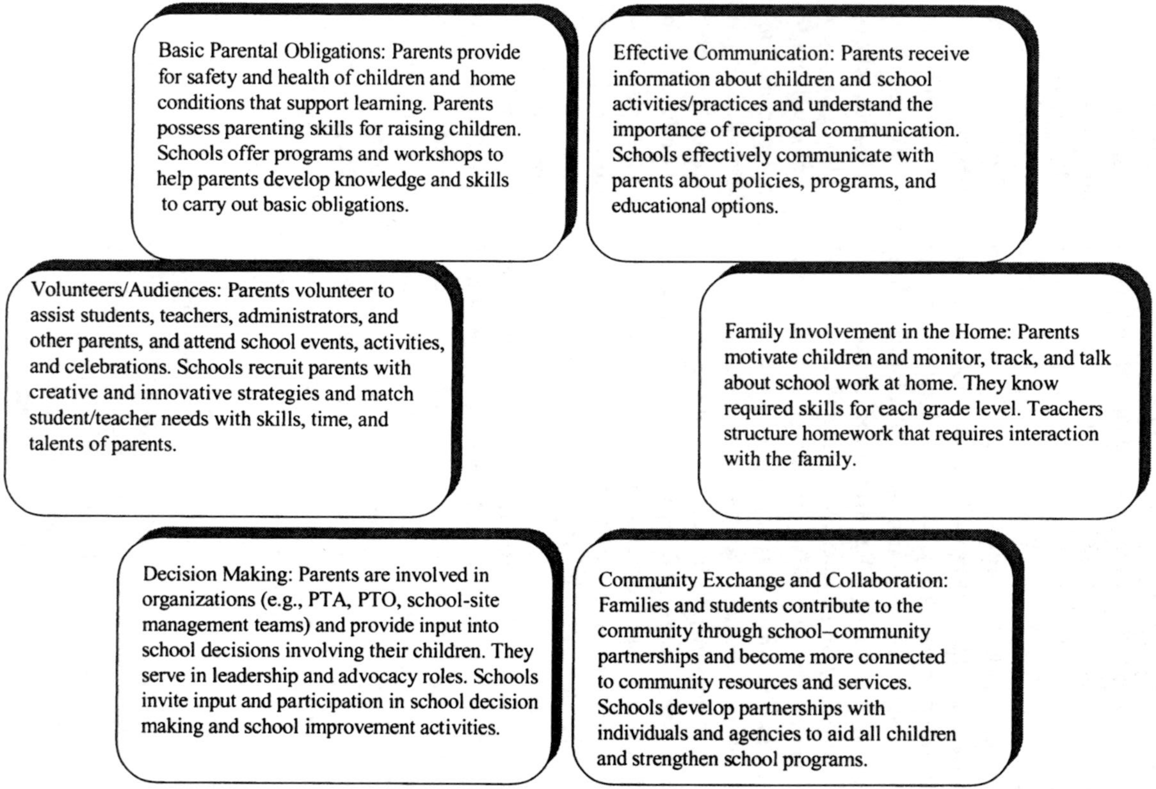

Basic Parental Obligations: Parents provide for safety and health of children and home conditions that support learning. Parents possess parenting skills for raising children. Schools offer programs and workshops to help parents develop knowledge and skills to carry out basic obligations.

Effective Communication: Parents receive information about children and school activities/practices and understand the importance of reciprocal communication. Schools effectively communicate with parents about policies, programs, and educational options.

Volunteers/Audiences: Parents volunteer to assist students, teachers, administrators, and other parents, and attend school events, activities, and celebrations. Schools recruit parents with creative and innovative strategies and match student/teacher needs with skills, time, and talents of parents.

Family Involvement in the Home: Parents motivate children and monitor, track, and talk about school work at home. They know required skills for each grade level. Teachers structure homework that requires interaction with the family.

Decision Making: Parents are involved in organizations (e.g., PTA, PTO, school-site management teams) and provide input into school decisions involving their children. They serve in leadership and advocacy roles. Schools invite input and participation in school decision making and school improvement activities.

Community Exchange and Collaboration: Families and students contribute to the community through school–community partnerships and become more connected to community resources and services. Schools develop partnerships with individuals and agencies to aid all children and strengthen school programs.

Figure 5.1 Epstein's reciprocal parental and school practices to support parental involvement.
From: Epstein, J. (1994). Theory to practice: School and family partnerships lead to school improvement and success. In C.L. Fagnano and B. Z. Werber (Eds.), School, family, and community internal team: A view from the firing line (pp. 39–52).

Homework Help: Parents work with children on homework designed by teachers to facilitate child–family interaction; parents may receive training on homework strategies and resources to support student learning.
Supportive Home Environment: Parents supervise and structure childrens' time away from school in ways that support their education.
Home–School Communication and Interaction: Parents communicate and interact with schools; parents also receive information about school programs, events, and policies.
Parent Participation in School Activities: Parents are involved in school organizations (e.g., PTA), serve on committees, and volunteer in classrooms.
Literacy Development in the Home: Parents engage literacy activities at home (e.g., reading to their children, providing reading material at home) in support of literacy development.
Parents as Tutors: Parents serve as tutors for specific subjects.
Parental Support: Parents provide emotional and academic support for children and express expectations and aspirations for child's current and future performance.
Out-of-School Learning Opportunities: Activities provided by parents support student learning and development (e.g., library trips, visits to museums, etc.).
Home Interactions About School Issues: Child–parent interactions focus on school related issues such as academic decisions or course placements.
Parents as Role Models: Parents reinforce the value of an education by serving as role models and sharing their positive experiences of education.
Parents as Educational Advocates: Parents are involved in educational change and reform efforts.

Figure 5.2 Parental connections with schools.
From: Jordan, C., Orozo, E., & Averett, A. (2001). Emerging issues in school, family and community connections. Austin, TX: National Center for Family and Community Connections with Schools.

involvement in education intends to delineate behaviors and attitudes of parents that enhance and support the formal education of children when it takes place outside of the home. Jordan et al. (2001) developed a list of ways parents connect with schools (Figure 5.2) that routinely appears in current parental involvement literature. Although Jordan et al.'s summary and Epstein's framework are not perfectly aligned, combined they reflect views most commonly advanced in parental involvement discourse.

EDUCATIONAL AND SOCIAL IMPLICATIONS OF PARENTAL INVOLVEMENT POLICY

Parental involvement as a policy initiative directed toward academic improvement is not without criticism. The roles and expectations of parents in relation to schools tend to be externally defined (i.e., defined outside of the family). As a result, the effect of cultural, social, and economic differences among families on school–family interactions becomes secondary to universal notions of appropriate parental responses to education. School personnel, then, may not recognize nor honor the different ways families choose to be involved in the education of their children, some of which may not involve direct interactions with schools. When the level or quality of parental involvement is based primarily on institutionally derived parameters, some parents will inevitably fall short of expected participatory parental involvement behavior. Unfortunately, these parents are often labeled as uncaring about their children in general and, more specifically, uncaring about the child's education.

deCarvalho (2001) proposed that parental involvement policies may well sustain a historic view of schools as institutions that promote the reproduction of social inequity through unequal educational outcomes. The whole notion of "parental involvement," she suggested, advantages White middle-class families who embrace values such as competition and the search for personal advantage. Given their educational backgrounds and social and economic resources, middle-class families have traditionally been able to use schools as a means for ensuring an advantaged position for their children. They are often in better positions than non-middle-class parents to take advantage of school governance positions and in the process maneuver school policy in directions that support goals they have for their children. In addition, specific kinds of skills are inherent in descriptions of parental involvement discussed earlier, skills that may be lacking among parents of certain socioeconomic and educational backgrounds.

According to Lareau (1994), problematic issues associated with parental involvement as an educational policy are too often absent from parental involvement discourses. Issues such as stress and workload placed on teachers charged to implement parental involvement strategies, the possibility of less positive interactions between teachers and parents (e.g., anger and reciprocal criticism that emerge among adults in children's lives), or the existence of differences in power between teachers and parents (which may differ based on the social and economic status of parents) are not addressed in standards for school–family interactions.

Parents' connections with schools have positive affects across numerous school-related areas (see Figure 5.3). Although there may be a tendency to view parental involvement as a composite behavior that in total influences all aspects of student achievement and performance in schools, certain parental behaviors have an overall more powerful effect on student achievement and performance than other parental behaviors. For example, supervision of children in the home (e.g., monitoring homework, supervising television time) is routinely believed to have a positive influence on student

- ❑ improved performance in specific subject areas (e.g., math, reading, language arts, etc.)
- ❑ improved attendance
- ❑ positive aspirations for attending college
- ❑ transition to regular classrooms from special education classrooms
- ❑ decrease in dropout rates
- ❑ improved attendance
- ❑ improved motivation
- ❑ more positive student–teacher relations
- ❑ avenues to address barriers to learning (e.g., physical or mental health conditions that interfere with learning

Figure 5.3 Positive effects of parent–school connections.
From: Jordon et al. (2001).

achievement. Fan and Chen (2001), however, found that parents' supervision in the home had the weakest relationship to students' academic achievement, whereas the aspirations and expectations parents have for their children had the strongest relationship to it. Research also suggests that specific parental behavior will affect achievement in specific academic areas with less impact in others. Okpala, Okpala and Smith (2001), for example, found no significant relationship between the number of hours parents volunteer in schools and mathematic achievement among elementary students, although they speculated that the presence of parents in schools as volunteers sends a positive message to both teachers and students.

Parents, based on any number of familial situational issues, may not choose or be able to connect with schools in the multiple ways suggested by federal edict, or by Jordan et al.'s summary or Epstein's framework. The ability of teachers and other school personnel to articulate the extent to which specific parental involvement dimensions correlate to specific aspects of academic achievement and performance outcomes provides parents options as to how they might best support the educational performance of their children.

> Inquiry and Reflection 5D: Interview three teachers. What are their views on the pros and cons of parental involvement as a support for children's education? How are they involved in partnering with parents? How has the focus on parental involvement influenced their work as teachers?

PARENTAL INVOLVEMENT ORGANIZATIONS AND PROGRAMS

Structured programs designed to facilitate parental involvement include those organized by parents and communities, as well as those organized by schools. One criticism of school-initiated parental involvement programs is that pressures felt by schools to involve parents have led to creation of programs and roles for parents that risk losing the voice of parents (Smrekar & Cohen-Vogel, 2001). Although programs organized by parents reflect a vision of parental roles in education as perceived by parents, it should not be assumed that all parent groups share the same vision for their role in education. Similarly, community-organized programs can impose external values that may not be shared by the population of parents they are meant to serve.

Parent–Teacher Associations and Organizations

The most established parental involvement organization, the Parent–Teacher Association (PTA), was organized by parents. In 1897, Alice McLellan Birney and Phoebe Apperson Hearst organized the National Congress of Mothers, a meeting attended by 2,000 participants. During its 1899 convention, this group adopted plans for a parent–teacher association, ostensibly as "schools for parents" (National PTA, 2005). By 1924, NCM had become the National Congress of Parents and Teachers (NCPT), with a broadened focus that included more interaction with educators and child development experts (Cutler, 2000).

NCPT membership was for the most part White, middle-class Protestant women. They were also a separatist organization, and African American mothers were not invited to be among their members. As a result, the National Congress of Colored Parents and Teachers (NCCPT) was organized in 1926, with state and local goals for the education of African American children that were similar to those of the NCPT. Although the two organizations had common goals, racism and the fear of lost membership motivated NCPT leadership to promote separate local chapters, although some chapters located in areas with integrated schools were counseled to make local decisions regarding racial separation. Given the state of race relations in the country during this period, the NCCPT found it did not have the power to command the attention of educators or policy makers. As a result, membership steadily declined, and by 1945, the organization as a national entity was essentially defunct (Cutler, 2000).

The NCPT became what is today the PTA, a national organization that views itself as the primary organization to speak on behalf of children and youth to agencies and organizations making decisions about children. They

Kansas Congress of Colored Parents and Teachers Meeting, Leavenworth, KS, 1952. The National Congress of Colored Parents and Teachers, organized in 1926, was defunct as a national organization by 1945. Many state organizations continued to meet to respond to the eductional needs of African American children. *Beatrice, Johnson Collection, Kansas Collection: Kenneth Spencer Research Library. University of Kansas Libraries.*

generally see their purpose as raising standards in home life, encouraging close relationships between schools and families, ensuring that laws exist to protect and care for children and youth, and developing ties between educators and the general public for the benefit of children and youth. In addition to school-level activities, the PTA addresses its mission and purposes through political lobbying at the national and state levels. For example, they successfully lobbied for measures to strengthen parental involvement provisions in the No Child Left Behind legislation to include the requirement that schools have written parent-involvement policies and that parents be involved in the development of schools' parental involvement programs. The PTA has a membership of well over 6 million parents, although this is a decline from a membership of 12.1 million 30 years ago. Rather than view membership decline as problematic, the PTA leadership believes advocacy efforts with a smaller group of parents offer a more strategic approach to accomplishing their goals (Parent Teacher Organization [PTO], 2005).

The PTA should not be confused with the PTO. PTOs are generally organized by parents who prefer to center their efforts and resources on local school needs, although members have taken steps toward organizing nationally through the National PTO Network. A national network will allow organizations that primarily function independently to benefit from shared information and resources. Although many PTOs operate independently of PTAs, some exist alongside PTAs in the same school, and parents may be members of both groups. Some parents question the expense and benefits of being a PTA member, and others have broken ties with the PTA due to positions taken by the organization on issues such as the use of vouchers (opposed by the PTA) and the organization of gay and lesbian PTA units (PTO, 2005). Even so, PTAs and PTOs are currently the largest and most organized parent organizations.

Parental Involvement in School Governance

School-site Based Decision-Making (SBDM) bodies emerged in the mid-1960s based on the belief that student performance could improve if parents, teachers, administrators, and communities had more authority to govern local school sites. To date, the extent to which SBDM bodies impact student performance remains equivocal. A number of issues surround the SBDM concept that ostensibly impact school-site decision-making bodies' influence on school policies and subsequently student performance. First, socioeconomic status often defines who participates in school governance. For example, middle-class parents are more likely to be members of SBDM bodies in schools attended by children of different socioeconomic levels. Unequal power and influence among parents potentially leads to approval of polices that lack the voices and perspectives of some parents. In this instance, the needs of children and families from low socioeconomic backgrounds may not be met. SBDM bodies made up of middle-class parents may find it beneficial to maintain the status quo or may not fully understand the needs of families who are different from their own.

Unequal power also exists between school personnel and parents. In a clear sense, the power of SBDM bodies to affect change is mitigated by the power states have over the operation of schools, as well as the extent to which principals support goals that may be generated by the group. Finally, for many SBDM bodies, the lack of clarity in roles and expectations results in confusion over what they are to accomplish, particularly in instances where principals, and to a lesser extent teachers, do not value the contribution these bodies could make. SBDM as a parental involvement strategy appears to work best when parents have had training directly related to the roles they are to play, have support, and are able to work collaboratively with principals and other school personnel.

Parent Education and Family Literacy Programs

The major goal of family education and family literacy programs is to provide parents with skills and knowledge meant to have a positive influence on the education and development of their children. The programs may be federally funded (e.g., Even Start funded by No Child Left Behind) or may be funded by private foundations. Schools and community organizations that offer parent education programs provide a number of topic-specific classes, such as those focused on understanding child and adolescent development, information on how to handle problematic situations (e.g., effective discipline practices), or information on issues such as child abuse or neglect. Parent education programs may also provide more academically based information to parents, although these experiences are more often offered by family literacy programs. Parent education programs are different from family literacy programs in that the former may attract parents at all socioeconomic and educational attainment levels. Family literacy programs are directed toward economically disadvantaged families headed by a parent or guardian having lower levels of educational attainment. The goal of these programs is to alter intergenerational family literacy patterns through interventions with both parents and children.

Comprehensive family literacy programs include components that focus on early childhood education, activities between the child and parent, parenting skills, and basic skills for parents (leading to completion of a General Education Development [GED] certificate). Family literacy programs honor the notion of parents as the first teachers of their children, hence, the focus on working with both children and families simultaneously. A primary problem experienced by organizations that offer family literacy programs is the retention of families considered to be in need of program services (e.g., teen parents, families for whom English is a second language). Family literacy programs are also challenged to offer approaches to literacy development and parenting education that will not conflict with cultural norms of various groups. As a result, literacy program facilitators are encouraged to move away from deficit evaluations of families who are not White and middle-class. Many family literacy programs operate on an assumption that all families bring strengths to learning situations and that these should be incorporated into family literacy programs. As a result, these programs will likely differ from community to community, as program facilitators attempt to find processes that will address literacy development needs of various groups of families (Padak, Sapin, & Baycich, 2002).

Parents as Teachers (PAT), initiated in Missouri in the 1970s, is a parent education and family support program focused on working with families from pregnancy until children reach kindergarten. Today PAT is an international program with the primary goal of supporting child development and school achievement through parent education. The impetus for the program was educators' desire to improve readiness among children entering kindergarten. Based on the belief that family involvement was crucial to children's development of academic skills, the program was developed to help parents understand their role in children's development from birth.

PAT is based on the notion that parents are children's first and most influential teachers and that experiences in the early years provide the foundation for success later in school and life. Although the program prides itself on responding to needs unique to families within specific communities, all programs have core components in common. These include personal visits from parent educators who provide age-appropriate development information to parents; group meetings where parents learn from and support each other; screening for the purpose of identifying developmental delays, health issues, or vision or hearing problems; and a resource network where parent educators help families learn how to access needed resources (Parents as Teachers, 2004).

Father Involvement Programs

Most often, parental involvement is simply a euphemism for mother involvement in education. Reay (1995) discussed the overwhelming tendency of parental involvement literature to be gender neutral, when in reality mothers are more apt to be the involved parent. Increasing the level of father involvement in education is not a new issue; this topic appeared on the agenda of the 1899 convention agenda of National Congress of Women, but a renewed focus on father involvement has evolved with the overall parental involvement project.

Fathers in certain family situations appear to be more involved than fathers not having these family characteristics. For example, fathers with higher levels of educational attainment and fathers in families where children attend private schools are more involved in their children's education. Additionally, men whose wives have full-time jobs and those in stepmother–child households have increased levels of involvement in education, as do men who are routinely involved with the child's activities outside of school. Overall, nonresidential fathers tend to be less involved in their children's education (Nord, Brimhall, & West, 1998).

The limited amount of parental involvement literature on parents' involvement in education at home that is not school driven applies to father involvement as well. Thus, educational support roles played by fathers in the home may also be underreported. It is also the case that fathers are more likely to be involved in some school-driven activities more than others (e.g., attending performances, conferences, or participating on SBDM teams and other councils or boards). In an effort to increase father involvement among economically disadvantaged families, a number of family literacy and family education programs are reaching out to fathers. They are attempting to remove barriers, such as discomfort on the part of providers when working with fathers, to have fathers play a more active role in their children's education and development (Turbiville & Marquis, 2001). Young fathers with low levels of education are particularly targeted as part of the family literacy projects.

CONCLUDING COMMENTS

Parental involvement in education has changed over time, shifting from parents as primary educators, to parents as responsible for choosing adults to educate their children, to parents having little say in who educates their children. Interestingly, No Child Left Behind attempts to increase parental power in education through measures such as the requirement that teachers provide unambiguous information on student performance, the mandate that schools provide information on teacher qualifications, and the right of parents to remove children from low-performing schools. Federal intervention in school–family relations has focused on prescribed roles for parents, and corresponding roles for teachers in the parental involvement project for more than 40 years. Like any political issue, federal parental involvement dictates have been influenced by the social and political climate of the nation at the time legislation was passed. Although federal funding influences state and local school district parental involvement efforts, federally prescribed roles for parents are less effective.

Even as legislated meanings of parental involvement persist, researchers continue to seek consensus on meanings that address both the complexity of parental involvement as a social construct and the particular elements of parental involvement activity that have a direct and positive impact on the children's education. In the interim, parental involvement programs will likely continue to exist. The fact that these programs differ in terms of purpose and focus speaks to the complexity of the involvement of parents in children's education. According to Zuniga and Alva (1999), collaborative efforts between parents and schools must include multiple opportunities for parents to recognize and expand on their skills and knowledge. Teachers will need to recognize and value strengths and resources parents bring to educational settings and may have to look beyond actions, processes, and resources familiar to them in traditional school–family interactions. The explicit roles of teachers in parental involvement efforts signal an additional responsibility for the position of "teacher" to an already full agenda. Although studies on the effect of parental involvement continue, preliminary results suggest that the education of children is enhanced when adults in their lives work collaboratively to ensure that their educational needs are met. Partnerships between teachers and parents (both mothers and fathers when possible) reduce assumptions that each has of the other while increasing shared meanings and expectations among adults in the children's lives.

GUIDED OBSERVATIONS

5E. Describe parental involvement activities and organizations existing in your field placement school. What are the goals and purposes of these organizations? Who is involved? Who are the leaders?

5F. Attend a PTA, PTO, or site-based decision-making body meeting. What evidence (if any) suggests that certain groups of parents (with respect to ethnicity, socioeconomic background, educational attainment level) are more present and have more power in these meetings than other groups of parents?

Chapter 6

Parental Attributes: Influence on Interactions With Schools

Parents are adults who possess a variety of educational backgrounds, experiences, personalities, values, and beliefs, all of which influence their ways and means for parenting and consequently their interactions with schools. Teachers and other school personnel, however, are expected to work collaboratively with all parents of children in school settings, regardless of individual attributes parents may possess. As alluded to earlier, parents and educators having similar socioeconomic, cultural, language, and educational backgrounds tend to have a less difficult time collaborating than parents and educators who differ along these lines. Similarity in backgrounds often results in similarity in expectations of children's performance, greater ease in communication, and smoother routes to family–school partnerships. Furthermore, school personnel will likely develop more harmonious relationships with parents possessing attributes that align with the norms of school cultures and the process of schooling in the United States.

In an increasing number of schooling situations, educators will not share the same background characteristics or values and beliefs with parents and families with whom they must collaborate. School personnel in these situations will likely confront the intersection and possible conflict between personal beliefs and professional expectations as they attempt to work with a diversity of parents and families.

Parental attributes that educators are likely to encounter as they attempt to build alliances with parents are explored in this chapter. The first section reviews approaches to parenting, as well as the impact various approaches have on teacher–family relations and student performance in schools. Although it may be surprising to many educators, feelings parents have about themselves as individuals and feelings they have about their capability as parents will likely emerge as an issue in teacher–parent relations. An understanding of parenting self-efficacy and parent self-esteem will help teachers reflect on the impact of parents' feelings about self on teacher–parent relations.

Throughout the text thus far, social and cultural differences have been addressed as a means for broadening teachers' understanding of these differences, and the influence they will have on school–family relations. This theme is continued in this chapter with a focus on the influence of socioeconomic status and educational attainment on school–family interactions. The concluding section of this chapter addresses the challenging and complex topic of child maltreatment. Unfortunately, some parents neglect or abuse their children, and given the amount of time teachers spend with children, they are often the ones to discover this devastating event in the lives of children and youth. According to the Family Resource Coalition (1996), "building and maintaining genuine partnerships with parents is a process of continually seeking to understand assumptions and to share meanings and expectations" (p. 12). Understanding some of the attributes parents bring to the partnership is a first step to building partnerships for the benefit of children and youth.

APPROACHES TO PARENTING

The approach parents take to raise children is influenced by their socioeconomic and cultural background, their personality and mental health, and even the parenting practices modeled to them when they were children. Approaches to parenting play a part in parent–school interactions in that some approaches are compatible or complement school policies and practices, whereas others may appear to be in opposition to or in conflict with school practices.

Parenting Styles

Baumrind (1991, 1996) organized parenting behaviors into four **parenting styles** (Table 6.1) that researchers use routinely to predict developmental and academic outcomes among children. The permissive, authoritarian, authoritative, and uninvolved parenting styles reflect differences along two major dimensions of child-rearing practices. Varying degrees of parental

TABLE 6.1
Parenting Styles

	Permissive Parents	*Authoritarian Parents*	*Authoritative Parents*	*Uninvolved Parents*
Responsiveness	High	Low	High	Low
Demandingness	Low	High	High	Low
Psychological/ Emotional Development	**Parents:** child centered, lenient, encourage self-regulation in children, avoid confrontations	**Parents:** punitive disciplinary practices; expect obedience without questioning authority; more controlling; autonomy not emphasized	**Parents:** expectations clearly communicated and monitored; self-regulatory and socially responsible dispositions expected; disciplinary practices are supportive	**Parents:** rejecting and neglectful
	Children: high self-esteem; good social skills; tend to have behavior problems	**Children:** low self-esteem, poor social skills; fewer behavior problems	**Children:** socially competent; few behavior problems	**Children:** socially in-competent; more behavior problems than children from other parenting style homes
School Performance	Poor school performance	Perform moderately well in school	School performance better than children from other parenting-style homes	Poor school performance

From: Baumrind, 1991, 1996; and Darling, 1999.

responsiveness and demandingness influence children's behavior. Parental responsiveness refers to practices in which parents are attentive to children's needs and demands, while they support development of individuality, self-regulation, and self-assertion in children. Parental demandingness refers to practices parents engage as means for integrating children into the family and community. Parents monitor and supervise children's behaviors through direct confrontation and by using consistent and contingent disciplinary actions. At the same time, the role of children in the family may result in expectations for higher levels of maturity that may not exist for children in families in which parental responsiveness is more prominent.

In addition to the responsiveness and demandingness dimensions of child rearing, parental practices are further defined by the extent to which parents wish to control children's psychological and emotional development or allow for psychological autonomy. Parenting practices such as withdrawal of love, shaming children, or making them feel guilty are more often associated with controlling behaviors, whereas explanations, reasoning, and discussions of expectations are associated with behaviors that allow for psychological autonomy. Parents' practices with respect to responsiveness and demandingness and to psychological control and autonomy place them into a parenting style category.

Inquiry and Reflection 6A: If you are a parent, which parenting style discussed best fits your approach to parenting? If you are not a parent, which parenting style fits the approach taken by your parent(s)? Upon reflection, are there parallels to parenting style (or the style you experienced as a child) and the ways in which you approach children in the classroom?

Parenting Styles and the Cultural Context of Parenting

The use of parenting style topology as a means for evaluating parental effectiveness without taking into consideration the cultural context in which parenting takes place is problematic (Baumrind, 1996; Chao, 1994). Authoritative parenting, which is most common to and effective for White middle-class families, is routinely cited as the most effective among parenting styles. Expectations that all parents adopt authoritative parenting practices regardless of the environment in which they parent is unrealistic and ignores the culturally specific goals of parenting. Furthermore, cultural practices parents adopt to raise children able to negotiate aspects of a specific living context are minimized by expectations that all parents adopt a specific approach to parenting (Baumrind, 1996).

In a summary of the literature on several ethnic minority-family parenting patterns, Jambunathan, Burts, and Pierce (2000) proposed that African American parents are more authoritarian and thus generally more strict compared with White middle-class families. They have been portrayed as expecting high levels of obedience, with low levels of reasoning and tolerance for input from children. In an effort to teach children skills needed to survive in hostile environments, African American parents may emphasize achievement and a strong work ethic as means to counteract racism when it serves as a barrier to progress. For example, traditional African American parents may communicate to their children the old aphorism that Blacks have to possess twice as much education and skills required for certain jobs and positions to be considered for employment. Additionally, parents following more traditional African American parenting customs will likely emphasize respect for authority figures, promote the value of religion, and inculcate in children an obligation to support and care for extended family members. Disagreement exists in the literature with respect to communication styles among African American parents, with some researchers suggesting that African American parents incorporate high rates of verbal communication into their parenting practices and others suggesting a high rate of nonverbal communication (e.g., eye contact, body stance, or facial expression that communicates expectations for behavior).

Traditional Asian American parents are characterized as more permissive when children are young, then moving to more authoritarian parenting practices as children mature. A strong sense of obligation to family is instilled in children, and shaming and guilt may be used as a means for ensuring that children adhere to parental expectations. Even though authoritarian parenting is believed to be predictive of poor achievement, many Asian American children perform well academically. Caution must be taken, however, in generalizing expectations of high academic performance among all Asian American children. Such attitudes might result in some children not receiving help or support needed to improve performance. Still, pointing to the academic success of Chinese children, Chao (1994) proposed that it is likely that White children raised in authoritarian homes will perform more poorly academically than ethnic-minority children who are raised in authoritarian homes. Aspects of parenting engaged by ethnic-minority parents that have a positive impact on academic achievement may not be addressed by the authoritarian–authoritative parenting concepts. According to Chao, research on approaches to parenting could be enhanced as researchers are more attentive to the impact of cultural frames of references on larger theoretical frameworks.

Latino parents have alternately been described as permissive, authoritarian, and authoritative. In their study, however, Jambunathan et al. (2000) found Latino parents were less likely than other ethnic-minority parents to expect the high level of maturity in children that is required for role flexibility typical in multigenerational and other extended-family arrangements. Latino parents were more attuned to the developmental needs of their children, behavior that resonates with the high responsiveness typical of authoritative parenting. They were also less supportive of corporal punishment than Asian American and African American parents, which is also in keeping with more responsive parental attitudes. Still, Latino families have been noted for familism, with a strong commitment to large extended-kin networks. One might speculate that the degree of responsiveness expressed by Latino parents reflects expectations of children in the extended-family network that does not call for the role flexibility that characterizes other ethnic-minority families. In fact, there is some indication that adults focus on the well-being and development of children in Latino families with less focus on children's responsibility to adults (Chahin et al., 1999). Although these characteristics might point to parents who are permissive, Chao's caution that evaluating parenting practices of ethnic-minority parents without attention to other cultural aspects of parenting must be noted. Indeed, conflicting reports of Latino families in the literature may well point to attempts to explain parenting that takes place in these families by placing their practices into theoretical frameworks that do not fully capture the complexities of parenting behaviors that actually take place.

Tension arises when parental approaches to child rearing conflict with school policy, practices, and expectations of children and youth. Disagreement between schools and the home could conceivably exist around appropriate adult–child communication, discipline practices, importance of school attendance, or even the level of difficulty of academic work to which the child should be exposed. The mother in Case 6A, for example, expresses beliefs about corporal punishment that are in direct opposition to school policy and practices. As a another example, Feng (1994) reported that some Asian American children may feel confused by the informal teacher–student interaction existing in some schools, particularly given the expected reverence to adults instilled in children in some Asian American families. As a final example, developmental expectations of children may differ between the home and the school, with school personnel (or the parents in the home) determining that certain behaviors are developmentally inappropriate, given the child's age.

Case 6A: Discipline Practices

Toni arrived at her son's middle school, belt in hand, and demanded a private room in which to whip the boy for not attending school. In her judgment, this reaction was supported by her views of the importance of education and what her actions must be to ensure that her children receive at least a high school diploma. She recounts the school's reaction to her desire to discipline her son this way:

I proceeded to go up there and they said, well Mrs. Howard, you can't do this. And I said, I can to, because it will be a cold day in hell before the cops brought my child in here (i.e., the school) on two good healthy legs for skipping school! (—Toni, a low-income single mother)

Inquiry and Reflection 6B: Toni's views (Case 6A) on corporal punishment conflict with school practices and policies. What is your personal reaction to Toni's demand to discipline her son through corporal punishment? How would you react to a similar situation professionally?

PARENTING SELF-EFFICACY AND SELF-ESTEEM

Parents are individuals with past and present experiences that influence how they feel about themselves generally, as well as how capable they feel in certain situations. These attributes emerge outside of roles as parents but will influence both child–parent and parent–school interactions. **Parenting self-efficacy** can be described as parents' evaluation of their ability to perform a range of parenting behaviors that support the social, emotional, and educational development of children. Mothers who feel more competent in their roles raise healthier children, even when child rearing takes place in high-risk environments. It is often assumed that low-income mothers, given their limited socioeconomic resources, feel less competent and have a lower sense of parenting self-efficacy than middle-class mothers (Raver & Leadbetter, 1999). In a study of mothers raising children in serious economic hardship situations, however, Raver and Leadbetter found that these mothers viewed themselves at self-efficacy levels similar to mothers from more advantaged backgrounds. Teachers and other helpers may assume that low-income and other mothers in stressful situations implicitly have low levels of parenting self-efficacy and are in need of help or support. Teachers' good intentions may be viewed as unwarranted interference by these mothers, however. In fact, it is often the case that raising children may be the one area over which these mothers feel control, and, as a result, an area that actually contributes to feelings of self-worth (Dorsey, Klein, Forehand, & Family Health Project Research Group, 1999). Although those wishing to help mothers in stressful and life-threatening circumstances (e.g., living in poverty, living with HIV/AIDS) may feel compelled to provide direct service to children, Dorsey et al. suggested that it is better to help parents learn how to use social support in ways that enhance their feelings of parenting self-efficacy.

Parenting self-efficacy can also be influenced by family structure and changes in the family's economic situations. In their study of the impact of economic pressure on parental self-efficacy of African American and White low-income families, Elder, Eccles, Ardelt, and Lord (1995) found that family hardship and economic pressure diminish parental self-efficacy, although the nature of that diminution differs by family ethnicity and family structure. Black families in their study experienced both direct and indirect effects of hardship primarily because they had fewer resources on which to draw prior to the onset of additional hardships. The direct impact of fewer resources, combined with an indirect impact of depressed feelings about the family situation reduced Black parents' sense of efficacy in managing their children's experiences. Feeling discouraged about the family situation was the primary source for diminished parental self-efficacy among White parents. The direct impact of hardship was minimized by the greater access to services experienced by White parents.

The presence of a supportive partner acts a buffer to the emotional stress that accompanies economic duress in Black families. Caution must be taken in assuming that all African American single mothers in hardship situations experience a loss of parental self-efficacy, however. Levels of personal competence, access to resources, and types of adaptive strategies possessed by single parents should be considered in determining the extent to which problematic situations would diminish a sense of competency in caring for children.

Parents also vary in terms of the level of **self-esteem** they bring to the act of parenting. Self-esteem, often used interchangeably with self-worth, may be defined as the evaluations of self made by an individual and the associated feelings about those evaluations. Parental self-esteem has been linked to educational expectations parents communicate to children and youth. A strong link also exists between parental expectations of student performance and student achievement.

Kaplan, Liu, and Kaplan (2001) were interested in the intersection of parental self-feelings, parental educational attainment, children's expectations of themselves, and children's academic achievement, based on the proposition that parents' feelings about their own educational attainment and about themselves could influence the nature of educational expectations communicated to children. According to their findings, highly educated parents with low self-esteem may put pressure on children to perform, in effect using their children to work through self-expectations. Also, parents with low levels of education and low self-esteem may not be as concerned with their children's poor academic performance, as they may communicate to children the importance of excelling in areas other than education. Children living in homes where parents have higher levels of educational attainment may be influenced in a positive way by resources in the home, even if high educational expectations are not communicated. In contrast, children living in homes with parents having low levels of education attainment will not benefit from resources that might support noncommunicated expectations. In some cases, parents having high negative self-feelings about their situation and low educational attainment will embrace education as a

Case 6B: Parental Expectations of Children's Performance

I want her to get that GED. I want her to go to college.... I talk to her about this.... I told her I don't want her to turn out like me. I don't want her to turn out with no education. I don't want her to end up in low-income housing. I want her to do what is best for her. (—Harriet, single low-income mother of one daughter)

Hopefully, the way things are going now I hope he makes it all the way through and takes up some college 'cause he's a very bright kid and he seem like he's willing to learn. (—Laura, single low-income mother of one son)

I tell her... she can look around here (mother's living conditions)... get a better job if you go get a better education and don't be like me, going to high school and some college and quit... you don't have to be staying in conditions like what I'm doing. (—Ella, single low-income mother of three daughters)

means for their children to have a better life. Such is the case of the mothers in Case 6B, all of whom ostensibly have negative feelings about their position in life but who have high expectations and aspirations for their children.

In general, parents having healthy self-esteem, a high sense of parenting self-efficacy, and coping skills for dealing with adversity appear to have the most positive impact on the social, emotional, and educational development of their children. School personnel will undoubtedly encounter parents having low self-esteem or low parenting self-efficacy as they interact with a diversity of parents. Some parents appear to be more focused on their personal sense of self-worth than that of their children. Others will want parenting advice from school personnel, and, as mentioned earlier, still other parents appearing to have low self-esteem or low parenting self-efficacy may resent what they may determine as intrusion of school personnel into an area intimately intertwined with their feelings of self-worth. Clearly this is a sensitive area for school personnel, particularly because the goal is to develop positive working relationships with other adults in children's lives, not to alienate them. A combination of effective listening skills and list of supportive resources may enhance teachers' abilities to develop positive and appropriate relationships, when considering issues of self-efficacy and self-esteem.

Inquiry and Reflection 6C: Interview your mentor or cooperating teacher for situations where issues of self-esteem or parental self-efficacy have emerged as important components in teacher–parent interactions. How did he or she handle these situations? What would you do in similar situations?

INFLUENCE OF SOCIOECONOMIC STATUS AND EDUCATIONAL ATTAINMENT OF PARENTS

Parents' socioeconomic status and level of education may be viewed as attributes that influence school–family interactions. Educators are being asked to work with all families, some of whom may hold beliefs about the role of education in their children's lives that differ from those held by school personnel. Some educators believe families having a low socioeconomic status do not value education. Although these families may view the function and purpose of education differently from middle- and upper-class families, they believe education is important. Gorman (1998) found that middle-class families tend to value the credentialing function of an education. Education is a means to ensure that their children are able to live at the social and economic position the parent experienced. Many school structures (i.e., grades, honors classes, honor role) support the educational goals of these families. Educated adults in middle-class families are aware of the skills and educational experiences needed to maintain a middle-class lifestyle. They are likely to be adamant that schools provide these experiences and will make sure that their children take advantage of them.

By contrast, some working-class and low-socioeconomic-status parents tend to focus on children learning common sense, self-confidence, and taking advantage of the applied aspects of an education. Thus, they may not always be aware of the competitive subtleties inherent in an education for credentialing purposes. While some working-class families in Gorman's study believed college was a preferred avenue to high-paying jobs, others felt a college degree was not necessary. In Case 6C, Toni describes a situation her daughter experienced that could easily be interpreted as a class-biased incident. She does not approach the school and insist that her daughter be able to pursue a medical science class that could possibly open doors

Case 6C: Educational Opportunity Loss

She tried to go for this science, medical class... the last year of school, and because she didn't wear the right clothes and where we came from... that stopped there. Living out here (low-income housing) stopped her. They didn't want her in that class... she didn't wear the proper clothes, she didn't speak properly—I don't know how well she is supposed to speak. Because of her clothes, the other kids didn't want to work with her. And I've told her how to avoid them kind of people. I mean I've told her your clothes are clean, paid for, and bought. I told Tammy, I said tell you what, make them give you the test Tammy. And then you ace it. And then you tell that class where to stick it... well who the hell's teaching snobs here? We're out to teach children... what is this with uppity nose and everything? (—Toni, low-income single mother) to health-related college scholarships. Rather, her focus is on the human relations aspect of the scenario. In this instance, her goal is that her daughter teach a lesson to those who ostracize her. One can speculate that some middle-class parents would have taken their concern or complaint directly to school personnel with a request for an explanation of what had transpired, particularly if the class influenced future options for their child.

Most research suggests that two-parent families at higher socioeconomic levels, with higher levels of educational attainment tend to be more involved in their children's education both at school and at home than families not having these characteristics. In addition to more resources outside of schools, middle-class families generally have more access to teachers and other school personnel through informal networks and formal networks. Because most educators are middle class, there is an increased likelihood that middle-class families and teachers will share the same community. Also, parents who are more involved with schools through formal networks such as the PTA, school-site councils, or other volunteer efforts have an additional access to teachers and other school personnel through their work in schools. Access leads to better lines of communication, more avenues to information, and subsequently to advantaged schooling situations for children and youth whose parents are in the "inner circle" of school processes.

Although families of color and those having less education, limited financial resources, and limited English proficiency may have fewer interactions with schools, this should not be translated to mean that they are less concerned and less interested in the education of their children. As Heymann and Earle (2000) pointed out, discussions of parental involvement that position all parents on an even playing field when it comes to opportunity for involvement ignore the realities of differences in the occupational lives of some working-poor families. In their study, families having a low socioeconomic status did not have flexible work schedules or jobs with paid leave that would allow them to be involved in their children's education at school.

Other experiences among parents described as socially and economically disadvantaged contribute to notions that partnerships with these parents are the most difficult to develop. Many of these parents have had negative schooling experiences themselves and increasing numbers of parents have no experience with schooling in the United States. In some instances, parents who have had a negative school experience view schools as places that do not have genuine concern about them or their children. Additionally, linguistic differences serve as a barrier to building school–home connections between school personnel and parents who speak little or no English. The same linguistic barriers often exist between school personnel and parents who do not speak standard English.

Differences in expectations between parents with limited school experiences and school personnel may lead school personnel to judge parents to be disinterested in their child's education. For example, some parents believe if schools don't call, there is no need for them to insert themselves into the business of schools, which they believe to be the education of their children. School personnel may expect parents to help their children with homework in homes where parents do not have the language or literacy skills to offer such support. Furthermore, parents may conclude that their low level of literacy precludes them from offering much of value to the classroom. Too often, lack of knowledge about the way schools work leads to friction between school personnel and parents, resulting in feelings among parents that they are not welcome at school.

School personnel who do not find ways to establish relationships with families having a low socioeconomic status prior to the event of problematic situations find themselves in an untenable position when school-related problems arise. Attempts to involve parents at this point may result in missed meetings and general unresponsiveness on the parents' part, which unfortunately confirms beliefs among some school personnel that the parent really doesn't care (Raffaele & Knoff, 1999).

Some teachers prefer working in school environments populated by students from middle-class or higher homes, believing they will be able to teach without interference from the host of problems presented by children and families living in poverty. Unfortunately, some teachers working with poor children distance themselves emotionally and professionally from these students and their families, leaving a void in possible connections between adults in the child's life. Still others abhor poverty and harbor disdain for the poor. They have decided that moral and dispositional differences separate the haves and have-nots and, in this vein, basically absent themselves from critical assessment of the causes and consequences of poverty. These teachers miss the opportunity to work with low-socioeconomic-status parents who want their children to develop skills and knowledge needed to navigate and negotiate circumstances associated with being poor. Teachers able to replace dispositional explanations for social stratification with a clearer understanding of the structural factors that influence the social and economic positions of families are in a better position to engage practices with the potential of increasing continuity between the homes of children living in poverty and their schools. To build connections that lead to shared responsibility in children's education, a climate of mutual trust and respect must exist. Educators who are acutely aware of their evaluative beliefs with respect to social class are better positioned to make decisions as to whether they will be able to work with families spanning the range of socioeconomic and educational backgrounds. As suggested by Raffalele and Knoff (1999), school–home partnerships are not an end; rather, they are the means for ongoing relationships between adults who share the responsibility for children's education.

ABUSIVE AND NEGLECTFUL PARENTS

Some parents mistreat children by abusing them sexually, emotionally, or physically or neglecting them in ways that disregard children's physical, emotional, or educational needs. Sexual abuse of a child includes fondling their genitals, engaging them in intercourse, incest, or sodomy, or causing the exploitation or exhibitionism of a child through prostitution or involvement in the development of pornographic material. Physical abuse includes hitting, kicking, biting, burning, punching, shaking, and in other ways causing physical harm to a child, whether intentional or not. In some cases, parental acts meant to punish or discipline children and youth may constitute physical abuse. Some parents engage in psychologically or verbally abusive behavior that causes serious behavioral, cognitive, or emotional disorders in their children. These might include extreme disciplinary acts such as locking a child into a room without food or water, scapegoating or belittling a child, or engaging in routine rejecting behaviors. Parental behaviors that result in physical child neglect include abandonment, refusal to seek timely and appropriate medical care, inadequate supervision, or kicking a child out of the home and not allowing him or her to return. Emotional neglect includes behaviors ranging from allowing children to use drugs and alcohol, to ignoring the child's need for affection, to abusing a spouse in the child's presence. Finally, parents can be guilty of educational neglect if they allow children to be truant, fail to enroll school-age children in school, or fail to attend to the special education needs of children. (U.S. Department of Health and Human Services, 2002).

Child maltreatment (Figure 6.1) occurs in families across socioeconomic and ethnic–cultural lines. It is often more difficult to detect maltreatment in middle- and upper-class families, primarily because these families have the resources to hide abuse and neglect more effectively. Families in certain ethnic–cultural groups may engage in behaviors that are cultural norms but by legal standards constitute abuse or neglect. According to the Children's Bureau of the U.S. Department of Health and Human Services, approximately 879,000 children were victims of maltreatment during 2000, with approximately 1,200 dying as a result of abuse or neglect. Of those abused, 84% were abused by parents, with mothers acting alone responsible for 47% of the neglect incidences and 32% of the physical abuse cases. Relatives, babysitters, foster-care parents, and other caretakers are also perpetrators of child maltreatment. Teachers and other professionals reported more than half of the abuse and neglect cases during this period. (U.S. Department of Health and Human Services, 2002).

Cohen (1999) outlined four risk factors that set the stage for possible child maltreatment: parental mental health, family stress, children's personal characteristics, and the social and cultural context in which parenting

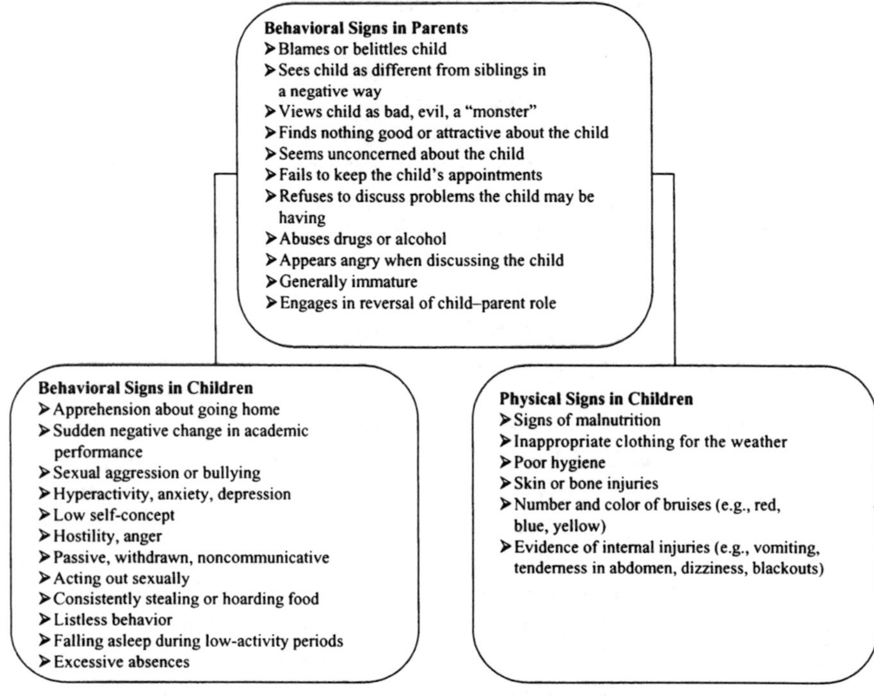

Figure 6.1 Signs of child maltreatment.
From: U.S. Department of Health and Human Services, 2002.

takes place. The degree to which these factors exist in the home situation, along with the particular interaction among the factors, influences whether child maltreatment will actually occur. Parental mental health may result in a predisposition for child maltreatment, particularly during the postpartum period or in homes where there are infants or children in the early stages of adolescence. Parents who were maltreated as children are considered at risk for maltreating their children, along with parents who have a limited understanding of developmentally appropriate behavior for children. In some instances, a predisposition toward maltreatment may be influenced by the age of the mother. Adolescent mothers are at risk for mistreating their children in cultures where teen mothers are an exception and not the norm. This is not the case in cultures where mothering traditionally begins in adolescence.

A second risk factor for child maltreatment relates to the amount of stress in the family or home life. Situations such as conflict and tension among parents in the home; parental isolation or lack of support from friends, neighbors, or relatives; and unemployment or other sudden changes in family life (e.g., death, divorce, illness of a family member) are among the factors that can lead to mistreatment of a child. Domestic violence can also lead to child maltreatment. Sometimes children are unintended victims of the abuse of a spouse as they attempt to intervene. In other instances, the child is abused in ways similar to that of the abused adult. Although immigration is also listed as a possible risk factor for child maltreatment, cultural differences in child-rearing practices limit definitive labels of child maltreatment in immigrant parental interactions with children.

A third risk factor relates to characteristics of the child, with some children being at a higher risk for maltreatment than others. Children who were premature at birth influence parental behavior well beyond the period of infancy in that parents have difficulty finding the right balance between overstimulation and understimulation when interacting with these children. Parental behavior intended to adjust to infants who are not as hardy or alert and more difficult to quiet than full-term babies, transforms into confusion over appropriate parental behavior as the infants grow into childhood. Children having health and psychological problems, as well as children with physical and mental disabilities, are at increased risk of maltreatment, as are children whose temperament is at odds with that of a parent.

A final factor that influences child maltreatment focuses on the social and cultural context in which parenting takes place. Cultural norms dictate agreed-on attitudes toward children, the family, and violent behavior. Certain norms lean more toward the possibility of maltreatment occurring, however. For example, some cultural groups may accept corporal punishments as an appropriate way to discipline children. Some may honor the sovereignty of the family in determining what should transpire within the family unit. Still other groups may believe violence is an acceptable way to solve conflicts. The interaction of these circumstances with other risk factors increases chances that maltreatment will take place.

Although victims of abuse or neglect exhibit a range of symptoms in school, their parent or parents may minimize or deny symptoms teachers observed. In some cases, they present themselves as caring parents, but teachers may observe that they also appear defensive or evasive. All states have some type of law that requires teachers to report suspected abuse and neglect, and most school systems have policies and procedures for addressing suspected abuse and neglect situations. Still, some teachers are reluctant to get involved with child maltreatment cases because they fear confrontation with angry adults, have concerns over personal safety, or believe nothing will be done after the case has been reported, among other reasons. It is also common for teachers to have friendships or other relationships with the abusing parent. Failure to report suspected child maltreatment places teachers in jeopardy of not adhering to state law and district and school policies. More important, however, teachers miss the opportunity to contribute

> Inquiry and Reflection 6D: What are the policies for reporting suspected abuse or neglect in your school? What types of school or community supports are available to your school community to help prevent child maltreatment? What services are available to parents who abuse or neglect their children?

to the safety and well-being of children, which in some cases could potentially save a child's life.

Schools are often involved in cases of abuse or neglect beyond the reporting stage by offering special services that support both the child and the family. As a preventive measure, schools may offer programs and services, often in collaboration with community agencies, for families at risk for child maltreatment and may also offer programs for abusing parents. These may include skill development lessons for children (e.g., socialization skills, problem-solving skills, and self-protection training), parenting courses for adolescent parents, and public awareness programs meant to increase sensitivity about child abuse and neglect. (U.S. Department of Health and Human Services, 2002).

> Inquiry and Reflection 6E: Should parents who abuse or neglect their children be punished, incarcerated, or banned from interacting with children? Should these parents receive counseling and support as a means for reuniting the family?

CONCLUDING COMMENTS

An intricate combination of socioeconomic and educational background, personal beliefs and behaviors, and mental and physical well-being interact to influence parenting among individuals, and subsequently their interaction with schools. Teachers will constantly confront the intersection between personal beliefs and professional expectations, as they attempt to work with the diversity of adults who parent today's children. Even though teachers are expected to work collaboratively with parents on a consistent basis, the amount and nature of parental interactions with schools are influenced by parental attributes and characteristics. In some instances, parental attributes actually manifest as barriers to school–parent interactions. Understanding how parental attributes intersect with schools as social institutions having specific norms and traditions is a first step to moving beyond barriers. Beyond that, being aware of the types of supports available for parents in schools and communities and developing effective avenues to communication that are respectful may aid educators' efforts to build stronger and more effective ties with parents.

GUIDED OBSERVATIONS

6F. Based on the ethnic–cultural makeup of a classroom, which parenting styles would you expect students to experience? Can you identify differences in classroom behavior among students that suggest they may experience different parenting styles?

6G. As noted in Cases 6B and 6C, parents have different expectations of the impact schooling will have in the lives of their children. Attend a parent conference scheduled by your mentor or cooperating teacher or one requested by a parent. What types of goals do parents express for the role of education in the lives of their children?

Chapter 7

Authority and Advocacy: Who Is Responsible for What?

In complementary U.S. Department of Education surveys, parents and teachers disagreed on the extent to which schools reached out to parents and, conversely, the extent to which parents took advantage of opportunities generated by schools for them to be more involved in the education of their children. Topics surveyed included school efforts to communicate with parents; provision of resources to assist parents in parenting or to participate in their children's education; volunteer opportunities; and the involvement of parents in school governance, policy, or other decision-making activities. Generally, school personnel reported more frequently that certain parental involvement practices existed, whereas parents more frequently reported that such practices did not exist. At the same time, parents reported that parents were more involved in parental involvement school activities than did school personnel (U.S. Department of Education, 2001).

The lack of mutual perspectives between parents and school personnel as reflected by the survey is consistent with a history of school–family interactions that has vacillated between periods of cooperative, if not collaborative relations and periods of adversarial and conflictive associations. Issues of authority, control, and responsibility have been major sources of friction between the two groups. As a result, a shadow of discord that has existed since the institutionalization of public education and the professionalization of teaching serves as a backdrop for calls of improved parental involvement in the education of children and youth today.

This chapter takes an in-depth look at the impact of social, legal, and educational policy on teacher–parent relations, as well as ideological differences that often influence relations between the two. The first section of the chapter examines the matter of authority and control in the education of children and youth. Parental and school authority are affected by power-laden education processes and practices, educational reform proposals, and federal and state laws. Examples of school practices will be reviewed for the purpose of understanding the power position of parents juxtaposed to that of school personnel and the overall effect of these power arrangements on school–family relations. The second section of the chapter addresses the issue of advocacy. The need for advocacy is based on the premise that the educational well-being of children is not being met by the responsible party, thus making it necessary for another party to act on children's behalf. In this vein, advocacy may emanate from a parent, a teacher, or even an organization, as a means to ensure that an improved educational situation occurs. The final section focuses on parental perceptions and beliefs about their roles and responsibilities in the education of children. Parental understanding of schools and the process of schooling is important to address because of the close association between perception and behavior. Whereas Chapter 5 addressed educator-generated roles and responsibilities for parents, this chapter focuses on parental beliefs about their educational roles and responsibilities, as well as the expectations they have of schools.

POSITIONAL AND RELATIONAL SCHOOL AUTHORITY

As established in earlier chapters, mid-19th century social and economic changes served as a precursor to public schools becoming the major agency for educating children. Cutler (2000) noted that the informal interactions and understandings between parents and schools were eventually replaced with well-defined boundaries susceptible to bureaucratic and legal dictates. Teachers were clearly in a position of authority over parents in guiding the cognitive and moral development of children. Furthermore, during the early 1900s, public schools took on a "social welfare" agenda with visiting teachers, vocational counselors, and school nurses extending the boundaries of schools' authority into the home. According to Cutler, educators and social reformers intended to increase families' capability to prepare children for school by improving mothers' knowledge of child development and appropriate homemaking. It can be argued that school officials relied on **positional authority** as a source of power when interacting with certain parents, but were able to combine positional and **relational authority** when working with others.

Positional authority is the formal authority granted as a result of one's position (e.g., school administrator or teacher). Evidence suggests that teachers and school officials influenced educational situations based on power emanating from positional authority early in the development of public schools. Parents and schools did not always agree on which aspects of child rearing and education should be shared between families and schools, and which should be the domain of one institution over the other. Some parents were not passive bystanders of educators' and reformers' efforts to control children's lives outside of schools and perceived the work of educators and other professionals into their home lives as intrusive. Moreover, as early as the mid-1800s, parents, primarily mothers, desired a stronger voice in the educational lives of their children, and often challenged schools on issues such as discipline, school facilities, and the curriculum (Cutler, 2000). Yet school officials' positional authority allowed for implementation of educational policies at schools and intervention on behalf of schools in the home despite parental protests and dissatisfaction.

It is also possible that school officials used relational authority to influence educational situations. Relational authority is granted as a result of personal characteristics possessed by individuals, such as expert knowledge or interpersonal skills. Situations can be influenced without positional authority only when others willingly cooperate without feeling forced to do so. Some parents acquiesced to school dictates, possibly feeling that as experts, teachers and other school officials were implementing policies and practices in the best interest of children.

The use of relational and positional authority are important to address in a climate where parental involvement and empowerment are being emphasized. The power to influence parents' involvement may emanate from either authority location. However, particular involvement activities may be structured so that the positional authority of teachers and other school officials remains in intact. According to Waggoner and Griffith (1998), parental involvement can be thought of as normalized or taken-for-granted social interactions between parents and schools, with schools in the position of assigning appropriate in-school activities to parents. This notion is in keeping with Cutler's (2000) account of efforts by mid-19th-century school officials to eliminate acrimonious interactions between schools and disenchanted parents by finding ways to include parents into the organizational framework of the school. Then, as is the case today, schools were able to define and control what it meant for parents to be involved in the education of their children, whether these conceptions fit with parents' understanding and desires of their involvement or not (Waggoner & Griffith, 1998).

Inquiry and Reflection 7A: Interview a teacher to determine his or her perspectives regarding the appropriate roles of teachers when working with parents. Analyze responses given to discern the relational and positional authority aspects of the teacher's beliefs. Are you more comfortable with authority emanating from relational or positional locations?

Teachers' Professionalism and Autonomy

Teachers may be granted relational authority by parents and the general public when they are viewed as professionals with expertise in educating children. Positional authority is granted by the school district and state in which they teach. In this instance, they have the authority and responsibility to implement district and state policies and carry out practices whether or not they or parents agree with them. The authority given teachers to direct the education and development of children exists with a long-standing and continuing debate over the status of teaching as a "true" profession. Teaching has been characterized as lacking the rigor in training, uniqueness in service provided, accountability, and autonomy attributed to other professions (i.e., doctors or lawyers).

The legitimacy of teaching as a true profession is being supported by a number of initiatives that address shortcomings believed to contribute to teachers' secondary professional status. For example, teacher education programs accredited by the **National Council for the Accreditation of Teacher Education (NCATE)** are guided by a common set of standards for teacher preparation (i.e., standards derived from Interstate New Teacher Assessment and Support Consortium principles); most states require acceptable performance on professional knowledge or teaching content exams (or both) before awarding a teaching license, and teacher effectiveness is being evaluated in terms of teacher impact on student learning. Additionally, a major step toward an enhanced professional status for teaching was the establishment of the **National Board for Professional Teaching Standards (NBPTS)** in 1987. The NBPTS, which is primarily controlled by practicing teachers, developed standards of practice for exemplary teachers as well as a rigorous process that allows teachers to pursue national certification voluntarily.

Reformers do not necessarily agree on the best route to improved professionalism among teachers, although most believe change is needed for enhanced achievement among all children. For example, some reforms call for teachers as experts to use their judgment to make teaching and learning decisions in the classroom (Dodd & Konzal, 2002). Teachers are also being asked to contribute to the body of knowledge on effective teaching through **action research,** rather than relying solely on the knowledge generated by education researchers. Teacher authority and autonomy inherent in these proposals are believed to be curtailed by the standards-based curriculum movement and a focus on student standardized test performance of interest at the district, state, and federal levels.

Standards-based education holds teachers accountable for students meeting specified standards that are often determined by performance on **high-stakes tests.** The results of student performance on standardized tests have a tremendous impact on students, teachers, and schools. Low-performing students risk grade-level retention or having their high school graduation postponed. Depending on the state, low-performing schools (i.e., those having substantial numbers of students not meeting standards of performance) have experiences ranging from **reconstitution,** the process by which states take over schools and reopen them with a new staff, to requirements to develop school improvement plans that will result in improved student performance. School performance is also a federal issues, because the No Child Left Behind legislation requires that each school make **adequate yearly progress (AYP)** according to state benchmarks.

Teachers are criticized or stigmatized when their students perform poorly on standardized tests. Critics of high-stakes tests argue that teachers' autonomy and creativity are threatened (and thus their status as true professionals diminished) when they are excessively concerned with students' test scores. The influence of high-stakes testing on teacher autonomy is also felt when school districts concerned with test performance dictate approaches to teaching (e.g., some districts may decide to focus on phonics to improve students' reading ability) and in the process further encroach on teacher autonomy. Proponents suggest that all professionals are accountable for professional standards and that the impact of teaching on student learning and performance is an acceptable area of accountability for teachers as professionals.

Notions of teacher professionalism and reforms to promote it are occurring alongside advocacy for parental involvement. Some reformers believe increased levels of empowerment for teachers and parents will result in a redistribution of power between the two groups, with the outcome of improved education of all children. Empowerment, they propose, can be accomplished by redefining roles of both groups in ways that lead to a partnership for the benefit of children's education. For some reformers, teacher empowerment relates directly to teachers' professionalism because their expertise is emphasized. This view may compete with reformers' parent–teacher partnership goals because teachers may view parents as clients or consumers of education more than partners (Bauch & Goldring, 1998).

A level of autonomy is part of a teacher's professional identity that remains difficult to erase, even when reduced by educational policy. Teachers still control their classrooms and make numerous decisions that affect the lives of children and youth. Parents may feel unwelcome in this environment, making it difficult for them to perceive themselves as partners with teachers. In fact, Cutler (2000) stated that teachers believe "they have the authority to manage parental inquires and even dismiss complaints (*by parents*) about judgments they (*teachers*) make or the methods they use" (p. 2). Such attitudes may in fact fuel the lack of involvement among some parents.

Other reformers argue that giving parents more control will improve education by breaking up the excessive authority of schools. Participation on school councils is one means for increasing parental empowerment. Parents are reticent about serving as members of these bodies for a number of reasons, however—some related to a lack of understanding of school operations and an uncertainty in an arena where decisions are made based on what they deem to be professional expertise or knowledge (Bauch & Goldring, 1998). As addressed in Chapter 5, under No Child Left Behind guidelines, parents have the right to know about teachers' background and training and the right to remove their children from low-performing schools. This legislation provides parents additional power to evaluate and act on their perceptions of teachers' professionalism and effectiveness. It appears, however, that some parents are less interested in having a voice in teachers' professionalism and are willing to defer to teachers as experts, while holding them accountable for students' learning and school performance.

Teachers enjoy positional authority given by states and school districts. They are not, however, totally autonomous in terms of educational decisions they are able to make. Teachers able to combine relational and positional authority will likely have more productive relationships with parents because the former suggests that parents believe teachers to possess a level of expertise and skill that will benefit their children. Teachers who rely predominantly on positional authority will likely have less effective relationships with parents.

Curriculum, Assessment, and Academic Placement

Although teachers deliver school curricula, the authority to determine what is taught resides with the school district and the state. States have the legal right to develop curricula and the right to ensure that it is being implemented in their public and private schools. Local school districts, however, are able to supplement state-mandated curricula to address local needs. States also present school districts with a list of acceptable textbooks from which districts may select. School districts normally have policies for selection and review of books. Curriculum decisions teachers make are thus influenced by the state-developed curriculum and, as suggested earlier, tests that are required by the district and the state. Many states have moved to standards-based curriculum and assessments in which what is taught and the evaluation of how effectively it is learned is guided by a set of state-generated standards. Even though parents have access to curriculum standards and assessment results, they have less input on state-level curricula and assessments. Local districts, in the process of complementing state curricula with material to address local needs may encourage parental input on curriculum issues through site councils for example.

Parents have additional avenues for influencing curriculum, however. Although they do not have the authority to choose what is taught, they have registered complaints to teachers, school officials, and school boards about curricula and materials used to support what is taught, and have also used the legal system for remedy of their dissatisfaction. School curricula and materials believed to go against a family's values or religion may be the basis for a complaint.

For example, the Office of Intellectual Freedom of the American Library Association reports that parents initiated book challenges far more frequently than any other group or individual between 1990 and 2000 (e.g., parents, 3,891 complaints; pressure groups, 175; religious organizations, 108; school board members, 232). When parents initiate a book challenge, they are attempting to remove or restrict materials they find offensive from the curriculum or the library. Nevertheless, states have the right to implement curriculum based on their beliefs that the health and welfare of students are served, even when parents disagree. Table 7.1 provides an example of the books most frequently challenged by parents in 2003.

Parents may also attempt to influence curriculum by actions that affect curriculum delivery or the placement of students in differentiated learning situations. Middle-class parents tend to favor a differentiated curriculum inherent in school tracking, for example, because they ensure that upper-track courses and learning experiences are available to their children. They

TABLE 7.1
Most Frequently Challenged Books of 2003 (Reason for Challenge)

Alice Series (sexual content, offensive language, unsuitable for age group)
Harry Potter Series (wizardry and magic)
Of Mice and Men (offensive language, unsuitable for age group)
Arming America: The Origins of a National Gun Culture (inaccuracy)
Fallen Angels (racism, sexual content, offensive language, drugs, and violence)
Go Ask Alice (drugs)
It's Perfectly Normal (nudity, homosexuality, sexual content, sex education)
We All Fall Down (offensive language, sexual content)
King and King (homosexuality)
Bridge to Terabithia (offensive language and occult/satanism)

may advocate for these courses through formal routes such as positions on school councils or committees. Also, parents who are more involved with schools form informal social networks with teachers and each other that serve as communication routes for information on curriculum and placement issues. As a result, these parents simply have more information about the curriculum and know how to make it work for educational goals they have for their children.

Parents have little influence on district assessments; however, many parents rely on assessment information from schools to determine how well their children are performing. Some parents may complain about teacher-driven assessments, but this information, especially grades, also provides parents additional information about how well their children are progressing. Parents do not always understand standardized performance results, nor are they necessarily clear about the educational implications of test results. Likewise, parents may not understand the influence of the combination of letter grades and test results on placement in differentiated curricula situations (e.g., an advanced-track middle school student placed on the honor roll will have educational opportunities at the high school level and beyond that far exceed opportunities available for Debbie (Case 7A), whose honor status occurred because of grades in remedial courses). Given the lack of knowledge about the way schools work, and absent informative social networks, some parents defer to teacher expertise even when assessment results communicated to them do not match their perception of their child's capability.

Although teachers and other school personnel have the authority to recommend student placement, parents have the right, in some instances to override teacher recommendations. For example, parents have little authority when it comes to school decisions to retain students, and some schools have strict guidelines for the placement of students in gifted and talented programs, even though parents may advocate for their child's admission. On the other hand, some schools allow students to enroll in upper-track classes without requiring certain achievement scores, and parents may advise their children to do so.

Case 7A: Middle School "Honor Student" With Low Reading Skills

I had a parent... conference and they talked about what she was doing... because she was behind in her reading.... I got her a dictionary where she can look up words at home.... She's real slow in reading... like I say, she's been real good in her schooling, except she needed the tutoring in her reading. But other than that, she's been real good. Even in her grades... she's a A–B honor roll (student), so I'm real proud of her. (—Harriet, single low-income mother of one daughter)

Inquiry and Reflection 7B: Parents may not understand the intricacies of assessments, particularly in terms of educational opportunities for their children. Design a list of "talking points" you would cover when explaining Debbie's educational performance (see Case 7A) to her parent.

Attendance and Discipline Authority

Every state has compulsory school attendance laws that require children in a specific age range to be educated, whether in public schools, private schools, or home schooling. Educators in public schools expect children to attend school on a regular basis. Attendance has long been tied to state funding and some states continue to use schools' average daily attendance to allocate state funds. More recently, educators have become concerned about the effect of chronic absenteeism and tardiness on standardized test performance. Students potentially miss critical instructional time when they do not attend school or are routinely late. Furthermore, teacher time is taken away from other students when they must help chronically absent students complete work missed. Students who miss school are not only disadvantaged academically, but also pose social threats to their community because they have increased opportunities to engage in substance abuse or commit crimes.

Absenteeism and chronic tardiness result from home-based reasons ranging from the inability to get up on time to students feeling they do not have appropriate clothing for school. High school–age single parents may have difficulties with child care or transportation. In some cases, parents condone absences, feeling that the child missing school is justified by a family need or situation. Some students are absent for school-based reasons, which may include feelings of marginalization because of curricular practices and policies (e.g., tracking), feelings of isolation related to a lack of connection with teachers and other students or negative interactions with peers (e.g., being bullied or socially ostracized). Regardless of the reasons for truancy or chronic tardiness, parents are held liable, even when they are unaware that their child is consistently absent or tardy.

Inquiry and Reflection 7C: Interview the person responsible for truancies and tardiness at your observation site. What are the major reasons for truancy and tardiness at the school? How are parents involved in addressing issues that contribute to truancy and tardiness?

Schools have punitive and supportive policies related to tardiness and truancy that are directed toward both students and their parents. Students who are truant or chronically tardy may be suspended or even transferred to alternative schools or special programs. Sometimes the accumulation of absences leads to automatic failure. Some communities have school-hour curfews that allow police to detain children seen on the streets during school hours. Punitive policies directed toward parents have included mandated parent-education programs, court appearances, cuts in public assistance benefits, Saturday detention, jail sentences, and fines (Pardini, 1995). Schools have also instituted more supportive measures to reduce instances of truancy and tardiness. Wake-up calls to students, school calls to inform parents of students' absences, parent counseling, and workshops to ensure that parents understand the educational and legal consequences of truancy are among the more supportive practices schools use to reduce truancy and chronic tardiness. Supportive policies are not always embraced because some educators may question whether schools ought to be responsible for making sure parents meet obligations to monitor their children's school attendance.

Discipline polices are often a source of contention between schools and parents. Schools are responsible for ensuring the safety of all students and school personnel and for making sure that the school climate is conducive to learning. Many schools inform parents and students of expected school behavior, often in the form of brochures or handbooks that outline school policies. Teachers may have classroom rules with related consequences for breaking rules that in some instances have been generated along with students. In this way, some levels of discipline will take place without communication with parents. More serious or continuous infractions often require the involvement of parents to improve school behavior. Teachers become frustrated when they feel they are not getting support from the home with misbehaving children and youth. As suggested earlier, the lack of a relationship between teachers and parents subsequently results in unreturned phone calls, refusal to attend conferences, and lack of reinforcement of school rules and expected conduct by parents. The apparent lack of cooperation between parents and teachers conceivably increases misbehavior among students.

A number of school districts have adopted zero tolerance policies for student behavior involving substance abuse and potential violence against other students and school personnel (see Case 7B). Zero tolerance polices have been criticized by parents, students, and various agencies as being arbitrary, unfair, and unreasonable and reportedly have the effect of limiting students' and parents' right to due process (Henault, 2001; Keleher, 2000). This policy, meant to ensure a safe climate in schools, is ostensibly used more frequently to discipline children of color. Policy guidelines are used to expel or suspend children of color at higher rates than white children. Also, many question whether administrators are using reasonable professional judgment to expel or suspend children for relatively minor offenses

Case 7B: Zero Tolerance Expulsions

In Jonesboro, Arkansas, a first-grader was suspended for 3 days for pointing a breaded chicken finger at a friend like a gun.

In Puyallup, Washington, an eighth-grader was suspended for sharing Midol. She was also required to meet with a drug counselor.

In Hawaii, a 17-year-old class president was suspended for giving classmates alcohol at his parents' house before their senior luau.

In Pennsylvania, a 13-year-old boy was expelled for making a list of his enemies, which a classmate of his found in the trash and showed to a teacher. The list made no references to hurting anyone.

In Georgia, a sixth-grader was suspended because the thin metal key chain attached to her Tweety Bird purse was considered a weapon.

(Keleher, 2000; Harvard Civil Rights Project, 2000). Only half of the states in the country require alternative educational assignments for suspended or expelled students, which means that the education of these students is disrupted under the policy. Additional negative outcomes of zero tolerance policies are that they criminalize children and often lead them to distrust those charged with their education (Harvard Civil Rights Project, 2000); these policies may also lead parents to question whether school actions serve the best interests of their children.

Inquiry and Reflection 7D: Does your observation school or district have zero tolerance polices? What types of misbehavior fall under these policies? Are you aware of students in the school or district who have been expelled under them? Given the offense, do you believe expulsion was warranted?

The issue of trust between teachers and parents is complicated by the fact that teachers are legally responsible for children during the school day, serving in ***loco parentis*** (i.e., in place of parents) while children are in their charge. Parents may bring a liability suit against a teacher or the school district for negligence if they believe the teacher or other school personnel failed to protect their child from injury during the school day or while the child is under the school's supervision. At the same time, a number of cases exist in which teachers and other school personnel have pressed legal charges against children for assault and other charges in an apparent belief that teacher and parent will be unable to work through the offense of the child. Disagreements between parents and teachers over whether the best interest of children has been served (either as a result of behavior on students' part or that of teachers') are perhaps some of the most difficult to reconcile. School or district policy often supercedes the desire of teachers to compromise; however, there are also cases in which neither parent nor teacher is interested in arbitration. In these instances, school or district policy will determine whose position or perspective will be honored.

ADVOCACY

Advocacy is a process used by individuals or organizations to speak out or take action for or against issues, policies, practices, values, or attitudes. Normally advocates have a targeted audience and may advocate by use of direct action or education. Advocates may act on their own behalf or may take action for those they believe to be marginalized or disempowered. Schools can be affected by advocacy from individuals, groups, or agencies that wish to mitigate positions on educational policies and practices they oppose or strengthen those they support. Individual parents may advocate for their children or may join with other parents to advocate collectively for an agreed-on position. Agencies and organizations advocate for children and families and may initiate campaigns at the local or national levels to press for educational practices and policies in keeping with the mission and goals of the organization. Teachers, too may advocate for individual students in their classrooms or may be members of professional organizations that speak out for or against policies affecting their profession. Not surprisingly, rights and responsibilities of individuals or groups are often at the center of advocacy campaigns and are thus important to consider in school–family relations.

Advocacy for Parental Choice

A number of organizations and parent groups advocate for parents' freedom and right to make educational decisions and choices for children. From the perspective of many parental choice advocates, educational decisions are the responsibility of parents and not the state. Advocates for home schooling, for example, propose that parents have the right to choose what, when, and how their children learn. Parents, according to home-schooling advocates, should have the right to inculcate family values, including religious values, without interference from the state. Home schooling is a choice made by a growing number of parents, even though educators and others may question the broad nature and quality of education received by home-schooled children (see Table 7.2). In 1999, an estimated 850,000 students were being home schooled, accounting for 1.7% of children in Grades K through 12 (Bielick, Chandler, & Broughman, 2001).

TABLE 7.2
Home Schooled Students' Characteristics (Percentage of total)

Ethnicity	*Income*	*Parents' Educational Attainment*	*Community*
White: 75.3	≤25,000: 30.9	High school or less: 18.9	Urban: 53.5
Black: 9.9	25,001–50,000: 32.7	Some college: 33.7	Urban place: 14.3
Hispanic: 9.1	50,001–75,000: 19.1	Bachelor's degree: 25.1	Rural: 32.4
Other: 5.8	Above 75,000: 17.4	Graduate/professional: 22.3	

From: Bielick, Chandler, & Broughman, (2001).

Nearly half of the parents home schooling their children felt they could give the child a better education than they would receive in public schools. Religious reasons (38%) and poor learning environments at school (25%) were other reasons parents chose to educate their children at home. Public schools support the education of children, even when they are home schooled. Some children spend part of their time being educated at home and part of their time being educated in schools. Schools also provide parents with books and other materials, places to meet, and opportunities for home schoolers to take part in extracurricular activities.

According to some parental rights advocates, parents should have the right to enroll children in private schools or parochial schools and use their tax dollars to support their children's private education, not the education taking place in public schools. These advocates support a free market model of schooling where schools compete for students through the quality of their programs. Some proponents of public support for private education feel there is an inherent inequity when parents must support public schools not attended by their children. Currently, **tuition tax credits** exist in several states (e.g., Arizona, Florida, Illinois, Pennsylvania, Minnesota). Parents can deduct from their state income tax some or all private school tuition. Some states also allow tax credits for corporations who donate funds for scholarships to support private school tuition or funds in support of promising public school programs. In states where tuition tax credits do not exist, public support for private schools may take the form of transportation for private school students on public school buses, school lunches, and textbook loans.

Some parental choice advocates argue that low-income parents deserve the same opportunity as financially able parents to choose private over public schools for their children. They support the use of **school vouchers,** which are publicly funded scholarships that allow eligible public school students to attend a participating private school chosen by students and parents. Criticisms of vouchers originate from opposite sides of the issue. Advocates who support parental choice maintain that choice without direct parental responsibility to pay will eventually result in state oversite of private institutions. Because state governments are the source of voucher funds, critics fear that governmental regulations will eventually impinge on the autonomy of private schools. On the other side of the voucher issue are those who feel the use of vouchers undermine efforts to improve public schools. Public funds used for vouchers, in their view, should be used to ensure quality public schools.

Charter schools are yet another alternative to public education where issues of parental rights and responsibilities emerge. These schools are publicly funded yet independently managed and are free from many state regulations. Proposals for charter schools may be submitted by parents, community leaders, businesses, school districts, municipalities, and, in some instances, institutions of higher education may be involved with charter schools. The "charter" outlines the school's mission, programs, goals, students to be targeted for the school, and processes to evaluate school success. The flexibility possible for charter schools makes them attractive to parents, particularly parents of children who have not been successful in more traditional school settings. The response to the question of who is responsible for what among parents choosing nonpublic school settings for their children ranges from parents being totally responsible for children's education to parent's being responsible for choosing an appropriate educational environment for their child.

Advocacy Within Public Schools

When compared with private and parochial schools, responsibility and freedom to choose are not as far reaching in public schools. Indeed, much of the parental involvement literature prescribes the nature of parental involvement in public school settings, and parental responsibility is even outlined in major legislation (i.e., No Child Left Behind). The question of who is responsible for what may not always be agreed on by parents and schools. The outcome of this difference in perception is reflected by parental apathy, anger, or lack of participation. It can also lead to advocacy, as one party or the other seeks change. Parents may attempt to serve as advocates for themselves and for their children in public school settings in ways not defined by schools and the law.

Poor or ethnic-minority parents may engage in advocacy to mitigate school actions that result in disempowerment and disrespect, based solely on class, culture, and socioeconomic position (Bloom, 2001). These actions may take place individually or in groups and may involve community organization support. In fact, community leaders or organizations may routinely act as advocates for parents unable to advocate effectively for themselves because of language, lack of understanding of school ways, cultural dictates, or sense of lack of power when interacting with schools. Powerful parent organizations (e.g., PTA, PTO) may also advocate for their children by ensuring certain learning environments, curricula, or extracurricular activities exist in schools. Parents, within organizations or as spontaneous collectives, have even been known to influence teacher employment as they advocate for or against a position based on perceived influence on their children or the school environment.

Teachers also serve as advocates for children and families, sometimes as a professional requirement and other times on the basis of personal or professional values or perspectives. For example, teachers are required to advocate for children in instances of child abuse or neglect by reporting suspected incidences to appropriate authorities. Professional risks are involved when teachers personally choose to advocate for certain positions or actions. In some cases, teachers take a stand or action on behalf of students based on a personal worldview that may clash with that of parents. The possibility of teacher–parent conflict increases in these instances, and teachers may find themselves embroiled in predicaments without legal, administrative, or other professional support. Information on the social and legal implications of the cause advocated for is warranted, as well as the need to seek support from administrators and community organizations.

Broader advocacy campaigns for the health, education, and well-being of children conducted by child advocacy organizations or agencies may provide research, promotions, or directives and may have varying levels of influence on the relations of teachers and parents. Activities and education-related literature generated by broader advocacy groups may support the efforts of parents, teachers, and community leaders as advocates.

PERCEPTIONS OF ROLES AND RESPONSIBILITIES

Parental perceptions and beliefs about roles and responsibilities of adults in the educational process are important because they account, in part, for the range of parental behaviors and the level and nature of involvement teachers will likely observe. Strained and ineffective home–school relations exist when teachers and parents have different beliefs of the appropriate roles and responsibilities of each other. Parents differ in their perception and understanding of the schools and the schooling process. The perceptual framework parents bring to the school setting is influenced by a variety of factors, including the parent's social and cultural background, current familial configuration, and the parent's experiences as a learner in educational settings. Educators and policy makers who develop parental involvement strategies may be guided by the assumption that the roles and responsibilities inherent in those strategies meet with perceptions held by all parents of behaviors that are feasible, necessary, and appropriate for the effective education of their children. Despite the desire by schools for parental attitudes and behaviors that correspond to the work of schools, parents' perceptions serve as a stronger basis for parental school-related actions and efforts than the desires of schools.

Parental Role Construction

In their review of theory and research related to why parents become involved in the education of their children, Hooever-Dempsy and Sandler (1997) found that parents' role construction (i.e., parental beliefs about what they are supposed to do to support the education of their children and the corresponding actions deemed to be important, necessary, and permissible on behalf of their children) played a major role in parental involvement decisions. They suggest that parental involvement programs ignoring this critical component of parental belief systems will meet with limited success. Parental involvement is enhanced when roles parents construct for themselves are consistent with roles expected of them by significant groups with whom they interact (e.g., schools, family, workplace). If groups have similar role expectations, parents experience both clarity and support for their parental involvement actions. Parents experience conflict and even confusion about their roles when lack of agreement among various groups for parental roles exist, which in turn influences the nature and level of involvement (Hoover-Dempsey & Sandler, 1997).

DIMENSIONS OF PARENTAL PERCEPTIONS

Parents view schooling and their relation to schools in multiple ways. These perceptions have a profound effect on parents' school-related behaviors. In fact, parents' understanding of schools is located within a perceptual framework that has been structured by a combination of accumulated life experiences and current living circumstances. Parents return to this framework to interpret school-related situations and to generate behavior believed to be appropriate, given the school-related situation presented (Winn Tutwiler, 1992). This view of parental involvement is in keeping with findings of a parent survey that suggests parents make decisions about the nature and level of involvement with schools based on personal life circumstances (Grossman, Osterman, & Schmelkin, 1999). The six dimensions of parental perceptions described in the following paragraphs provide examples of areas influenced by parents' perceptual frameworks.

Communicating Education Expectations

Parents have different beliefs regarding responsibility for communicating to children and youth the possibility of positive outcomes of an education. On the basis of their experiences, some parents have little confidence in the possibility that education can influence life chances. There is an underlying belief that the parent will not be able to advocate for the child in educational environments, nor does the parent trust that schools will necessarily promote success for the child. Hence, they see few life possibilities for their children and are noncommittal in expressing a positive outcome for their future. In other instances, the need for an education is communicated by parents to their children and in some cases to the school. Parents feel it is their responsibility to voice their hopes for their children and the role of education in that endeavor. Moreover, parents are aware of the kinds of behaviors and actions required of both the child and the school for education to make a difference in the child's life. The requisite actions and behaviors are communicated to the child, and parents serve as advocates for the child's education, even when children protest and teachers appear less interested in the parent's involvement (e.g., at the middle or high school level; DeMoss, Vaughn, & Langenbach, 1996).

Connecting With Schools

Parents are drawn to schools for a variety of reasons. Parents may visit schools for award programs, class parties, parent–teacher conferences, or for discipline issues. Parents in Wanat's (1997) study intimated that they attend school events essentially to show support for their children, even when they believe the event to have little value in terms of student learning. Sometimes parents feel it is necessary to initiate contact with the school. They may feel the need to inform the school or be informed by the school regarding a matter that directly affects their child. Most parents in Wanat's study (1997) did not believe it was the school's responsibility to "recruit" them to be involved with their children's education. When teachers are accessible, good listeners, and willing to ensure parents are made to feel comfortable, parents will tend to connect with them given the mutual interest in children.

Other parents may believe a direct request is necessary for them to come to visit the school building. If the school does not initiate contact, the parent is not likely to interact with the school. Disinterest may not be the reason for failure to initiate contact. Some parents may focus their actions with the child around educational issues in the home and assume all is well if the school does not contact them regarding a school-related issue. Other parents have multiple demands on their time and attention (e.g., excessive work or mere survival issues for the family in some cases). They feel that if there were a problem, schools would let them know.

Parental Influence on School Success and Failure

Parents possess varying perceptions of factors that influence success and failure in school settings. Children's attributes and behaviors are dominant factors in school success for some parents, whereas others center on actions taken or not taken by schools as the main reason for children's failure or success. In the latter case, parents are heavily reliant on schools for the total education of their children and may not see themselves as instrumental to the child's success or failure. The perception that children's success or failure hinges predominately on what transpires at school could translate into minimal extension of schoolwork in the home. Furthermore, parents may not see the value of nonschool activities (e.g., church, athletics, or theme-focused clubs) for students' overall academic success and may not seek out these activities for their children.

Parents who focus on students' personal attributes and behaviors as contributing to school success or failure are likely to ensure that children are engaged in activities that support academic success. Parental practices fitting this type of involvement in the education of children often takes place outside and independent of the school's purview. Indeed, some parents may not distinguish between school involvement and home involvement, because they believe being involved in a child's life is valuable whether it is inside or outside of schools (Wanat, 1997).

Influence of Parental Attributes

Parents hold beliefs regarding the influence of their attributes on children's education and development. Embedded in these beliefs are perceptions of circumstances parents believe they control or should control. The influence of parents' self-efficacy and self-esteem in the parenting process has been noted elsewhere in this text. Some parents are aware that they possess personal attributes and the social capital to aid and contribute to their child's education and do not hesitate to use them for that purpose. Parents may also be aware of personal attributes and circumstances that complicate the child's life in general, which may lead to complications in the child's education and development. At the very extreme of these instances, parents may engage in self-effacing conceptions (e.g., "I can't help her with that 'cause I'm terrible in math").

Schools have an opportunity to play instrumental roles in supporting parents who believe they have little to contribute to their child's education. Although teachers and other school personnel may find it more expedient to work with parents having attributes and assets that overtly support the work of schools, helping all parents contribute to children's education can be rewarding. All parents have strengths and are able to contribute in some way. Even parents in ostensibly challenging living situations have personal attributes that potentially have educational benefit for their children.

School–Home Boundaries

Another way to understand parental perceptions and behaviors toward schools is to investigate their beliefs regarding the appropriate domain of the school, juxtaposed to that of the home. Some parents tend to be more relational and are comfortable with or may expect fluid boundaries between the home and school. Depending to some extent on the socioeconomic status of the family, parents welcome or allow schools and other agencies to assist in issues and activities involving the child, some of which are traditionally viewed as the domain and responsibility of the family. Relational parents perceive themselves as having a mutually supportive relationship with the school and will often expect teachers to care not only about the child in the classroom but also the child's family and community.

Still other parents tend to be more transactional, erecting rigid boundaries between the home and the school. Attempts by the school or other agencies to ignore these boundaries could meet with anger and resentment by the parent. Transactional parents perceive themselves as having an "agreed-on arrangement" with the school—they send their children to school and the school educates them. In this manner, the school and family exist parallel to each other. Certain aspects of the child's family life is inaccessible for school inspection or intervention. Tangible results, in the form of academic symbols of the child being educated are expected. Transactional parents perceive problems in the education of the child as emanating from difficulties with the child and the school and not the parent. Hence, in the face of school-related problems, they are likely to act as "brokers," negotiating with the school, the child, or both to return the "arrangement" to a functional status. Transactional and relational perceptions are viewed as two points on a continuum of beliefs that result in a range of behaviors among parents. Still, they require different approaches from teachers and school personnel, particularly if the goal is to build a workable relationship between the school and the home.

Sense of Community

The neighborhood or community where the child spends time away from school can be judged by parents as having a negative or supportive impact on the child's education and development. Although some parents who are critical of their community will choose to relocate (if they are able to do so), others see themselves as part of the community and are willing to take part in fomenting needed changes. Rather than leave, community-committed parents are interested in ways the neighborhood can change—not only for their own children, but for the children of the community as well. They may speak of aspects of the community that enhance rather than detract from the child's development, even though there are community issues needing attention. Parents wanting to relocate may perceive that any number of community characteristics are having a negative influence on their children, an influence that neither the parent nor the child will be able to deflect. As a result, parents may think it best to escape the community context completely or keep the child away from its negative conditions as much as possible.

Of course, the different perspectives parents have on their community have an impact on schools. Community-committed parents may be committed to the school located in that community as well. Conversely, parents seeking to relocate will likely not be committed to the school, and may even view the school as the adverse condition they wish to escape.

Inquiry and Reflection 7E: Use the six dimensions of parental perceptions as a tool to understand a parent's beliefs about his or her appropriate role with schools. During a conversation with a parent, inquire into his or her beliefs along each of the dimensions. How are the parent's school-related behaviors exemplified by his or her beliefs?

CONCLUDING COMMENTS

Power and authority are unavoidable elements of parent–teacher relations. Positional and relational powers available to teachers play significant roles in the quality of relationships they are able to develop with parents. Positional authority comes with expectations from parents and society at large that teachers will have a positive impact on student learning. Relatedly, parents extend relational authority when they feel teachers will attend to the educational, and possibly social and emotional well-being of their children, and sometimes of the whole family. Some parents are unwilling to support either authority position operating in public schools. Many believe public schools have an extraordinary and possibly unnecessary amount of authority over the education of children and youth, and many are not persuaded that the education available in public schools is the best education for their children. These parents often seek alternatives to public schools, with the support of organizations that work for federal and state legislation to sanction this option.

Parents and teachers in public school settings bring a host of perceptions, values, and beliefs to the task of developing collaborative relationships for the benefit of children and youth. Teachers' beliefs about the position of teachers and parents' understanding of their roles and responsibility as parents do not always mesh. In the end, both groups have to believe there is value to the relationship and be willing to communicate their understanding of the school–home to each other. Parents are not likely to initiate this conversation. Given the charge to teachers to work more closely with the home, the instigation for this type of discourse will likely come from teachers.

GUIDED OBSERVATIONS

7F. Attend a PTA, PTO, or school site–based decision-making group meeting. What types of issues are discussed (e.g., school policy, student academic performance, school material needs, school social activities)? What are the levels and nature of parental and staff input in group deliberations?

7G. Record incidences of disagreements among parents, the community, and your observation schools. Who are the advocates for children or youth in these situations? How are the disagreements resolved?

Part III

CREATING MUTUALLY RESPECTFUL AND RESPONSIVE FAMILY, COMMUNITY, AND SCHOOL PARTNERSHIPS

The benefits of educators connecting with families and communities have been well documented. The nature of that interaction has changed, however, and educators are being called on to reconceptualize their practice to accommodate new roles families and communities play in the education of children and youth. Part III of this text addresses three skill areas that support anticipated changes in educational practice related to family–community–school partnerships: skill in communicating with parents and communities in ways that suggest mutual, albeit different, roles in the education of children and youth; skill in using the diversity of experiences students bring to the school setting to support learning; and skill among educators in assessing the needs of the context in which they work, as a means for working collaboratively with families and communities to generate solutions that address those needs. In many ways, it will be incumbent on future teachers to draw from skills common to other professions (e.g., counselors, social workers) to be effective teachers.

Chapter 8 addresses the importance of effective communication with families and communities. Traditional modes of communication between schools and family continue to be important in many school settings. The effectiveness of these strategies must be evaluated in light of needs of today's families, however. The types of barriers to communication that often exist between schools and families and communities representing multiple ethnic, cultural, and socioeconomic backgrounds are addressed, along with the importance of teachers developing skill in crosscultural communication. Chapter 8 concludes with a discussion of working with angry parents.

The importance of teachers learning how to incorporate into teaching the knowledge and experiences that *all* children bring to school settings has become more apparent. Teachers first have to believe that all homes and communities can contribute to the social, emotional, cultural, and educational capital needed to support school learning. Chapter 9 focuses on the influence of family and community on school learning by exploring the basis for the diversity of experiences students bring to the school setting. The importance of school–home–community collaboration is underscored, and an enhanced conception of collaboration is proposed—one that includes the use of cultural reciprocity, the development of trust, and increased ingenuity on the part of teachers, when thinking about family and community resources to support learning. The final chapter of the text presents a set of exercises designed to guide teachers' development of the Family, School, Community Profile, an evaluative document of family–community–school dynamics existing in specific community–school contexts. It also provides teacher candidates an opportunity to engage in self-reflection around school–family–community issues. The completed profile easily becomes a portfolio section documenting teacher skill and knowledge associated with school, family, and community dynamics.

Chapter 8

Communicating With Families and Communities

Communicating with parents has become an increasingly important teacher role. Effective family–community–school connections require expanded communication skills among teachers and other school personnel. This chapter focuses on three aspects of communication important to this connection, beginning with the value and status of traditional modes of school–family communications (e.g., parent–teacher conferences, parent nights, school newsletters, etc.). The dynamics and effectiveness of these meetings and activities are discussed, as well as the skills teachers bring to these interactions.

Barriers to communication between educators and families and communities with whom they wish to connect are the second focus of this chapter. This area is particularly important as educators attempt to communicate with families and communities representing multiple ethnic–cultural, socioeconomic, and language backgrounds. Cross-cultural communication modes are addressed as means to facilitate educators' ability to engage in sensitive and responsive communication with individuals from numerous backgrounds.

Finally, teachers and other educators are likely to encounter parents or other community members who are angry or critical, who use profanity, or who engage in behaviors believed to be inappropriate and counterproductive. Educators must find ways to communicate and work with these individuals as well. The chapter concludes with suggestions and strategies to address these situations.

SCHOOL–FAMILY COMMUNICATION PRACTICES

Teachers communicate with parents in multiple venues and for multiple reasons. While traditional school–family communication practices continue to exist, some have been altered, and new communication practices have emerged to address family change. Parent–teacher conferences, newsletters and notes to parents, parent orientations and back-to-school nights, phone calls and home visits, and grades and other forms of progress reports are among the traditional strategies used by schools to communicate with parents. Many school districts continue to use these strategies, and many are beginning to use technology as a means for improving communication with parents.

Parent–Teacher Conference

Parent–teacher conferences are most effective when viewed by parents and teachers as opportunities to ensure that complementary approaches are taking place in the school and the home to support students' growth and development. Teachers are able to present information on what is being taught and students' progress toward meeting academic goals, and parents should have the opportunity to discuss their goals for their children. Both parent and teacher can discuss students' emotional and social dispositions at home and at school because these characteristics influence academic growth. Schools have incorporated a number of changes that enhance the effectiveness of parent–teacher conferences. School districts having substantial numbers of parents who do not speak English may employ interpreters to facilitate communication. As means for minimizing the transportation difficulties experienced by some parents, schools may provide transportation to teacher–parent conferences and may also provide child care. Finally, many schools offer flexible conference schedules to accommodate families where both parents work.

Parent–teacher conferences may be structured in a number of ways; however, conferences that allow for ample time and privacy to discuss throughly students' performance, progress, and needs will likely be the most effective. Arena-type conferences where parents must seek their child's teacher in large settings such as a gym or lunchroom are used by some middle and high schools. Georgiady and Romano (2002) suggested this practice is ineffective because of the lack of an assigned time for parents to meet with teachers, the tendency of parents to rush interactions with teachers when others are waiting, and the hesitancy of parents to discuss certain issues because of a lack of privacy. They also question the effectiveness of the all-day conference where parents are informed that conferences will take place

Parents form opinions about the well-being of their child based on what teachers communicate about the student.
Back-to-School Night, Pauline A. Shaw School, Boston, MA.

but are not given a specific time to meet with teachers. Like the arena-type conference, teachers will not know how many parents will attend the conference and will likely feel pressured to complete a conference if other parents are waiting.

Although time and structural arrangements constitute physical influences on communication between parents and teachers during conferences, the language teachers use influences the emotional tone of the conference and can invite or disinvite effective communication with parents (Table 8.1). Language that is accusatory, offensive, or disparaging about students or their family serves only to anger, embarrass, or humiliate parents. Parents form opinions about the well-being of their child based on what teachers communicate about the student. As a result, teachers must find ways to communicate areas that are going well with students and those in need of improvement in ways that invite parents to discuss strategies that support improved educational situations for their children. Teachers' ability to listen to parents is just as important as the language used during the conference. Teachers can gain important insights about students based on the way parents talk about their children, questions that are asked, and concerns expressed during the conference. In the end, parents and teacher should leave the conference

TABLE 8.1
Disinviting Versus Inviting Language

Disinviting Language	*Inviting Language*
Lazy	Can do more when he or she tries
Uncooperative	Should learn to work with others
Stubborn	Insists on having her own way
Rude	Inconsiderate of others
Cheats	Depends on others to do her work
Liar	Doesn't always tell the truth
Below average	Working at his own level

From: Georgiady and Romano (2002).

feeling that a positive working relationship has been established between adults in the child's life.

Student-led conferences have been adopted by some teachers. The primary purpose of this conference model is to have students take responsibility for communicating to parents what they have learned. Teachers using this process believe preparation for the conference aids students' organizational skills and enhances communication skills as students describe their work, and in the case of older students, their academic performance to parents. Although a primary goal of the student-led conference is to increase parents' conference attendance, students may also conduct the conference at home if parents are unable to attend the scheduled conference period. In these cases, parent are offered the option of having an additional conference with teachers.

Teachers will want to be aware of the impact of this type of conference for some ethnic–cultural groups. While the development of children in leadership roles aligns with individualistic value structures, this aspect of child development may conflict with parent–child roles established in some families, particularly those having collectivistic values. In these families, children will be expected to look to parents for leadership and guidance (Quiroz, Greenfield, & Altchech, 1999). Teachers, however, can seek ways to bridge cultural traditions so that dominant-cultural strategies are combined with those that are familiar to parents of nondominant-culture traditions. For example, teachers could hold group conferences for parents with similar language backgrounds and for whom English is the second language. A group conference that builds on collectivist values will likely be less threatening and allow parents to gain insights and information from one another as questions and discussions ensue during the conference. An adult interpreter from the community could be invited to the meeting, rather than relying on children to interpret English to their parents (a common practice for parent–teacher conferences between teachers and non- or limited-English-speaking parents). The teacher could present general information to the group and then allow children to share their work and perhaps give parents a tour of the classroom. A conference so structured honors the schools' need that children be involved in parent–teacher conferences as it integrates different values into the process of conferencing with parents (Quiroz et al., 1999).

Back-to-School Nights and Organized School Meetings

Back-to-School Nights are important events in that teachers have the opportunity to present their goals for the year to parents. This first formal meeting between parents and teachers often sets the tone for parent–teacher relations throughout the year. Elementary teachers, in particular, attempt to present an inviting classroom environment so that parents have an idea of the climate in which the child will spend a large portion of the day. The teacher presentation, however, is critical for all teachers. The content of this message should leave parents with the feeling that their child or young person will have a successful academic year under the charge of a caring, knowledgeable, and skillful educator. A number of teachers have moved to Power-Point presentations, with handouts for parents to refer to later.

For many teachers, back-to-school night attendance is a sign of parental interest. Some teachers may use this night as an opportunity to engage parents as volunteers, but many are more concerned that parents show an interest in teachers' academic goals and expectations for children for the year. Absent parents miss this important message. Given its importance, teachers may have to use additional means (i.e., home visits, Web sites, newsletters) to get the message to parents.

Schools also sponsor a number of additional school meetings, some of which involve selected teachers. Whether they are involved in the meeting or not, teachers should be aware of the meeting's purpose, just in case parents need additional information about the session. Special information nights might focus on a particular discipline or skill area. For example, math or technology nights might introduce parents to new materials or a change in the curriculum. Schools may also have math nights designed to teach parents a skill or concept so that they are better able to support their children through homework.

Other organized school meetings might focus on changes in the status of the school community. Information sessions on changes in district attendance boundaries that might affect the school attended by a child or a district's decision to close a school are representative of this type of organized meeting. Additionally, meetings or orientations for parents at school-level transition points, such as the transition from elementary to middle school or middle school to high school are common to many school districts. For the most part, attendance at organized school meetings is optional, with schools having varying levels of success at persuading parents to attend these meetings. Some schools use creative means for increasing parental attendance at these events. Combining information sessions with some type of student performance (e.g., drama presentation or musical performance), turning the event into a community meal-sharing time, or developing a contest between classes based on the number of parents attending an event are among strategies that have been used to increase parental attendance at school-sponsored meetings.

Home Visits

Home visits have served as a strategy for schools to communicate with parents for centuries. They were previously viewed as an opportunity for teachers to teach parents how to raise children in ways that supported the work of schools and how to conduct school-related activities in the home. Although some educators continue to view the goal of home visits in this way, many now see them as a means for teachers to learn more about students and their parents. In some instances, home visits serve as an opportunity for teachers to introduce themselves and their goals and expectations to parents in a one-time visit arrangement at the beginning of the year. Teachers also have the opportunity to learn of goals and/or concerns parents have about their children's education. Other home visits may be ongoing, conducted several times during the school year.

The home visit provides an additional avenue for teachers to build a level of trust and rapport with parents. Teachers who conduct home visits communicate care and concern to parents about the school-age child and children observe a home–school connection in which two adults are focused on them. Just as important, teachers who reach out to parents using this approach communicate a desire to develop a relationship. The existence of a relationship between parent and teacher allows teachers to rely on relational authority when it comes to communicating to parents the importance of school–family partnerships in children's education.

Even though the home visit can have a positive effect on school–home relations, some teachers are hesitant to embrace this activity because of concerns of safety, fear over parental reactions, time constraints, and a lack of knowledge as to how to conduct a home visit (Taveras, 1998). **Home–school liaisons** are normally familiar with the school neighborhood and parents and can serve as a support for teachers who are ambivalent about a neighborhood or parental reaction. The liaison can also provide teachers with information that will aid in conducting a productive home visit.

Home visits are more common for early childhood teachers and teachers of elementary-age children. Some districts have experimented with forms of home visits that are appropriate for parents of young people at any age or grade level. Ziegler (2000) described a home visit at which teams have been organized to visit homes and communities. In addition to visits made to focus on school issues related to an individual child, this type of home visit may also have the goal of ensuring a school presence in the community, to provide information, and to encourage parents to become more involved with the school.

Phone Calls, Notes, and Newsletters

Phone calls home have been mainstays for teachers as a means for communicating with parents. Teachers may call to report misbehavior or missed work, and some teachers call to report academic progress or positive change in a child's behavior. Some teachers make their home telephone numbers available to parents so that parents can initiate phone calls as well. Calls home have lost some of their effectiveness because of family change and diversity. Teachers who would like to reach parents during the school day often face the fact that parents or guardians work. They must then decide whether to call a parent at work; to attempt to reach a parent later in the day, perhaps after school; or to call a parent in the evening. Additionally, given the diversity of socioeconomic levels among families, it should be expected that some families will not have phones or that phone service is frequently interrupted. The phone call home may also be ineffective with non-English-speaking parents and with parents having limited English proficiency. When teachers are able to communicate with a parent by phone, the effectiveness of the call in aiding desired outcomes among students varies. Teachers who find themselves calling the same parents repeatedly for the same reasons might reflect on the possibility that the phone contact is less productive compared with other communication modes.

Written communication to parents in the form of notes and newsletters is a common practice among individual teachers and schools. Notes may provide parents with information regarding student problems and successes. They may also serve as a vehicle to welcome new families to a school. In an effort to start the year on a positive note, many teachers write notes or letters to parents to introduce themselves and to state their goals for the school year. Teachers who use notes as a means to report problems run the risk of the note never reaching home. As schools move toward the use of technology as a mode of communication, notes homes are being used less frequently.

Newsletters may be produced by an individual teacher, a group of teachers (e.g., those at the same grade level or a high school department), or by the total school. They are used not only to report important school events to parents, but may also include parenting information, questions or exercises that call for a response from parents, and learning activities to be shared by parents and children. Newsletters provide a vehicle for discussing school policy issues and may highlight school, teacher, or student achievements. In addition, newsletters may include Web sites to which parents may refer for information or activities with children. To increase possibilities of parents reading the newsletter, they should be sent at scheduled times so that parents learn to expect them. This may serve as a remedy to one problem associated with newsletters—that of the communication never reaching students' homes. Some schools post newsletters on Web sites to increase chances that newsletter information reaches parents.

Schools or teachers who use newsletters as means for communicating with parents must take into consideration literacy and language issues when deciding on the value of the newsletter as a communication tool. Parents for whom English is the second language should be able to access information contained in the letter. Furthermore, schools having large numbers of students with parents who are poor readers will want to consider whether these parents are able to access the information as well. Newsletters lose their effectiveness as a communication tool when inaccessible language or jargon that is unfamiliar to parents is used. Complex or abstract language is not necessary to communicate important messages to parents. Also, parents are more likely to get "hooked" on newsletters when there is a personal element in the newsletter, and they can look forward to reading something about a teacher or student, for example, whom they know.

Technology and Communication

A growing number of schools use technology as means for communicating with parents. Teachers may create distribution lists that include parents having access to e-mail. The distribution list allows teachers to notify parents quickly of events, as well as to survey parents for input on any number of issues. Parents can also e-mail teachers directly and have access to other parents in their child's classroom. Some teachers may have a Web site where parents can get information about assignments and classroom or school policies and events. A shortcoming of the use of e-mail and Web sites is that some parents may not have access to the Internet or may be uncomfortable using technology. A survey of parents' access to and comfort with technology before embarking on a technology-based communication system is important. A number of strategies, such as a technology-training session for parents or, where necessary, providing hard copies of some materials, may be needed to ensure that all parents can access information.

Inquiry and Reflection 8A: Access Web sites for two schools located in your observation site community. What type of information is communicated? Is the information presented so that it is accessible to a diversity of parents? What is communicated about the school? What is unnecessary, and what could be added?

Integrating technology into home–school communication practices may be particularly helpful at the middle and high school levels, when reduced contact between teachers and parents is accompanied by reduced contact between parent and child (Strom & Strom, 2002/2003). Adolescent students are less dependable as conduits of written or verbal information to parents from schools and may even intercept negative information meant for parents. Strom and Strom described a program where palm pilots and pagers were used to communicate both negative and positive messages to parents using codes that aligned with specific issues or behaviors. The use of these technologies received positive evaluations from both parents and teachers because of both the immediacy of messages and the confidence that the messages actually reached the parent.

Grades and Progress Reports

Report cards are the most traditional format for communicating information to both parents and students about students' performance and social and academic development. According to Munk and Bursuck (2001), report cards are intended to communicate information regarding students' strengths and weaknesses, level of motivation and work habits, and achievement in specific curricular areas. In some cases, information on students' overall performance and ability communicate the need for academic or social support beyond that available within the regular classroom structure. Parents may sense this need, but may feel powerless in effecting a changed learning environment for their children (see Case 8A). The expectation is that parents and school personnel would work together for appropriate solutions.

Letter grades are familiar to parents; however, the meaning intended by teachers when submitting grades and parents' understanding of the meaning behind the grade may not always match. In a study of parents of secondary students, Munk and Bursuck (2001) found that parents, in general, believed grades were too general to provide sufficient information regarding students' performance. Based on their responses, it appeared parents questioned the accuracy, fairness, and usefulness of grades, due primarily to a lack of understanding or awareness of the processes used by teachers to

Case 8A: "They Just Let Her Went"

> *First she was in the second... and they passed, they let her went, they just let her went to third grade.... The man that was s'posed to been helping her... he say he doesn't like keeping kids behind... at the time I felt like she wasn't ready to go to third grade.... I was telling him she needs to stay in that grade... make her learn more... then she would know everything... but they say she'll pick up.... Her port card, evertime she got her port card, it was all Fs. I mean all of em.... She was still behind her grades and stuff, and she still is. She haven't move up none... They pass her to fourth grade, and why they do it, I don't know.* (—Fern, single mother of three living in poverty)

determine grades. Furthermore, despite the tendency of some teachers to do so, parents appeared not to be interested in students getting higher grades because of effort or as a means for increasing student motivation. Teachers having multiple meanings for specific grades (e.g., a grade of "C" may represent students' effort, or it may represent the level or quality of knowledge and skills) may lull some parents into complacency about a child's progress, where additional academic support might be warranted. According to Munk and Bursuck (2001), communication between parents and teachers could be enhanced by teachers providing the criteria or purpose for giving certain grades before actually submitting the grades.

> Inquiry and Reflection 8B: The mother in Case 8A believes her daughter is not performing well. Despite her protests, the daughter is twice passed to the next grade. The mother is distressed about these events. What are the possible areas of communication breakdown between the mother, teacher, and the school?

Rates of response in the Munk and Bursuck study were higher among parents of high-achieving students, low-achieving students, and students with disabilities than they were for parents of average-achieving students. Rates of return could indicate that the former groups of parents have heightened interests in grades, but for different reasons. Parents of high-achieving students are more apt to be interested in grades because of the impact on future employment and educational opportunities. Grades, for these parents, not only allow them to track students' performance, but also serve as a communication tool for future employers and postsecondary schools. Rates of return by parents of lower achieving students and those with learning disabilities could indicate that these parents perceived the distributed survey as an opportunity to express frustration or concern over grades received by their children.

Some schools incorporate alternative or authentic assessments (e.g., the use of a portfolio of student work) believing parents are provided with more in-depth information about what children know and are able to do. It is important in these instances to explain to parents through meetings or other mechanisms how to understand and interpret students' progress, based on alternative assessment tools. Although some parents may initially be skeptical of a progress report that goes beyond the more familiar report of grades or a report card, many parents come to appreciate the more detailed information about children's performance available from authentic assessment documentation.

In addition to report cards and alternative and authentic assessment processes for communicating students' progress and performance, many teachers and schools use technology not only as means for reporting grades, but also as a vehicle for providing information about assignment due dates and assignments students may be missing. Through use of Web pages, teachers are able to communicate detailed and frequent information about students' progress and performance, both of which appear to have a positive impact on students' achievement (Rogers, 2000).

Although teachers are guided to use multiple measures to determine students' academic performance and progress, performance on standardized tests is frequently uppermost in teachers' minds because of the high-stakes nature of this assessment for schools, teachers, and students. As discussed in Chapter 7, standardized tests have become primary measures of teacher and school accountability. Under No Child Left Behind schools must demonstrate adequate yearly progress with rising achieving levels for all children. If a school fails to make progress for 2 consecutive years, students must be offered the opportunity to transfer to a better performing school, and the district must provide transportation. Schools failing to show progress for a third year must provide supplemental services chosen by parents.

Schools must ensure that parents have adequate test performance information. This information should be communicated in the form of district "report cards" that provide test performance information at the class, school, and district levels. Test information must also be disaggregated by race, socioeconomic level, disability, and English proficiency. In a study conducted by Donegan and Trepanier-Street (1998), teachers and parents differed in terms of beliefs regarding the use of standardized tests to compare teachers, administrators, school districts as a whole, and individual schools within the same district. Although teachers strongly opposed the use of standardized for these purposes, parents strongly supported this use of standardized test results. In many communities, test results are published in local newspapers, thus giving parents information needed to compare test performance among schools in a district.

In an era where accountability is at the center of many educational discourses, teachers and other school personnel are challenged from professional, legal, and ethical perspectives to communicate performance information that allows parents to make educational decisions for their children. For many in the educational community, grades and other measures of student performance are secondary to performance on standardized tests. The extent to which parents compare and contrast grades and standardized test performance has not been fully researched.

Communicating Sensitive or Unpleasant Information

Teachers are often the bearers of unpleasant information to parents and may feel hesitant, afraid, or uncomfortable when faced with this particular communication task. Letting parents know about bad or inappropriate behaviors, that children or youth are failing or will be retained, or sharing sensitive information (e.g., child's involvement with substance abuse) is never easy, yet it must be accomplished in a straightforward and honest way. Ramsey (2002) suggested that teachers never be vague when communicating potentially painful news, even as they are aware that parents may exhibit a range of emotions in response to what they are hearing. Parents may be angry, devastated, cooperative, defensive, or in a state of denial. The teacher's role, however, is to present honest information in clear and straightforward language (i.e., avoid being coy, using jargon, or presenting too much or too little information). If the goal is to work with parents for the best interest of the child, it is also not helpful to be arrogant, patronizing, or blaming. Ramsey noted the importance of teachers providing information such as students' rights, legal implications of students' behavior (or implications for school or district policies where appropriate), choices available, and resources (school, community) that might offer help.

COMMUNICATING WITH COMMUNITIES

In addition to strategies for communicating with parents, teachers and schools must be aware of messages communicated to the school and district community. Perceptions held by the community at large influence the kind and level of support extended to public schools. Public engagement as an educational reform strategy focuses on increasing community discussions about public schools, with the goal of increasing support for public education (Kernan-Schloss & Plattner, 1998). A first step in initiating community discussions is to listen well to communities, so that community priorities are clear. This is not an easy task in that teachers and schools often have multiple publics within a community, and it is often the case that differences in perceptions of how well schools and teachers are performing their responsibilities will exist among these groups. Past school efforts to manipulate public expectations is becoming less desirable and is being replaced by strategies to manage communities' need for information on district goals, processes and progress in reaching those goals, and what is to be expected during the process as districts move toward reaching goals.

Inquiry and Reflection 8C: Search a local newspaper for school district issues over the past year. Describe the issue and the school district's response. In your view, did this response enhance or damage community support for the district?

Although district goals are highlighted here, teachers play two important roles in communicating with communities. First, many parents rely on teachers as a source of information. Therefore, it is important that teachers be informed about district goals and strategies so that they are able to communicate accurate information to parents and the community. Second, teachers may find themselves acting as spokespersons to community organizations or at public meetings because they are often perceived as a credible source of information for what is happening in the classroom. For many community groups, student achievement is often the bottom line. Teachers, and sometimes their students, can provide examples to community groups of ways in which schools are addressing student achievement goals.

Schools comprising both majority and minority communities must find ways to communicate with both, even when they have different needs and expectations of teachers. For some communities of color, even seeing a teacher in the community beyond the school walls or school day communicates the teacher's desire and willingness to develop a relationship with the community. Teachers willing to interact with communities of color in this way improve the likelihood of developing relationships that lead to a level of respect that influences behavior of children and their parents. Some communities of color expect that professional boundaries (as perceived by teachers) should not get in the way of building relationships with the community. Relationships, for some communities of color, are based on trust and mutual comfort and are not limited by boundaries established by the teaching profession. Teachers able to establish trust with communities of color find themselves able to rely on both positional and relational authority when interacting with parents and children from minority ethnic–cultural backgrounds.

CROSS-CULTURAL COMMUNICATION

Multicultural perspectives are addressed in teacher education courses at varying levels, and most programs attempt to expose preservice teachers to diverse teaching and learning environments through field and clinical experiences. Still, too many teacher education programs are pervasively **monocultural** in their outlook and promote individualistic values as perservice teachers learn what it means to teach and what it means to learn. Knowledge of what to expect of parents in the educational process is based on individualistic value orientations as well. As a result, many teachers continue to bring cultural assumptions to teacher practice that serve as barriers to communication with certain families. Teachers seeking to build or improve on relationships with parents are encouraged to develop a habit of reflecting on the impact of their beliefs and behaviors on the quality of communication with parents and make modifications that facilitate improved interactions (Lupi & Ton, 2001). Individualistic and collective cultural patterns are often at the center of conflicts between the home and school during home–school communication. When working with families who adopt nondominant-culture family patterns, teachers' intended meanings are sometimes misinterpreted, and generally accepted patterns of social interaction are often ineffective (Quiroz et al., 1999). As teachers work with diverse groups of parents, they should anticipate that diverse communication patterns will play a role in different communication episodes.

Communication Patterns

Schools, as dominant-culture-based institutions, have historically been less tolerant of thought, behavior, and communication patterns different from dominant-culture norms. Communication across cultures does not, however, have to be limited to dominant-culture communication patterns (Ting-Tommey, 1999). Ting-Tommey proposed five assumptions of cross-cultural communication to be considered when entering communication episodes with individuals having cultural backgrounds and preferences different from one's own:

1. Varying degrees of cultural group membership differences and similarities exist when individuals from different cultural groups communicate. Group membership factors affect the communication process on either a conscious or unconscious level.
2. Simultaneous encoding and decoding of verbal and nonverbal messages take place during cross-cultural communication. Encoding and decoding processes can lead to a shared understanding of what is being communicated or to cross-cultural misunderstanding.
3. Unintended clashes occur during cross-cultural communication. **Pragmatic variables** of communication are determined by cultural scripts and

differ among various cultural groups. Appropriate communication variables for one culture will appear rude or inappropriate to another.

4. Cross-cultural communication is context and interactive-situation bound. It is influenced by the cultural norms, beliefs, knowledge, and experiences of the interacting individuals, given the context and situation of the interactive episode.

5. Cross-cultural communication takes place within social systems where interacting individuals have been socialized by socializing elements that differ at macro levels (e.g., family, education, religion, socioeconomic system) and micro levels (e.g., day-to-day interaction with individuals in our living environments), as well as by the media. Individuals, however, are not locked into points of view resulting from their socialization and are thus able to make a choice to use different cultural lenses to understand different cultural perspectives.

Teachers able to interpret verbal and nonverbal communication patterns among diverse groups of parents will likely open channels for more effective communication and interactions. One way of understanding the relationship between family diversity and communication patterns is to think of communication within frameworks that align with collectivistic or individualistic value orientations discussed earlier in the text. Groups oriented toward individualistic values likely adopt more **low-context communication patterns,** whereas collectivistic-oriented groups lean toward **high-context communication patterns.** Meaning within a low-context communication framework is expressed through explicit verbal messages. A preference for direct talk, verbal self-enhancement, talkativeness, and **person-oriented verbal interaction** (i.e., emphasis on unique personal identities, with less attention to formalities and roles or status of those communicating) predominates in situations and communication episodes where individualistic values are the norm. Additionally, speakers are expected to express clear verbal messages.

Conversely, nonverbal communication (e.g., pauses, silence) plays a larger role in meaning making within a high-context communication framework, as does the respective roles and positions of the communicators during the communication episode. Within high-context communication episodes, the listener is expected to interpret the meaning of the message from what is said as well as what is not said directly. A preference for indirect talk, silence, and **status-oriented verbal interaction** (i.e., status or power associated with individuals' roles are important, with appropriate language and **paralanguage** given the respective status of those communicating) can be associated with situations and communication episodes where collectivistic values predominate. These opposing communication frameworks are best viewed as a continuum of communication preferences, with individuals from both value orientations incorporating some of each (Ting-Tommey, 1999).

Pragmatic variables, such as the opening and closing of conversations, the leader of discussions, and changing subjects are also culturally determined, yet play an important role in the quality of communication between teachers and parents. Even the tone of voice and candidness of the message content can be culturally dictated. Families from non-dominant-culture and minority language backgrounds may not be familiar with dominant-culture pragmatics. This unfamiliarity with rules of speaking may lead to hesitancy to speak up at a parent–teacher conference, for example. Relatedly, teachers may wish to be aware of the impact of the level of familiarity displayed during teacher–parent interactions. Jokes, for example, may be misread (or misunderstood) or felt to be inappropriate for someone holding the position of teacher. DuPraw and Axner (1997) discussed six cultural pattern differences that potentially influence cross-cultural communication (Table 8.2). As with all references to group characteristics, the location of individuals along the Assimilation–Enculturation Continuum (see Chapter 3) should

TABLE 8.2
Influences on Cross-Cultural Communication

Attitude Toward Conflict ■ Conflict viewed as negative by some groups, positive by others ■ Preference for face-to-face resolution by some, open conflict embarrassing or demeaning to others	*Approach to Task Completion* ■ Build relationships before work on tasks (Asian, Latino); for others, relationships are established in the process of completing tasks (European Americans)
Decision-Making Styles ■ Majority rules for some groups (dominant-culture value); for others, consensus is preferred (some Asian American groups) ■ Decision making delegated for some groups, others value personal decision making	*Attitudes Toward Disclosure* ■ Frankness about emotions and discussing personal information or reasons behind conflict is inappropriate for some groups ■ Questions probing about personal situations is viewed as intrusive by some groups
Approach to Knowing ■ Some groups prefer cognitive approaches to knowing (European), others symbolic imagery and rhythm (African), and still others knowledge gained through transcendence (Asian) ■ Approach to knowing influences approach to problem solving	*Different Communication Styles* ■ Differences in meaning behind the same word or phrase ■ Differences in communication intensity (e.g., raised voices for White Americans signify conflict; for African Americans or Jewish Americans, raised voices are part of friendly conversation)

From DuPraw and Axner (1997). Working on common cross-cultural communication challenges. http//www.wwcd.org/action/ampu/crosscult.html

be considered. As an example, ethnic-minority parents who are more assimilated could exhibit communication patterns typical of dominant culture parents.

Inquiry and Reflection 8D: Using the six influences on cross-cultural communication (see DuPraw & Axner, 1997), conduct an in-depth study of cultural patterns along the six areas suggested for two ethnic–cultural groups that are different from your own.

Communication and English-Language Usage

Given the diversity among families today, teachers will need to communicate with parents having a range of English-language capabilities. Parents may be bilingual, thus able to speak English (at varying skill levels) when conversing with teachers, while preferring to speak their first language among members of their ethnic–cultural group. It is also appropriate to view English dialects as part of a bilingual capability. For example, some African Americans speak standard English in formal conversations (e.g., parent–teacher conference) but may switch to **Ebonics** (an English dialect) when conversing with a group of African Americans. Ebonics, however, may be the only form of language used by some African American parents. Some parents may speak a mixture of English and another language (e.g., Spanish), which makes for a more challenging communication episode for those not having facility with Spanish, for example. In other cases English-language pronunciation among parents for whom English is not the first language may make it difficult to understand all that is being communicated.

Teachers often make judgments of parental capability based on parents' ability to use "standard English." Parents using incorrect grammar, those with limited English skills, and those who do not speak English are judged to be less able to support children's academic and social development than parents able to engage in clear oral and written English language when communicating with teachers. As Ting-Tommy pointed out, however, "on linguistic grounds, all languages are created equal" (1999, p. 93). Although teachers may prefer the use of standard English, the essence of parental messages should not be ignored or minimized simply because parents are not using standard English. Neither should poor English usage skills be translated to meaning a parent cares less about the education of his or her children. The parent in Case 8A is clearly concerned about her daughter's educational experience, even though the message is not communicated in standard English. Teachers may have to listen more carefully to understand the message that is being communicated.

Inquiry and Reflection 8E: Assume the parent in Case 8A communicates her concerns to you at the beginning of the school year. Describe this parent's concern in a memo directed to all parties within the school you believe can offer information and/or support to her, her daughter, and you as the child's new teacher.

English-language usage will not be the only communication issue at hand when communicating with parents having limited English proficiency. Lack of facility with English is complicated by a lack of knowledge about the way schools work. Although this may be expected of recent immigrant parents, parents who have lived in the states for a number of years but who were not educated in U.S. schools may also have limited understanding of schooling in this country. Furthermore, parents who were educated here but who had poor schooling experiences may still be unaware of the complexities of schooling in the United States. The primary goal when working with parents from diverse language backgrounds is to establish a process for engaging in meaningful and respectful communication. To develop workable strategies, the suspension of judgment about parents based on their ability to use standard English is likely a first step. Sometimes an interpreter is necessary, keeping in mind that it may be more appropriate to contact an adult interpreter rather than rely on a child. Other times, more careful and intent listening on the teacher's part is warranted. Providing open and clear explanations of the relationship between what is being communicated and broader schooling practices will support parents in becoming more informed collaborators in the education of their children.

COMMUNICATING WITH ANGRY PARENTS

Teachers will work with angry or out-of-control parents at some point in their teaching careers. Parental anger may occur as result of information communicated during a conference or phone conversation, or anger may come about as a result of a perception on parents' part that their children have been treated unfairly or disrespectfully or put in harm's way. Parents may take offense to intentional or unintentional negative remarks made by teachers. From the parents' perspective, such remarks reflect negatively on parenting capability or on a personal characteristic. Some parents express complaints to the principal (or even to the superintendent, school board, or the media). Others express their anger by refusing to interact with teachers or the school. Still other parents confront teachers directly and may even appear at the classroom door without notice, either during or after the school day.

Confrontational episodes with angry parents are more apt to occur around holiday seasons, when the economy or other social forces are affecting the sense of well-being among families, or when disruptive home situations (e.g., parental separation or divorce) increase family stress. In some cases, parents simply do not trust that teachers and other school personnel have the best interest of their children at heart. Their mistrust of teachers make for a more volatile teacher–parent relationship that can more easily erupt into anger episodes.

Angry parents may yell, use profanity, or threaten teachers, and, in some instances, parents have actually physically assaulted teachers. It is important that teachers feel safe and that they are aware of school plans and policies for security and safety in situations involving angry parents. Teachers have to develop a sense of when to work with an angry parent, when to call for help, and when to simply walk away. It is important to understand that parental anger is a sign of a problem. Even so, teachers are not devoid of emotional responses to parental anger and may feel afraid, defensive, or angry themselves. Teachers may feel unappreciated or hurt, particularly if they feel they have extended extra effort to help or support a student. Despite the natural instinct to feel personally attacked, it is important to remember that angry parents confront teachers professionally and not personally. Listening is probably the best initial response to an angry parent. Teachers able to hold their emotions in check are better able to listen objectively to what is being communicated and to think clearly about how best to respond. Reacting defensively or becoming angry in turn not only interferes with the teacher's understanding of what has made the parent so upset, but also interferes with the possibility that the parent merely wanted to vent (Ramsey, 2002).

In the process of listening, teachers will have the opportunity to learn why the parent is angry, with the underlining assumption that the parent has an unmet need or expectation. Teachers also will want to determine the parent's view of what has or has not been done, as well as what the parent expects teachers can do about the situation. The worst response to parental anger is to minimize the parent's concern or to respond in a patronizing manner. Often parental anger is based in erroneous information, but teachers may want to hear the parent out before rushing to provide correct information. As difficult as it may be, teachers should consider finding a point of agreement, even when the parent is wrong. An intact relationship with the parent may be more valuable in the long run than being right and putting the parent in his or her place.

Teachers who agree to unreasonable demands or make promises they cannot keep only make matters worse. In the short run, they may be able to calm the parent and defuse a difficult and likely uncomfortable situation. In the long run, they risk a subsequent anger episode if they are unable to follow through on promises. It is far better to have the parent agree that

ANGER

ANGER

ANGER

ANGER

ANGER

(Is a sign that a problem exists)

Parents will likely exhibit anger when

- ☞ they feel hurt
- ☞ their needs are not being met
- ☞ they sense they are being disrespected
- ☞ they are frustrated about not getting what they want
- ☞ they perceive they or their children have been mistreated
- ☞ they feel ignored or that issues important to them are not being addressed
- ☞ they feel they have lost control over factors affecting situations important to them

Figure 8.1 Reasons parents exhibit anger.

more time or information is needed to find a solution to their concern or frustration. Even though teachers are encouraged to remain calm and be good listeners, it is also recommended that they look for opportunities during anger-charged conversations to explain their point of view tactfully and assertively.

CONCLUDING COMMENTS

Effective and respectful communication with families and communities has become an integral component of teacher practice. Although a number of traditional processes for communicating with parents persist, even these are being altered to ensure that communication occurs with broader numbers of parents. Teachers are being called on to expand their communication skills so that culture and language differences cease to be barriers to communication. This change calls for teachers to be aware of personal language biases. It also calls for teachers to be reflective about judgments and assumptions made about parents based on parental facility with the English language. Finally, although the topic is not routinely addressed, teachers should expect that they will work with angry parents. In a sense, knowing more about families and communities not only will support teachers' work with diverse families, but will also aid teachers on occasions when they must work with parents who have lost control and confront teachers in anger-tinged communication episodes.

GUIDED OBSERVATIONS

8F. Describe the ethnic–cultural, socioeconomic, and language background characteristic of the community in which your observation site is located. How does your school respond to the varying communication needs of the community? Are the strategies used effective?

8G. Collect copies of written communication used by your school to communicate with parents. Provide a written analysis of these documents in light of the ethnic–cultural, socioeconomic, language, and the educational level of parents that make up the school community.

8H. Sit in on parent conferences arranged by your observation site mentor or cooperating teacher. Look for nonverbal communication and signs of anger among parents. How does your mentor or cooperating teacher work with these communication issues?

Chapter 9

Collaborating With Families and Communities: Support for Teaching and Learning

Most teachers, along with society at large, agree that children's homes and communities affect school performance. Judgments made about home and community characteristics can lead, however, to conclusions that certain home and community environments simply cannot provide the social, emotional, cultural, and educational capital needed to support school learning. It has long been known that teachers have low expectations of children and youth from ethnic-minority and low-socioeconomic homes. Some teachers likely have similar expectations of parents in these homes. Teachers' belief systems affect not only teacher–student interactions but teacher–parent interactions as well. Deficit evaluations made by teachers of some homes and communities contribute to barriers to home–school–community collaborations directly focused on school performance.

The predominant thinking on family and community involvement in education emerges from an **"educentric"** perspective (Dunlap & Alva, 1999). A tendency on the part of teachers to view parent and community involvement in education from perspectives that reflect only school values, goals, and priorities is limiting in that it interferes with teachers' ability to understand goals parents may have for the education of their children.

Because teachers continue to believe that homes influence school performance, then it is incumbent on them to have a clearer understanding of how different home environments actually contribute to student learning. Teachers will need to be prepared for the fact that home contributions will take different forms—and will likely reflect the diversity existing in their classrooms. This chapter first explores the influence of home environments on student learning. A discussion of the diversity of experiences students bring to the school setting will follow, along with an examination of how diverse experiences can be used to support learning. The second section of the chapter focuses on school–community connections and the challenges and potential positive outcomes when schools and communities collaborate to support children and families.

FAMILY INFLUENCES ON LEARNING

It is clear that learning, motivation, and performance are influenced by the home environment. Given the level of diversity in the United States today, we should expect that all children arrive at school "ready to learn" with different kinds of prior knowledge and experiences that potentially support school learning. An alternate interpretation—that children from some homes arrive at school lacking appropriate skills and knowledge and thus are ill prepared to learn—rests on beliefs that children must have predetermined knowledge and experiences to be successful in school. Some families may be aware of the type of skills and knowledge expected by schools and will seek ways to ensure that their children have them. Other families may not be aware of such concerns or have no need for these in their everyday lives. Important for teachers to remember, however, is that the home is not only the first site for learning knowledge and skills; it is also the place where children learn how to learn (Nieto, 1999).

Approaches to Learning

The culture of the home plays an important role in student learning. John Ogbu (1978, 1994) conducted extensive research on the social adaptation of minority groups in countries having dominant and minority cultures. Ogbu suggested that voluntary minorities (for example, groups choosing to immigrate to the United States for economic opportunity or political freedom) have different perceptions, attitudes, and strategies for interacting with the dominant or host culture than will involuntary minorities. Involuntary minorities are groups who were unwillingly incorporated into the United States through enslavement, conquest, or colonization and were denied true assimilation into the dominant culture way of life (e.g., African Americans, Mexican Americans, Native Hawaiians). Voluntary minorities tend to compare their situation here in the United States with that of group members in their homeland and believe that they are much better off in the United States. Moreover, they view differences between themselves and the dominant culture as temporary barriers that can be overcome. Conversely,

World Views

Different groups develop different ways of viewing the world.

Worldviews influence

*** Values**

*** Skills**

*** Ways of making meaning of people and situations**

Figure 9.1 Worldviews.

involuntary minorities have no group in other countries with whom to compare their current living situation and, according to Ogbu (1994), tend to develop ways of viewing the world that are in opposition to that of the dominant-culture. Ogbu suggested that oppositional frames of reference and oppositional identities lead involuntary minorities to the conclusion that institutional racism will serve as a barrier to progress that will not be superceded by education.

Differences in worldviews (Figure 9.1) are particularly important to note because they undergird differences in the values, skills, and ways of making meaning of people and situations transferred to children by parents. Although it is commonly known that customs and traditions that children embrace are influenced by these teachings, less attention has been paid to the fact that cognitive development is also influenced by worldviews. **Cognitive socialization,** the process by which children are socialized to acquire cognitive skills or patterns of intelligence that are functional within a particular culture differs from culture to culture (Ogbu, 1994). Thus, a child from a White middle-class family may possess cognitive skills and knowledge different from a Mexican-American child living in poverty. Differences in skills and knowledge possessed by one child may be prized over the skills and knowledge of the other, depending on the cultural context in which the evaluation or judgment is taking place.

Some educators suggest that an approach to learning or learning style can also be associated with one's cultural background (Table 9.1). This perspective has caused consternation among other educators. They fear teachers

TABLE 9.1
Approach to Learning (Learning Style)

* Negotiated activity and not a display of ascribed characteristics
* Pattern for processing information—not a measure of ability
* Preference for learning
* Observable across domain-specific competencies
Mediating Influences
* Family's position on the Assimilation–Enculturation Continuum (see Chapter 3)
* Gender
* Socioeconomic status
* Flexibility and adaptability of the learner

will use a learning style–culture formula to label children with a particular learning style solely on the basis of their cultural background. As suggested by Nieto (1999), conveniently deciding that a child has a particular learning style based on his or her cultural background leads to assessment and instructional strategies and adaptations that are overly mechanical and technical. Quoting the work of Deyhle and Swisher (1997), Nieto suggested that group tendencies for approaches to learning could serve as a framework to observe and gain more understanding of how an individual child approaches learning.

Funds of Knowledge and Culturally Responsive Teaching

Many children benefit from school structures and practices that support their cultural backgrounds and communication styles. Others are socialized to communicate and learn based on cultural and communication patterns not practiced in school settings. In fact, values honored in their homes may be disparaged at schools in ways that negatively affect their motivation and performance (Nieto, 1999). One step toward understanding differences in the social and intellectual resources existing in diverse home environments is to consider that all children have "funds of knowledge," the historically developed and accumulated skills, abilities, practices, and knowledge that are essential to household functioning and well-being (Gonzales et al., 1994).

Teachers need to seek actively to understand funds of knowledge possessed by children from cultural- and linguistic-minority homes. To become aware of funds of knowledge possessed by their students, teachers need to understand the social and labor histories of ethnic-minority families, how they develop social networks both within and outside of the home, and, for some, how the exchange of resources between families occurs. Some teachers may view these activities as well beyond the role of teachers, but consider the fact that this information is known for traditional dominant-culture families and consciously or unconsciously integrated into school and classroom practices. Similar information is needed for ethnic- and linguistic-minority families to access the source and nature of knowledge and skills existing in these families (Gonzales et al., 1994).

Home visits, family interviews, and student observations and interviews are among the ways teachers become aware of home-context knowledge and skills students from non-dominant-culture and non-middle-class homes bring to school settings. Beyond that, teachers will need to create and develop classroom practices—that is, to engage in **culturally responsive classroom practices**— to reduce the discontinuity between the home and classroom practices. Belgarde, Mitchell, and Arquero (2002) defined culturally responsive education as curriculum and teaching that validate students and allow them to co-construct knowledge in school settings. Teachers actively connect what and how they teach to the cultural and linguistic backgrounds existing in the homes and communities of their students. Students are thus able to use what they already know to construct new academic knowledge. A number of scholars believe teachers able to identify culturally relevant skills and prior knowledge that children bring to school are able to use this information to facilitate increased learning. These teachers are in a better position to help students make meaningful connections between the knowledge and experiences brought to school with expected learning within school contexts (Delpit, 1995a; Gay, 1993; Hollins, 1996; Zeichner, 1996). Culturally responsive teaching begins with teachers accepting and valuing the experiences and prior knowledge all children bring to school.

Home Language and Learning

Worldviews and beliefs are reflected in spoken language, thus making language an important part of learning. For this reason, it is extremely important that teachers know students' home language. Language is part of cognitive functioning in that it allows for categorization of experiences. As important, language allows us to shape ideas (Ting-Tommey, 1999) and organize unrelated experiences into coherent and understandable funds of knowledge. An increasing number of students come from homes where English is not the primary language spoken. Some teachers believe students must abandon their first language to learn English. According to Nieto (1999), however, Latino children from additive bilingual homes (i.e., homes where Spanish continued to be spoken after English was learned) performed better academically than children from homes where Spanish was replaced by English. It is likely that bilingual children have increased **metalinguistic awareness** that not only results in improved English skills but also serves to support learning in general.

The increased number of children from homes where English is not the primary language is occurring alongside children arriving to school from homes where standard English is not spoken. English dialects not only are functional and valued in students' communities, they also influence learning. The tenacity of Ebonics as a part of African American culture, for example, is evidenced by the fact that children from multiple locations (e.g., urban and rural communities) continue to arrive at school using Ebonics. Ting-Tommey (1999) stated that the "grammatical structure of a language ... shapes and constitutes one's thought processes" (p. 95). This notion is in keeping with a study cited by Nieto (1999) in which African American preschool children were able to recall more details with greater accuracy when allowed to retell stories using Black English.

Culturally responsive teaching includes consideration of students' home language in ways that address the communication discontinuities between some homes and schools. Given the importance of language in learning, teachers who reject students' home language may actually set up barriers to improved school performance. Some teachers completely reject English dialects and feel compelled to correct students when they use nonstandard English in the classroom. Given the connection between language and a sense of identity, these teachers risk sending messages that the student is devalued. Other teachers completely accept the dialect and miss opportunities to teach students how to use an invaluable tool (i.e., standard English), which is essential for school success. An approach in the middle, in many cases results in students being able to switch back and forth between a dialect and standard English. In this way, teachers accept students' home or community language and understand its value, while they correct students' language in school settings so that they learn to use standard English (Eggen & Kauchak, 2001).

CULTURAL RECIPROCITY BETWEEN SCHOOL AND HOME

Educational research is inundated with studies with comparisons between the performance of children from ethnic- and linguistic-minority families and those from low-income families and that of children from middle-class and dominant-culture families. Basically, these studies underscore the cultural and linguistic continuity between mainstream home environments and school and classroom practices. Ethnic- and linguistic-minority and low-income parents have been expected to make changes so that they send children to school ready to learn in ways schools are prepared to educate them. Today we are clearer about the need for schools to make changes along with parents to respond to the learning needs of all children.

Collaboration Through Cultural Reciprocity

Teacher and parent collaboration is accepted as necessary for effective education of children and youth. Collaboration through **cultural reciprocity** more explicitly describes the nature of school–family collaboration needed to disrupt the long-standing cultural and linguistic discontinuity between schools and some homes. Cultural reciprocity can be defined as the process by which teachers and other helping professionals become aware of cultural assumptions that guide their practice and the cultural values and norms of families with whom they work, as means for generating processes and practices to build bridges among different cultural perspectives. It begins with teachers' reflection on their beliefs and values about families, parents' role in education, the influence of home environments on students' performance, and the "taken for granted" or cultural assumptions on which those beliefs rest. This process is followed by work on teachers' part to learn the beliefs, values, customs, and traditions among families who are a part of the school community. A primary goal is to find culturally compatible ways to achieve the goals of schools, while incorporating and honoring the values and beliefs of diverse families. The lack of knowledge and acceptance of cultural values and customs different from one's own is the primary source of tension and misunderstanding between teachers and parents who honor non-mainstream customs in the home (see Case 9A). Parents may be judged as uncaring or negligent when they engage culturally constructed courses of action that do not align with school expectations.

Teachers able to learn and genuinely respect different worldviews and the values, beliefs, customs, and behaviors that emanate from them are in a

Case 9A: Native American Custom Misconstrued

A few years back, my mother died. . . . She had been sick for a long time and was staying in our home. In my tribe, when a relative dies, the funeral lasts maybe a week, ten days. In my tribal customs, we honor our dead longer than some other tribes and cultures do. And in this case, it is my mother, my kid's grandmother. We needed to take her body up to the reservation to bury her in the way of our people. . . . Sometimes it takes a few days to make the arrangements, and then we have many days of celebrating her life and bidding her farewell. I understand that where other kids are out of school one day, maybe two, my daughter's out of school for over a week. And the teachers think I'm encouraging my child to play hooky. When I called to tell them my kid was going to be out of school for a few days, I suspected they had pegged me as a bad mom. Here's one basic misunderstanding—the people at the school think I'm encouraging truancy, and I think I'm encouraging respect for the elders and respect for the dead. (—Elana Jordan, In Hanson (1997), *Way to the River Source,* pp. 47–48) better position to engage in cultural reciprocity between the home and school. Effective teacher–parent collaborative relationships allow for each member of the collaboration to contribute equally to mutually agreed-on goals (i.e., the education of children). The fact that parents need to understand school ways to be effective collaborative partners has been sufficiently addressed. The need for teachers to understand family ways is just as important for mutually respectful collaboration to take place.

Inquiry and Reflection 9A: Analyze your observation school's process for connecting with families. What evidence do you see of cultural reciprocity as a means for collaborating with parents? Do you believe a positive disposition toward cultural reciprocity could have changed the teacher–parent interaction in Case 9A?

Collaboration and Trust

Adams and Christenson (2000) defined trust in family–school relationships as "confidence that another person will act in a way to benefit or sustain the relationship, or the implicit or explicit goals of the relationship, to achieve positive outcomes of students" (p. 480). In an earlier study on the impact of parent and teacher trust levels on family–school collaborative relationships, Adams and Christenson (1998) found that parents generally have higher levels of trust in teachers than teachers have in parents. As proposed by Goddard, Tschannen-Moran, and Hoy (2001), trust emerges as people realize they need the help of others to create and sustain things they cannot acquire on their own. Parental trust in teachers may be indicative of their reaction to the positional authority granted teachers and the belief among some parents that teachers have the professional knowledge and expertise appropriate for the position. Even so, parents engage in personal risk taking (believed to be an essential component in trust building) by entrusting the education of their children and youth to an unknown entity (i.e., the teacher). Parent trust levels seem to be influenced by the amount of school involvement, with parents having low and moderate trust levels tending to be less involved in their children's education. In fact, there may be a reciprocal relationship between trust level and level of involvement (Adams & Christenson, 1998).

Unlike parents, teachers engage in minimal personal risk taking in parent–teacher relationships, which negatively affects their trust levels. The level of teacher trust is also affected by the tendency of some teachers to look for certain parental behaviors to determine whether the parent is trustworthy. Teachers, however, may not fully understand the circumstances of some parents' everyday living situations and may be alarmed or even disgusted by certain parental behaviors (Delpit, 1995b). The prospect of building trusting relationships with these parents may be diminished, primarily because of a lack of understanding of why parents behave as they do. Overall, the imbalance in trust levels between teachers and parents portends difficulty in developing collaborative relationships. Additionally, opportunities to build trusting relationships are hindered by limited interactions typical of many contemporary teachers and parents (Adams & Chistenson, 1998). Even though an imbalance in trust levels exists, both teacher and parents tend to have higher levels of trust at the elementary level. One explanation for decreased levels of trust among teachers and parents in middle and high school situations is that parents have more teachers, and teachers have more parents with whom to develop relationships and build trust.

Inquiry and Reflection 9B: Interview three teachers. What are their levels of trust with their students' parents? What are the characteristics of parents with whom they have the highest trust levels? Do their beliefs about trustworthy parents resonate with your beliefs?

Contrasting views exist with respect to differences in trust levels among parents across income and ethnicity lines. Adams and Christenson (1998) found no differences in trust levels that could be attributed to the socioeconomic status and ethnicity of parents. Others, however, have suggested that trust levels among ethnic-minority and low-socioeconomic parents can be influenced by past negative experiences in school situations. As indicated by Delpit (1995b), it is the perception by some parents that their concerns are not heard or respected or that the best interests of their children are not being served.

Trust levels between teachers and parents can be negatively affected when conflict arises between individuals from different cultural backgrounds because of differences in expectations around school-related issues. Trust tends to be withheld in cultural conflict situations where language, gestures, and accents unfamiliar to individuals on either side of the conflict exacerbate an already-tense situation. The lack of trust subsequently results in individuals cognitively, emotionally, and physically moving away from each other (Ting-Toomey, 1999), thus making collaboration a distant possibility until the conflict can be resolved. Goddard et al. (2001) found that cultural differences among families appear to influence teacher trust level. Differences attributed to social and economic class, however, seem to have a stronger impact on teacher trust levels than differences attributed to other aspects of cultural background. According the Goddard et al. study, the larger the proportion of children living in poverty in a given school, the lower teachers' perception of trust.

In the end, teachers must personally reflect on the level of trust they extend to parents and be aware of instances in which parents are not willing to extend trust to them, for it is clear that certain levels of trust must exist prior to developing collaborative relationships. Levels of trust affect the sense of community among individuals and the extent to which they are willing to cooperate with each other. Low-trust relationships tend to result in expectations of negative behaviors and can lead to blaming and accusations rather than collaboration (Adams & Christenson, 1998). Teachers wanting to increase trust levels with parents from diverse family backgrounds will need to learn what it means to be trustworthy and the nature of trust-based behaviors in various cultures (Ting-Toomey, 1999). Trusting and caring relationships between teachers and parents facilitate collaboration (Mapp, 2003). Adams and Christenson (1998) presented five imperatives for schools and teachers wanting to build trust between all families and schools:

1. Create opportunities for personal contact and interaction between parents and school personnel so that parents and educators can get to know each other.
2. Create opportunities for parents and teachers to be colearners as they study and discuss student-related issues.
3. Ensure that parents have meaningful input in policy and programs.
4. Ensure that schools have effective means for handling conflict between the school and the home.
5. Focus the trust and partnership between parent and schools on creating conditions that support agreed-on outcomes for children and youth.

Families as Resources

Much of the parental involvement literature points to resourcefulness of parents in terms of how parents can support the work of schools. Given this view, parents are judged based on the worth of their "assets" to the educational endeavor as determined by schools. Volunteering at school and extending the work of school to the home, for example, are certainly important contributions parents can make. Yet resourcefulness implies imagination, creativity, ingenuity, and originality—all of which promises enriched partnerships and outcomes when all parties are open to extending and accepting what each has to offer. The connection with parents as a resource for children begins with teachers' belief that parents have something to offer. With respect to their children, parents can offer information about the child or young person at home, serve as a partner for planning and problem solving on educational issues, and provide insight into family customs and beliefs that can in turn provide insights into student learning. They may also be interested in contributing to the vitality of the school as a whole when a welcoming and inviting climate permeates the environment.

Collaborating with parents in ways that make use of their resources and strengths leads to a sense of empowerment and well-being, which leads to positive effects on the social and emotional development of children and youth (Dunlap & Alva, 1999). It has been noted that effective parental involvement programs for low-income parents tends to be committed to reducing the gap between school and home by developing programs and processes that respond to and build on the "values, structures, languages, and cultures of students' homes" (Nieto, 1999, p. 171). Similar approaches can be advanced for all parents who feel disconnected to schools attended by their children.

Inquiry and Reflection 9C: Generate a "Dear Parent" letter or survey to be distributed at an open house or other school event. Include questions designed to provide you with insight into parental needs, as well as contributions parents are able to extend. Write a summary of parental resources or needs for your class.

School–Community Connections

The level and nature of interaction between schools and communities varies from community to community. Some schools are integral to the life of the community, with many of its activities centered at the school. This may be evident, for example, in communities where school events such as athletic competitions are supported by a total community. Communities where residents focus on the education of youth as an essential component of the well-being of children and the community as a whole support collectively the work of schools in ways ranging from support of bond issues to improve school buildings to support of individual school events. This level of collective support has been noted, for example, in African American schools prior to desegregation. Even as these schools were underfunded and understaffed, they were "embedded" in the community with teachers, parents, and other members of the community possessing a level of familiarity with the needs of children and collectively working to ensure their education (Dempsey & Noblit, 1996). Observe, for example, the clarity of purpose

Case 9B: Sumner High School Teachers' Creed—1950

As teachers in the community, we recognize the key positions we hold in the proper development of our youth. This development brings responsibility along several lines. . . . Just now, we sense clearly that we are entering upon new world conditions that demand an orientation of methods and new emphases, not only to be prepared for those forces affecting America as a whole, but especially to prepare our youth for the definite impact of integrating forces affecting our particular race. . . . Finally, we will never cease to hold before our pupils the great heritage they have received from our . . . ancestors in matters of opportunity for the individual and his need for vigilance in stamping out those destructive ideas that were meant to enslave us either individually or as a nation. (Sumner High School was established in 1905 in Kansas City, Kansas, as a result of calls by the White community to exclude African American students from the local high school, following the death of a White student at the hands of an African American student. After a distinguished history, the school was closed in 1978 following the federal mandate for school integration.)

and strong sense of connection with the community articulated by teachers at Sumner High School, a segregated school established in 1905 (Case 9B). A collective perspective on the role of education in the lives of children continues to be observable in many communities today despite the notion of communities in decline as suggested by Putnam (2000). Still, the level of anonymity existing in some communities may contribute to the lack of centrality of the community's schools in community life.

Inquiry and Reflection 9D: The teachers at Sumner High School envisioned themselves as instrumental to the broader development of youth in ways that took into consideration the cultural and social position of African American youth during the 1950s. What evidence is there at your observation site that teachers incorporate the cultural and social position of the student population into the mission of the school?

Strained relations between schools and communities are manifested in many ways. Some communities have large numbers of private or parochial schools, which may signal a level of discontent with local public schools among substantial numbers of community residents. Voting against bond issues in support of school plans, or constant criticism in the media are other indicators of lack of a community's support for its schools. As addressed earlier, a school district's communication with its community is vital to gain insights into parental views of the district, as well as to inform parents of initiatives designed to ensure quality education in the community.

Community Action and Schooling

Historically, grassroots initiatives have emerged to serve the needs of children, families, and their communities in opposition to school policy and practices. The Americanization of immigrant children in the early 1900s, for example, was met with criticism from developers of the settlement house movement, who accused schools of being too removed from the needs of the diverse student population it purportedly served. Jane Addams, a prominent settlement house spokeswoman, sought to bring the community and families back into the educative process, seeing the role of community involvement beyond participation by a few laypeople in the form of school boards. The Freedom School movement marks another instance in which communities stepped forward to educate, believing schools would not serve the needs of children and the African American community. Initiated in Mississippi in 1964, a primary purpose of Freedom Schools was to teach African American children reading and math.

Freedom Schools continue in many communities today, with culturally specific curriculum and education that reaches other ethnic-minority youth. Although some school personnel may see education as the key to escape for children and youth from troubled communities, Freedom School developers view education as the means by which children learn to become leaders who will eventually produce solutions to community problems. Freedom Schools are committed to a set of values that honor the role of parents in education, as well as the importance of the inclusion of cultural heritage in the education of children and youth. Core values of the Freedom Schools are the following:

- All children can learn when they are nurtured and taught by knowledgeable and caring adults who believe in them and who are committed to sharing with them the joys of learning.
- Children must be listened to, treated with respect, and offered opportunities to learn about their rich culture and heritage.
- Reading is one of several keys that unlocks the door to a child's potential.
- Parents are vital partners in their children's education. (Children's Defense Fund, 2003)

The call for community action continues today. Community leaders are being encouraged to take an active role in ensuring quality schools and to engage in community action to ameliorate the achievement gap where it exists. The Public Education Network, a national association with the goal of advancing reform of public schools in low-income communities, publishes an action guide directing community and parent leaders to use No Child Left Behind as a vehicle to improve educational possibilities for poor and minority children. Other initiatives operate out of churches and community organizations and are engaged in providing a wide array of educational activities for community youth. It is ill advised for teachers to assume disinterest on the part of communities and believe it possible to disengage children from their neighborhoods and communities. Communities play an important socializing role in the lives of children, and numerous efforts, unknown to school personnel, may exist within the community that serve the needs of families. It is advisable that school personnel be aware of these initiatives, with a goal of establishing connections where common goals exist.

School–Community Partnerships

Many schools are connecting with communities to support educational experiences of students or serve more effectively the needs of community residents. School–business partnerships exist in many communities, with businesses providing schools with supplies and other equipment, or they may encourage or support employees to become involved with schools as tutors or mentors. Some students benefit from school-to-work programs by which they are able to connect what they learn in the classrooms with real-world work experiences provided by businesses. A number of school districts have been awarded U.S. Department of Education 21st Century Community Learning Center grants that fund development of after-school programs. These programs are normally collaborative efforts that bring together schools, universities and colleges, and community agencies and businesses. They offer programs to children and youth during the hours between the end of the school day and the time a parent is home to supervise (Thompson & Winn Tutwiler, 2001). Service learning projects (e.g., a community project that connects classroom learning with a service meant to benefit the community) are yet another example of school-initiated projects that are designed to serve the community in some way.

Although most 21st Century Community Learning Center grants are awarded to school districts to develop educational programs beyond the school day, a number of community-based organizations offer educational opportunities for children outside of the school day as well. Many of these organizations are located in urban areas and may offer culturally relevant education as they contribute to the sense of community for community youth. It is common for these organizations to be looked on as grassroots entities that lack formal training required for the education of youth. Yet for many minority cultural communities, they offer learning experiences for children and youth who have not been successful in more traditional settings (Ball, 2002). According to Ball, educators often overlook the collaborative and resource potential of these organizations. Teachers seeking to increase their understanding of communities different from their own may find partnerships with these organizations helpful as they develop increased knowledge about the community in which their school is located.

Full-Service Schools

Some schools collaborate with medical, mental health, and social service communities to form full-service schools that collectively address both the instructional and noninstructional needs of children and families. In this way, doctors or nurse practitioners, dentists, and counselors or social workers, for example, join with educators to provide families with needed services. Some full-service schools are structured so that all services are offered on school premises, whereas others are structured using a school-linked model with some services being offered at a hospital or clinic (Swerdlik, Reeder, & Bucy, 1999).

This integrated model for family service is not without precedent; there have been many periods throughout history where schools have been the center for delivery of both instructional and noninstructional services. Even so, a number of implementation and administration issues exist with the contemporary version of the integrated service model. First, although all partners in full-service arrangements are focused on serving the needs of children and families, they may define and address these needs differently based on practices appropriate for their fields (Alva & Kim-Goh, 1999). Language or jargon, codes of ethics, and issues around consent and confidentiality all threaten the mutual goal of service provision among different professionals (Swerdlik et al., 1999). Added to these issues is the expectation that teachers will play a central role in the integrated service model, when most have had little education and training for this role (Palmer, McCorkle, Durbin, & O'Neill, 2001). Even so, expanded services in the form of full-service schools continue to grow, suggesting the need for skill development for teachers in this area at both the preservice and practicing teacher levels.

LIVING IN THE COMMUNITY

Many teachers choose to live in communities outside their school's community. Some teachers hesitate to live in their teaching communities fearing a loss of privacy. Others, particularly those teaching in low-income or communities of color, choose not to live in the school community believing the community will not meet their personal or family needs. Teachers who are not members of the community in which they teach risk knowing little of the community and context in which their students' early social, emotional, and cognitive development take place. Furthermore, teachers and the students and parents with whom they must build relationships have limited informal interaction outside the school building. Teachers who live outside the community have a more difficult time developing the level of understanding of community culture and traditions as experienced by the teacher in Case 9C.

It is possible for community residents to feel disconnected from schools where a majority of teachers are not community residents. A sense of ownership and involvement in the education of the community's children is often lost, particularly when shared meanings and agreed-on educational practices do not exist between the school and the community. In fact, parents and community residents may feel schools do not recognize the voices, traditions, and knowledge within the community. Some parents, for example, may prefer that a community leader (e.g., minister, clan leader, or elder) serve as a liaison between the school and the family, especially when they believe traditional school practices and policies will not adequately address their issues. Relatedly, some parents may be taken aback by some teachers' lack of a familial or familiar approach to teacher–community relations. This approach may be uncomfortable for the teacher, yet it may be grounded in the notions of schooling within a particular cultural community.

Many communities of color experienced a period when teachers were part of the community—that is, they were born within the community and to some extent "chosen" or "raised up" to teach because of their gifts. Based on research of African American teachers, Irvine (2002) found that many engaged in culturally specific teaching styles and demonstrated culturally specific beliefs about teaching as well. In addition to views of teaching associated with content mastery, they also viewed teaching as "'other mothering' and a calling, and as caring, believing, and demanding the best, and disciplining" (p. 145). These contemporary teachers believed they were part of the community where they taught. They worked to ensure that parents were involved and felt invited into the classroom. An element of trust and mutual respect existed between teacher and parent, as teachers worked to establish relationships with both parent and community (Ware, 2002). The decreasing number of teachers of color continues to be major concern of teacher educators and educational administrators and may be a concern for parents and communities as well. According to the U.S. Census Bureau, in 2004, 17.3% of teachers were teachers of color (8.4% African American, 5.5% Hispanic, 2.9% Asian, and 0.5% American Indian and Alaska native; U.S. Census Bureau, 2004). Even though parents may express dismay over the limited number of teachers of color in their schools, they recognize the importance of teachers, families, and communities working together.

Case 9C: Teacher and Neighbor

I have always lived in the small rural community where I teach. The benefits of living in the community are numerous. One of the key benefits is having a deep understanding of the traditions and culture of the community. This helps me relate to my students on a much closer level than most teachers who do not live in the community. I am very aware of the problems faced by the students and their families, as well as understanding the rivalries and history of the different families or cultures that exist in this area. I have always tried to incorporate the community's history and folklore into my curriculum. This allows students the ability to understand and celebrate the diversity of our small community. The Anglo, Hispanic, and Native American cultures found in this area are rich and colorful. The area's economic history is just as important and provides a unique connection to the past and the present.

Another important benefit is having the opportunity to establish close, working relationships with most of the families in the surrounding area. In fact, some of the parents of my current students were previous students of mine. These parents are familiar with my teaching style, discipline methods, and grading system. More importantly, living in the community allows me to attend a variety of programs not associated with the school and allows me to establish a relationship with students and parents outside of the school setting. We are able to relate as neighbors, community members, and mentors. Students get to relate to me on a wider level and get to know me as a person rather than just their teacher.
(—Paula Lujan, teacher, Saguache, CO, 2003)

The act of teachers being seen in the community, even when they do not live in the community, makes a powerful statement to parents and students alike. It signals a willingness to connect with the community and establish relationships beyond those the school dictates.

Teachers who are not members of the community where their school is located should be proactive in their efforts to become aware of the values and norms of the community, especially as these relate to the role of formal education in the child's life. The role played by schools in the life of communities may differ. Thus, schools embedded in a rural community may play a different community role than a school embedded in an urban ethnic–minority community. The more aware teachers are of these norms, the better able they will be to adopt teacher practices consistent with community norms and to incorporate content based on knowledge and traditions within the community.

Inquiry and Reflection 9E: Do you or would you live in the community where your observation site is located? If not, how can you develop the level of community connections that can be observed in Case 9C?

COMMUNITIES AS RESOURCES

Teachers should plan to access resources in the communities where their schools are located. Some schools are located in communities with universities, businesses, and museums, for example, that are willing to partner with schools. These organizations are rich in resources and can support many of the school's programs and learning goals. Many communities have organizations that may not directly partner with schools but still provide experiences that support the education and development of children and youth. Communities with opportunities for participation on organized athletic teams, in the arts (e.g., dance, choir, band, orchestra, drama), or in theme-focused clubs may supplement (or in some communities even take the place of) school-based extracurricular activities that are known to have a positive impact on student learning and development. These activities are often available throughout the school year and will be joined by a number of camps and learning opportunities during the summer or nonschool months.

Cost may be associated with many community-based activities, yet some parents may not be able to purchase these opportunities for their children. Communities and neighborhoods with large numbers of families living in poverty may not have available to them the outside-of-school activities

Community resources are relative to the context in which the resource exists. A valued and respected source of support in a community may not be readily known to an individual viewing "resources" from specific cultural and experiential lenses. *Courtesy of the East St. Louis Action Research Project, College of Fine and Applied Arts, University of Illinois at Urbana-Champaign.*

that are available in many middle-class communities. Still, park districts, YMCA/YWCA facilities, and Boys and Girls Clubs will often have low- or no-cost activities for children and youth from families unable to pay full price for outside-of-school activities. Low-income communities may also have community centers supported through organizations such as the United Way that provide activities and support for community families.

Teachers may be concerned where there seems to be a profound lack of resources in a given community. They may determine that support for children and families is minimal, particularly in neighborhoods where poverty, unemployment, and perhaps crime are apparent. Through reflection, however, it is hoped that teachers will come to realize that the notion of community resources is relative to the context in which the resources exist. Said another way, a valued and respected source of support in a community may not be readily known to an individual viewing "resources" from specific cultural and experiential lenses. Teachers are encouraged to begin by connecting with one obvious resource in the community. Based on this connection, they may learn of other resources, which may come in the form of individuals, agencies, and organizations. Even in the most destitute of communities, resources will exist to support the curriculum, student learning, and teachers' understanding of the norms and traditions of the community.

Inquiry and Reflection 9F: Conduct a scan of resources (e.g., organizations, agencies, churches, human resources) in the community where your school is located. Analyze the file for the level and types of community resources available.

CONCLUDING COMMENTS

Teachers have more contact with children than any other professional providing a service for children and their families. A family-centered perspective, as opposed to a school-centered perspective, is necessary to build a unique relationship among families, communities, and schools to benefit children. Sustainable collaboration requires partnerships in which goals and priorities have been jointly developed and a commitment to shared responsibility for reaching those goals established. Teachers who focus on collaboration primarily for the purpose of increasing students' academic achievement may be at odds with families and community entities that may have a broader view of reasons for collaboration (Jordan et al., 2001). In the end, collaborative relationships must be grounded in mutual trust and respect for the values, beliefs, and experiences of those in the collaborative circle.

Learning about a culture different from one's own is a difficult process. For the most part, children from cultural- and linguistic-minority homes must become bicultural to experience success in schools (Nieto, 1999). Children and youth unable to make this transition, as a group, do not perform as well as students whose home cultures are similar to that of their school. Teachers seeking to improve the educational experiences of children from non-dominant-culture homes should consider becoming bicultural themselves, even as they recognize the challenges of learning another culture. Nieto suggested that such an effort involves "direct, sustained, and profound" (p. 57) involvement in a culture different from one's own. Teachers should not allow surface observations of common behaviors, attitudes, dress, or language that are a part of a "youth culture" to persuade them that children are basically the same, regardless of the home culture. The notion of "sameness" teachers hold often precludes them from taking advantage of rich familial, community, and cultural resources that could be utilized to benefit student learning.

GUIDED OBSERVATIONS

9G. Observe students in your observation classroom to determine whether there are prior knowledge and approaches to learning that can be attributed to their ethnic–cultural background. Write a brief summary of your findings.

9H. How does your observation-site cooperating teacher work with students whose home language is different from standard English?

Chapter **10**

Family, Community, and School Profile

The purpose of this final chapter is to guide teachers' development of the Family, Community, and School Profile (FCSP). The FCSP is a teacher-generated evaluation of family–community–school dynamics existing in specific community–school contexts. It honors differences among school and community contexts and the need for teachers to understand the intricacies of a particular school–family community before deciding on school-focused actions needed to build on and improve school–family–community relations. The FCSP gives teacher candidates opportunities to engage in self-introspection around school–family–community issues as they become interacting members of a school–family community. When completed, it serves as a portfolio section documenting teacher skills and knowledge associated with school, family, and community dynamics. The Inquiry and Reflection and Guided Observation exercises included in each chapter support development of the FCSP.

The FCSP is based on the recognition that school, family, and community relations are influenced by the backgrounds and expectations of all adults interacting in the community–school environment. Completion of the FCSP contributes to insight into interrelationships among

- beliefs and perceptions about necessary and appropriate adult behavior (both school personnel and parents) in the educational lives of children and youth,
- communication patterns existing among adults in a given community,

- the community context in which adults interact, and
- available resources (community, cultural, economic) to support the work of educating children.

COMPLETING THE FCSP

Four components structure the FCSP: Teacher's Personal Belief System, Perceptions of Schooling, Family–Community Characteristics, and School and Family Communication Patterns. Information collected and analyzed in each of these areas can be used to develop a Family, Community, and School Profile Summary. Strengths (both existing and potential) as well as challenge areas in school–family–community collaborations emerge on evaluation of the summary. Based on the content presented in the text, teacher candidates can suggest strategies needed to ameliorate challenge areas, as well as actions needed to maintain or further develop collaborative strengths.

The matrix for each of the FCSP components includes guide questions. They are included to stimulate teacher candidates' thinking of relevant reflections, observations, and documentation to address specific FCSP components. When completing the profile, candidates should feel free to list salient aspects from any chapter exercise they feel relates to guiding questions listed for each component. Guiding questions are followed by *INTASC* principles and *NBPTS* propositions the question addresses. Inquiry and Reflection and Guided Observation codes follow, which allow the FCSP completer to draw from insights, information, and reflections generated while reading the text and completing exercises and observations related to text content. By referring to their previous responses, FCSP completers are able to construct evidence and documentation suitable for portfolio entries.

Following completion of each component matrix, teacher candidates plot summary statements on the Family, Community, and School Profile Summary matrix. FCSP components are interrelated, with one component providing information and insight into another. For example, guide questions support development of a summary statement regarding Teacher's Personal Belief System. The remaining FCSP components are then addressed from a Teacher Personal Belief System perspective as well (see Table 10.1).

This process is repeated for each component. When all components have been summarized, statements of strengths and challenges are made. Action statements to build on or improve family, school, and community collaborations complete the Profile Summary, which becomes a section of a portfolio as well. It documents teacher candidates' ability to evaluate school, community, and family interaction and make suggestions to build on or improve existing interactions. An example of a complete, but abbreviated, FCSP Summary is located on page 213.

TABLE 10.1
Profile Components Matrix: Teacher's Personal Belief System Component

Profile Components	*Teacher's Personal Belief System*	*Perceptions of Schooling*	*Family–Community Characteristics*	*School and Family Communication Patterns*
Teacher's Personal Belief System	Summary of beliefs drawing from the Guide Questions	Statements of beliefs that relate to perceptions of schooling	Statements of beliefs that relate to family–school–community characteristics	Statements of beliefs that relate to school–family communication patterns
Perceptions of Schooling	Statements of perceptions of schooling that relate to personal beliefs	Summary of perceptions of schooling drawing from the Guide Questions	Statements of perceptions of schooling that relate to family–community characteristics	Statements of perceptions of schooling that relate to personal beliefs

FAMILY–COMMUNITY–SCHOOL PROFILE COMPONENTS

Each FCSP component contributes to an understanding of the complex dynamics occurring when school, families, and communities interact for the education and development of children and youth. Discussion of important elements of each component follows.

Teacher's Personal Belief System

The Teacher's Personal Belief System FCSP component provides an opportunity for teachers to examine personal meanings attributed to "family," as well as beliefs about appropriate adult roles and responsibilities as these affect the education of children and youth. It has been documented that teachers' beliefs, values, and perspectives that are products of personal life histories are infused into professional praxis (Levin, 2001; Trupedo-Dworsky & Cole, 1999). Relatedly, personal beliefs about family, including biases and prejudices, influence professional interactions with families of children and youth in schools. Even so, these beliefs are rarely critically examined in terms of how they shape teacher–parent relations.

Examination of personal beliefs is especially important for preservice teachers (Grossman, Osterman, & Schmelkin, 1999). Given the strong emphasis on field and clinical components in most teacher education programs, preservice teachers have multiple early experiences that affect their impressions and opinions regarding parent–teacher interactions. These

TABLE 10.2
Teacher's Personal Belief System

Guide Questions	*INTASC Principles/NBPST Propositions*	*Inquiry and Reflections/Guided Observations*	*Profile/Portfolio Entry*
What meanings do I attribute to the term "family"?	Principles 9, 10 Propositions 1, 4, 5	1A, 1B, 1D, 1E, 1F, 6A	Introductory statement of the personal meanings attributed to family
What are the appropriate roles and responsibilities for families in the educational lives of children?	Principles 2, 9, 10 Propositions 1, 4, 5	1C, 1G, 3E, 2A, 5B, 7C	Statement of preassumptions of roles and responsibilities of families in the educational process
What biases or prejudices do I hold toward certain types of families?	Principles 2, 9, 10 Propositions 1, 4, 5	2C, 2D, 2E, 3A, 4E	Reflection on personal biases or prejudices toward certain families that potentially influence professional practice
How do staff members at my observation school view families and their contributions to the process of schooling?	Principles 5, 7, 9, 10 Propositions 1, 4, 5	2H, 5D, 7A, 8H, 9A, 9E, 9G	Analysis of the impact of views held by school faculty on families and family-school relations

early impressions often last throughout teachers' careers. Their *professional* evaluations of families are influenced not only by personal histories, but also by comments and opinions of mentor and cooperating teachers in school settings. The Teacher's Personal Belief System (see Table 10.2) component is an excellent tool for preservice teachers to begin to formulate a professional perspective regarding parent–teacher interactions that acknowledges the impact of personal beliefs on these relationships. At the same time, they may avail themselves of opportunities to reshape personal beliefs to address professional expectations that teachers develop effective relationships with parents of children from a variety of backgrounds.

Perceptions of Schooling

The Perceptions of Schooling component facilitates skill in accessing perceptions, beliefs, and knowledge held by parents and other adults in the school–family community regarding the role of families, schools, and communities in the education of children and youth (see Table 10.3). This

TABLE 10.3
Perceptions of Schooling

Guide Questions	*INTASC Principles/NBPST Propositions*	*Inquiry and Reflections/Guided Observations*	*Profile/Portfolio Entry*
Do parents at my observation site hold specific views regarding power and authority? Are there groups of parents who feel disempowered?	*Principles 5, 6, 9, 10 Propositions 3, 4, 5*	*4D, 5A, 5C, 5E, 5F, 7B, 7C, 7D, 7F, 7G*	*Documentation of beliefs about power and authority in a specific school context Documentation of levels and kinds of involvement among parents feeling empowered and those feeling disempowered*
How do parents view ➢ responsibility for communicating educational expectations ➢ responsibility for connecting with schools ➢ parental influence on students' failure or success ➢ influence of parental attributes on school performance ➢ school–home boundaries ➢ sense of community	*Principles 9, 10 Propositions 4, 5*	*7E*	*Documentation of views of parental perceptions of schooling existing in a specific school context*
Do parents from various sociocultural backgrounds differ in terms of perceptions of schools/schooling along ethnic–cultural and socioeconomic lines?	*Principles 2, 3, 5, 7, 8, 9, 10 Propositions 2, 3, 4, 5*	*1G, 1H, 2C, 3B, 5E, 5F, 6G, 7F*	*Documentation of sociocultural influences on parental perceptions schooling*
What evidence suggests that continuities or discontinuities regarding the process of schooling exist between parents and school staff?	*Principles 2, 5, 3, 7, 8, 9, 10 Propositions 1, 2, 3, 4, 5*	*5E, 6B, 8B, 8E, 9A, 9G*	*Description of continuities or discontinuities between parents and school personnel and the influence this situation has on school–home relations*

component is based on the idea that behavior is guided by perceptions and beliefs and that these in turn are influenced by adults' sociocultural backgrounds, former schooling experiences, and current living situation. Beliefs around issues such as power and authority held by the school and the family, the nature of child–adult relationships, and the meaning of "parental involvement," for example, will become clearer through implementation of the Perceptions of Schooling component.

Perceptual information provides educators the "why" of behavior among parents. Differences in perceptions regarding roles are often at the root of conflict and tension among adults in a child's community. Conversely, school communities where perceptions of adults are aligned or complementary tend to experience fewer clashes over what is best for the educational lives of children and adolescents. A focus on perceptions, rather than the manifestation of perceptions (i.e., behavior), provides an initial basis for understanding the cause of tensions existing in the school–community environment, as well as insight into information or resources needed to bridge gaps in connections among the school, home, and community.

Family–Community Characteristics

The primary purpose of the Family–Community Characteristics component of the FCSP is to gather information about the parents, families, and the surrounding community that are a part of the family–community–school triad (see Table 10.4). Teachers use a variety of strategies to collect information in two categories, beginning with parental attributes. Prevailing beliefs regarding parental attributes supportive of schools can limit teachers' motivation to investigate distinctive parental attributes that may be helpful in the schooling and educational process. The more teachers and other school personnel are able to view parental characteristics as "attributes," the better positioned they will be to think creatively and respectfully of ways to incorporate parental attributes into the teaching and learning process. Realistically, there may be critical areas of parental involvement that can be addressed by some, but not all, adults in the school–family community. Awareness of parental attributes existing in a school–family community allows school personnel to enlist support of a number of adults in the community for various educationally related needs.

The second category of Family–Community Characteristics component centers on cultural, economic, family structure, and parental educational level information for the community where the school is located. Although family demographic information is routinely available to school personnel, this section of Family–Community Characteristics guides preservice teachers to analyze this information in light of how family characteristics can be incorporated into the process of educating children and youth. The family is not the only focus for the Family–Community Characteristics component,

TABLE 10.4
Family–Community Characteristics

Guide Questions	*INTASC Principles/NBPST Propositions*	*Inquiry and Reflections/Guided Observations*	*Profile/Portfolio Entry*
What are the family structure and ethnic, cultural, language, and socioeconomic makeup of my school population?	*Principles 2, 3, 5, 7, 9, 10 Propositions 1, 2, 3, 4, 5*	*2F, 3B, 3C, 3D, 3G, 8H*	*Documentation of family characteristics existing in the school community*
What are the unique attributes of families in my school community that potentially support teaching and learning?	*Principles 2, 3, 5, 7, 9, 10 Propositions 1, 2, 3*	*2B, 2F, 3F, 6C, 6E, 6F, 9C, 9F, 9G*	*Documentation and analysis of family attributes existing in the school community* *Documentation and file of family resources and needs*
What are the characteristics of the community where my school is located?	*Principles 5, 7, 9, 10 Propositions 2, 3, 4, 5*	*4A, 4B, 4F, 9D*	*Documentation and analysis of characteristics of the community where the school is located*
What resources are available in the community where my school is located?	*Principles 5, 7, 9, 10 Propositions 2, 3, 4, 5*	*2G, 4B, 4C, 4H, 6D, 9F*	*Documentation and analysis of resources available in the community where the school is located* *File of available community resources*

however; community information, to include resources, as well as the existence of positive and negative community influences on the schooling process, is sought as well.

School and Family Communication Patterns

Communication is at the center of effective family–community–school relations. School personnel expect and often initiate communication with parents and vice versa. Yet patterns of communication are not always complementary, and this results in the needs or expectations of adults in the child's community remaining unclear and thus unmet. It is likely that adults in the child's community evaluate each other's trustworthiness and capability in situations affecting the child's overall well-being, based on modes and styles of communication. The School and Family Communication Patterns component generates information on the multiple communication

TABLE 10.5
School and Family Communication Patterns

Guide Questions	*INTASC Principles/NBPST Propositions*	*Inquiry and Reflections/Guided Observations*	*Profile/Portfolio Entry*
How does my school communicate with parents, and how do parents communicate with the school?	*Principles 6, 9, 10 Propositions 1, 4, 5*	*8A, 8B, 8F, 8H, 8G, 9A, 9G.*	*Description of school-to-family and family-to-school communication practices*
How does my school address varying language patterns observable among my students and their parents?	*Principles 6, 9, 10 Propositions 4, 5*	*8A, 8D, 8E*	*Documentation of language patterns existing in the school environment and school strategies used to communicate with linguistic minority families*
How does my school communicate with the community where the school is located?	*Principles 6, 9, 10 Propositions 4, 5*	*8C, 9D*	*Documentation of communication practices existing between the school and the surrounding community*
What evidence suggests that communications practices at my school are effective or ineffective?	*Principles 6, 9, 10 Propositions 4, 5*	*8A, 8E, 8F, 9A*	*Analysis of the effectiveness of communication practices existing in a school environment*

patterns and processes existing in family–community–school interactions (see Table 10.5).

Family, Community, and School Profile Summary: Abbreviated Example

The FCSP Summary is a very specific document (see Table 10.6). It is meant to reflect the children and adults of a specific teaching and learning community. The critical reflection required to complete the FCSP Summary is the bedrock on which collaborative relationships with parents and communities are built. Given the diversity among U.S. families today, educators must continue to be introspective regarding their personal and professional beliefs about school–family relationships, while reaching out to learn as much as possible about the families and communities who will be their collaborative partners in the educational process.

TABLE 10.6
Family, Community, and School Profile Summary

chool Context: [Include contextual information about the school.] Harmon Elementary is located in city with a population of 150,000. It is one of 10 K–6 schools in the city, and there are 300 students nrolled in the school. Of the school personnel (11 teachers, 1 principal, and a half-time counselor), two re teachers of color . . .

Profile Components	*Teacher's Personal Belief System*	*Perceptions of Schooling*	*Family–Community Characteristics*	*School and Family Communication Patterns*
Teacher's Personal Belief System	*I have flexible beliefs of what makes a family. Family diversity does not mean that the family is in decline.*	*Many parents at my school actively communicate educational expectations to their children; too many do not. This is particularly observable among low-socioeconomic-status (SES) families. I believe parents are responsible for communicating educational expectations to their children.*	*Most teachers at my observation site live outside the school community, which influences how much they know about the day-to-day experiences of the students. What is taught rarely includes the backgrounds of too many of the students attending the school.*	*Teachers at this school are able to reduce instances of parental anger by paying attention to parents' nonverbal cues.*
Perceptions of Schooling	*Parents at this school believe they influence the failure or success of their students. I believe parental input is essential for children to be successful in school.*	*Middle-class parents are highly involved in school activities. They prefer that teachers interact with them from a relational authority location. Low-SES parents are less involved. Teachers use positional authority when interacting with these parents.*	*There are clear indications that parents differ along socioeconomic lines regarding their beliefs about the role of education in the lives of their children.*	*Tensions exist around discipline polices. Parents, particularly middle-class parents, disagree with stay-after-school discipline policies. They have been very vocal in site-based decision making (SBDM) meetings and want to have the policy removed.*

Table 10.6 (continued).

Profile Components	*Teacher's Personal Belief System*	*Perceptions of Schooling*	*Family–Community Characteristics*	*School and Family Communication Patterns*
Family–Community Characteristics	*I lean toward cultural rather than structural explanations for poverty. Approximately 30% of the children attending this school live in poverty.*	*Family continuity with middle-class parents is clearly evident–there is evidence of more discontinuity with all low-SES parents (both White and ethnic-minority). In this school, there are many different perceptions of who is responsible for what in the educational lives of children.*	*My school has a very diverse community in terms of language, ethnic–cultural, social, and economic backgrounds. Many resources are available in the community from businesses, agencies, and organizations.*	*Low-SES parents rarely initiate communication with the school. Language-minority parents often attend parent–teacher conferences with their children acting as interpreters.*
School and Family Communication Patterns	*School staff are responsible for communicating with all parents.*	*Most parents at this school believe schools should be welcoming places with a strong sense of community. My school attempts to create a sense a community through communications sent to the home and through an interactive Web site.*	*Low-SES and language-minority parents feel unheard in the school community.*	*School communication processes assume a high knowledge level of how schools work. Technology is often used to communicate with parents.*
Strengths	*I value collaboration with parents and believe working with them is essential for children's school success.*	*A majority of parents value the notion of a "school community."*	*The school community is diverse. It is located within a community with many resources.*	*The school values communication with parents and has set up mechanisms to support this communication.*

Table 10.6 (continued).

Profile Components	*Teacher's Personal Belief System*	*Perceptions of Schooling*	*Family–Community Characteristics*	*School and Family Communication Patterns*
Challenges	*My views of families living in poverty could interfere with my ability to work with these parents.*	*School faculty do not use different approaches to connect with family, which may be needed given the diversity of families who are a part of the school community. As a result, too many parents feel they are not a part of the school community.*	*Too many teachers live outside of the community and are not aware of resources in the community to support instruction and family–school collaboration.*	*Communication mechanisms are ineffective because some, but not all, parents are being reached by these efforts. Too many parents are left "outside of the loop."*

Action Plan

1. Personal/Professional: Learn more about the causes of poverty and families who live in poverty.
2. Attend more community events and take advantage of my community resource file to support instruction and to improve my connections with families.
3. Make sure my communication strategies are in concert with the multiple and diverse communication avenues that exist with parents of my students.
4. Work with the SBDM to develop a year-long "Developing School Community" theme, with the goal of creating an environment where all parents feel invited.
5. Volunteer to work with an ethnic-minority organization concerned with parental empowerment.
6. . . .

Glossary

acculturation The process by which ethnic-minority families adopt language patterns, behaviors, and values that constitute dominant-culture norms to the extent needed to interact with dominant-culture social institutions, while maintaining certain aspects of family life that are closely tied to ethnic–cultural traditions.

Adequate yearly progress (AYP) Measures of the year-to-year achievement of students on state-dictated assessments, as required by No Child Left Behind. States develop target starting goals for AYP and raise the bar in gradual increments so that 100% of students in the state are proficient on state assessments by the 2013–2014 school year.

Aid for Dependent Children (AFDC) Program established as part of the Social Security Act of 1935 and repealed in 1996 that provided cash assistance to low-income families with dependent children.

assimilation The process by which non-dominant-culture families fully adopt dominant-culture behaviors, beliefs, language patterns, and values into their everyday lives.

bedroom communities Living places where substantial numbers of residents live in one community and spend most of the day working in another community.

biological construct A genetically determined characteristic.

charter schools Alternatives to public school that are publicly funded, independently managed, and free from many state regulations.

communal care Living arrangements in which adults are accountable for each other's children.

community kin Kinship networks on and across plantations, patterned after Africans before enslavement in the United States, that provided extended kin as a means by which enslaved adults accomplished responsibilities for child rearing and other domestic activities.

compensatory education Education and experiences meant to overcome or compensate for perceived deficits in a student's home background.

cult of true womanhood Early-19th-century view of women as pious, submissive, pure, domestic, and willing to sacrifice personal needs or desires to serve others.

cultural lag The tendency for new practices that address change in social institutions to follow the actual transformations in the institution. Understandings and practices associated with social institutions are disrupted, before new practices that address institutional change are firmly established, routinely implemented, and collectively accepted.

cultural reciprocity Process by which teachers and other helping professionals become aware of cultural assumptions that guide their practice and the cultural values and norms of families with whom they work, as means for generating processes and practices that build bridges between and among different cultural perspectives.

culturally responsive classroom practices Curriculum and teaching that validate students from various home environments and allow them to co-construct knowledge in school settings.

culture Learned system of beliefs and behaviors that are passed from one generation to the next.

deculturalization Processes and policies by the dominant culture of a society that force non-dominant-culture groups to abandon language and customs of the minority-group culture.

dominant-culture norms Cultural beliefs and practices of a society's most powerful group.

educational attainment The level of formal education acquired by an individual.

educentric The tendency to view parent and community involvement in education from perspectives that only reflect school values, goals, and priorities.

enculturalization Process by which ethnic-minority families engage family practices to ensure that children acquire beliefs, knowledge, and behaviors that allow them to function as a member of a specific ethnic–cultural group.

ethnicity Term used to refer to a shared or common ancestry, history, or culture among a group of people.

ethnic minority Individual or group having cultural distinctions different from the culture of the dominant culture in a society.

familism Strong value for and commitment to the family. For some families, familism is reflected by large extended-kin networks, high levels of contact among family members, and reliance on the family as a resource for solving problems.

fictive kin Unrelated relatives considered to be part of an extended-family network.

gentrification A process of community change through which housing in old neighborhoods is restored, often resulting in higher rents and the displacement of previous tenants who can no longer afford to live in the area.

ghetto A community enclave inhabited by a group sharing the same ethnic, cultural, socioeconomic, or religious backgrounds.

high-context communication patterns Communication in which physical settings, relational cues, or shared understandings contribute to meanings in the message communicated.

high-stakes tests Tests that determine whether students are retained or passed to the next grade level. At the high school level, high-stakes tests are used to determine whether students graduate.

in loco parentis Term used to describe schools' right to act in place of parents in certain situations.

intergenerational family A family structure consisting of grandparents and grandchildren only, with the child's parent not a part of the household.

latchkey children Term applied to children who return to unsupervised homes at the conclusion of the regular school day.

low-context communication patterns Communication where meanings communicated rely on the literal meanings of words more so than the context surrounding the words.

metalinguistic awareness An understanding of how language works and how to use language to further learning.

miscegenation Marriage between two people from different racial backgrounds.

monocultural A single, homogeneous culture without diversity. In the case of teacher education programs, the tendency to lean toward dominant-culture perspectives when preparing teachers—with limited or surface attention to multicultural perspectives.

mother blaming The practice of holding mothers solely responsible for the actions and physical and psychosocial conditions of their children.

mother practice The day-to-day actions and decisions engaged in by mothers on behalf of their children.

mothering A relationship characterized by the nurture and care an individual extends to children and adolescents to ensure their growth and development.

motherteacher Late-19th-century conception of teachers as having nurturing and supportive dispositions similar to those of mothers in the home.

multigenerational family Family structure that includes multiple generations as a functional household unit, to include grandparents, adult children, and offspring of the adult children.

National Board for Professional Teaching Standards (NBPTS) A primarily teacher-controlled board, organized to evaluate exemplary teachers along NBPTS standards for national certification.

National Council for the Accreditation of Teacher Education (NCATE) Accrediting body for colleges and universities that prepare teachers and other school professionals.

nuclear family Family unit consisting of a husband, a wife, and their children.

parenting self-efficacy Parents' evaluation of their ability to perform a range of parenting behaviors that support the social, emotional, and educational development of children.

parenting styles Typology of four approaches to parenting (permissive, authoritarian, authoritative, and uninvolved) that describes parental behaviors believed to predict developmental and academic outcomes among children.

person-oriented verbal interaction Communication interactions in which unique personal identities are emphasized, with less attention to formality and specific roles of the communicators.

positional authority Authority derived as a result of one's position in an organization.

psychosocial distance The lack of understanding occurring between parents and school personnel when substantial differences in background and experiences exist.

race A social construct commonly used to separate individuals and groups based on physical characteristics.

racial tipping The event of increased numbers of ethnic minorities locating to a predominantly White neighborhood, with the end result of White residents leaving the area.

reconstituted schools Schools that have been closed by a state because of consistently low standardized test performance by students and then reopened with a new staff.

relational authority Authority derived as a result of personal qualities (e.g., expertise, interpersonal skills) that one brings to an organization.

rural areas Census Bureau categorization of incorporated areas located outside of urban areas with a population of less than 2,500 people.

school consolidation Process of combining two or more smaller schools into a larger school, resulting in the closing of some schools.

school vouchers Publicly funded scholarships that allow eligible public school students to attend a participating private school chosen by students and parents.

Section 8 housing Privately owned housing where the rent is partially paid by the federal government.

self-esteem Evaluations of self made by an individual and the associated feelings about those evaluations.

social construct Attributed roles and behaviors delineated by a society for certain groups within that society.

social networks Connections among people that result in norms of reciprocity and trust among those who are a part of the network.

status construction theory Concept that describes the process by which evaluative beliefs about differences among people are created, shared, and maintained.

status-oriented verbal interaction Communication interactions in which the status and associated power of individuals' roles are important, with appropriate language and paralanguage determined by the respective status of those communicating.

tuition tax credits A benefit for parents choosing to send their children to private school that allows parents to deduct from their state income tax some or all of private school tuition

War on Poverty Phrase used by President Lyndon Johnson in 1964 to describe legislation and programs initiated to break the cycle of poverty for the nation's poor.

urban areas Census Bureau categorization of places and surrounding densely populated areas that collectively have 50,000 or more people.

urban places Census Bureau categorization of incorporated places having at least 2,500 people living outside of urban areas.

urban sprawl The spread of housing developments beyond densely populated city limits to sparsely populated rural areas.

References

Achs, N. (1992). Exurbia. *American City & County, 107*(7), 64–72.

Adams, K., & Christenson, S. (1998). Differences in parent and teacher trust levels: Implications for creating collaborative family–school relationships. *Special Services in the Schools, 12,* 1–22.

Adams, K., & Christenson, S. (2000). Trust and the family–school relationship: Examination of parent–teacher differences in elementary grades. *Journal of School Psychology, 38,* 477–497.

Alba, R., Logan, J., & Crowder, K. (1997). White ethnic neighborhoods and assimilation: The greater New York region, 1980–1990. *Social Forces, 75,* 883–912.

Albrecht, D. (1998). The industrial transformation of farm communities: Implications for family structure and socioeconomic conditions. *Rural Sociology, 63*(1), 51–64.

Alva, S. A., & Kim-Goh, M. (1999). Rethinking the role of universities in preparing undergraduates for interprofessional practice. *Teacher Education Quarterly, 26*(4), 89–97.

Amata, P. (2000). Diversity within single-parent families. In D. Demo, K. Allen, & M. Fine (Eds.), *Handbook of family diversity* (pp. 149–172). New York: Oxford Press.

America's Children 2000. (2000a). *Population and family characteristics.* Retrieved Sept. 5, 2000, from http://childstats.gov/ac2000/poptxt.asp

America's Children 2000. (2000b). *Indicators of children's well-being.* Retrieved Sept. 5, 2000, from http://childstats.gov/ac2000/poptxt.asp

America's Children 2004. (2005). *Economic security.* Retrieved March 30, 2005, from http://www.childstats.gov/ac2004/eco.asp.

Anyon, J. (1997). *Ghetto schooling: A political economy of urban educational reform.* New York: Teachers College Press.

Baca Zinn, M., & Eitzen, D. (1996). Diversity in families. New York: HarperCollins College Publishers.

Baca Zinn, M., & Wells, B. (2000). Diversity within Latino families: New lessons for family social science. In D. Demo, K. Allen, & M. Fine (Eds.), *Handbook of family diversity* (pp. 293–315). New York: Oxford University Press.

Bailey, J., Bobrow, D., Wolfe, M., & Mikach, S. (1995). Sexual orientation of adult sons of gay fathers. *Developmental Psychology, 31,* 124–129.

Bailey, S., & Mosher, E. (1968). *ESEA: The office of education administers a law.* Syracuse, NY: Syracuse University Press.

Ball, A. (2000). Empowering pedagogies that enhance learning of multicultural students. *Teachers College Record, 102*(6), 1006–1034.

Barrett, B., Shadick, K., Schilling, R., Spencer, L., del Rosario, S., Moua, K., et al. (1998). Hmong/medicine interactions: Improving cross-cultural health care. *Family Medicine, 30*(3), 179–184.

Barth, R., Courtney, M., Berrick, J., & Albert, V. (1994). *From child abuse to permanancy planning: Child welfare services pathways and placements.* New York: Aldine de Gruyter.

Bauch, P., & Goldring, E. (1998). Parent–teacher participation in the context of school governance. *Peabody Journal of Education, 73*(1), 15–35.

Baumrind, D. (1991). The influence of parenting style on adolescent competence and substance use. *Journal of Early Adolescence, 11*(1), 56–95.

Baumrind, D. (1996). The discipline controversy revisited. *Family Relations, 45*(4), 405–414.

Belgarde, M. J., Mitchell, R., & Arquero, A. (2002). What do we have to do to create culturally responsive programs?: The challenge of transforming American Indian teacher education. *Action in Teacher Education, 24*(2), 42–54.

Berger, P., & Luckmann, T. (1966). The social reonstruction of reality: A treatise in the sociology of knowledge. New York: Doubleday.

Bernal, M., & Knight, G. (Eds.). (1993). *Ethnic identity: Formation and transmission among Hispanics and other minorities.* Albany: State University of New York Press.

Berry, M. (1993). *The politics of parenthood: Childcare, women's rights, and the myth of the good mother.* New York: Penguin.

Bielick, S., Chandler, K., & Broughman, S. (2001). *Homeschooling in the United States: 1999.* NCES 2002–033. Washington, DC: U.S. Department of Education, National Center for Education Statistics.

Bloch, R. (1978). American feminine ideals in transition: The rise of the moral mother, 1785–1815. *Feminist Studies, 4*(2), 100–126.

Bloom, B., Davis, A., & Hess, R. (1965). *Compensatory education for cultural deprivation.* New York: Holt, Rinehart, and Winston.

Bloom, L. (2001). "I'm poor, I'm single, I'm a mom, and I deserve respect": Advocating in schools as and with mothers in poverty. *Educational Studies, 32*(3), 300–316.

Borders, L. D., Black, L., & Pasley, B. K. (1998). Are adopted children and their parents at greater risk for negative outcomes? *Family Relations, 47*(3), 237–241.

Boutte, G. (1997). *Visiting the souls of African American mothers: Dilemmas and issues.* Unpublished essay.

Burgess, E., & Locke, H. (1945). *The family: From institution to companionship.* New York: American Book.

Carnoy, M. (1999). The family, flexible work, and social cohesion at risk. *International Labour Review, 138,* 411–429.

Carolan, M. (1999). Contemporary Muslim women and the family. In H. P. McAdoo (Ed.), *Family ethnicity: Strength in diversity* (pp. 213–220). Thousand Oaks, CA: Sage.

Chahin, J., Villarruel, F., & Viramontez, R. (1999). Dichos y Refranes: The transmission of cultural values and beliefs. In H. P. McAdoo (Ed.), *Family ethnicity: Strength in diversity* (pp. 153–167). Thousand Oaks, CA: Sage.

Chan, S. (1998). Families with Asian roots. In E. Lynch & M. Hanson (Eds.), *Developing cross-cultural competence* (pp. 251–344). Baltimore: Brookes.

Chao, R. K. (1994). Beyond parental control and authoritarian parenting style: Understanding Chinese parenting through the cultural notion of training. *Child Development, 65*(4), 1111–1119.

Children's Defense Fund. (2003). Freedom Schools. Retrieved January 23, 2005, from http://www.childrensdefense.org/bcc_freedsch.php.

Childstats.gov. (2004). America's children 2004. Retrieved January 23, 2005, from http://www.-childstats.gov/ac2002/inde.asp.

Cohen, T. (1999). *Risk factor and determinants of child maltreatment.* Retrieved January 31, 2005, from http://66.127.183.74/articles/Article8.htm.

Conant, J. (1959). *The child, the parent, and the state.* Cambridge, MA: Harvard University Press.

Coontz, S. (1992). *The way we never were: American families and the nostalgia gap.* New York: Basic Books.

Coontz, S. (1997). *The way we really are: Coming to terms with America's changing families.* New York: Basic Books.

Crosbie-Burnett, M., & Lewis, E. (1993). Use of African-American family structures and functioning to address the challenges of European-American postdivorce families. *Family Relations, 42*(3), 243–248.

Cutler, W. (2000). *Parents and schools: The 150-year struggle for control in American education.* Chicago: University of Chicago Press.

Darling, N. (1999). Parenting style and its correlates. Washington, DC: Office of Educational Research and Improvement. (ED427 896)

deCarvalho, M. E. (2001). Rethinking family–school relations: A critique of parental involvement in schooling. Mahwah, NJ: Lawrence Erlbaum Associates.

Delgado, M., & Barton, K. (1998). Murals in Latino communities: Social indicators of community strengths. *Social Work, 43*(4), 346–357.

Delpit, L. (1995a). I just want to be myself: Discovering what students bring to school "in their blood." In W. Ayers (Ed.), *To become a teacher: Making a difference in the children's lives* (pp. 34–48). New York: Teachers College Press.

Delpit, L. (1995b). *Other people's children: Cultural conflict in the classroom.* New York: New Press.

DeMoss, S., Vaughn, C., & Langenbach, M. (1996). Parental perceptions of long-term involvement with their children's schooling. *NASSP Bulletin, 80*(583), 92–101.

Dempsey, V., & Noblit, G. (1996). The demise of caring in an African-American community, one consequence of school desegregation. In D. Eaker-Rich & J. Van Galen (Eds.), *Caring in an unjust world: Negotiating borders and barriers in schools.* New York: State University of New York Press.

Deyhle, D., & Swisher, K. (1997). Research in American Indian and Alaska Native education: From assimilation to self-determination. In M. W. Apple (Ed.), *Review of research in education.* Washington, DC: American Educational Research Association.

Dodd, A., & Konzal, J. (2002). *Beyond parental involvement: A new paradigm for parent, school, community relationships–stories, strategies, and promising practices.* New York: Palgrave.

Donegan, M., & Trepanier-Street, M. (1998). Teacher and parent views on standardized testing: A cross-cultural comparison of the uses and influencing factors. *Journal of Research in Childhood Education, 13*(1), 85–93.

Dorsey, S., Klein, K., Forehand, R., & Family Health Project Research Group. (1999). Parenting self-efficacy of HIV infected mothers: The role of social support. *Journal of Marriage and Family, 61,* 295–305.

Downey, D., Ainsworth-Darnell, J., & Dufur, M. (1998). Sex of parents and children's well-being in single parent households. *Journal of Marriage and Family, 60,* 878–893.

Dunlap, C., & Alva, S. (1999). Redefining school and community relations: Teachers perceptions of parents as participants and stakeholders. *Teacher Education Quarterly, 26*(4), 123–133.

DuPraw, M., & Axner, M. (1997). Working on cross-cultural communication challenges. Retrieved April 5, 2005, from http: www.wwcd.org/action/ampu/crosscult.html

Eckel, S. (1999). Single mothers. *American Demographics, 21*(5), 62–66.

Eggan, P., & Kauchak, D. (2001). *Educational psychology: Windows on classrooms.* Upper Saddle River, NJ: Prentice Hall.

Elder, G., Eccles, J., Ardelt, M., & Lord, S. (1995). Inner-city parents under economic pressure: Perspectives on the strategies for parenting. *Journal of Marriage and the Family, 57,* 771–784.

Epstein, J. (1994). Theory to practice: School and family partnerships lead to school improvement and success. In C. L. Fagnano and B. Z. Werber (Eds.), *School, family and community interaction: A view from the firing lines* (pp. 39–52). Boulder, CO: Westview Press.

Evans, W. P., Fitzgerald, C., & Dan Chvilicek, S. (1999). Are rural gang members similar to their urban peers?: Implications for rural communities. *Youth & Society, 30*(3), 267–282.

Family Resource Coalition. (1996). *Guidelines for family support practice.* Chicago, IL: Family Resource Coalition. ERIC Document Reproduction Service No. ED401020.

Fan, X., & Chen, M. (2001). Parental involvement and students academic achievement: A meta-analysis. *Educational Psychology Review, 13*(1), 1–22.

Feng, J. (1994). Asian-American children: What teachers should know. *ERIC Digest.* ERIC Document Reproduction Service No. ED369577.

Fetto, J. (1999). Wide open spaces. *American Demographics, 21*(10), 44–45.

Fetto, J. (2000). One size doesn't fit all. *American Demographics, 22*(5), 44–45.

Flaks, D., Fischer, I., Masterpasqua, F., & Joseph G. (1995). Lesbians choosing motherhood: A comparative study of lesbian and heterosexual parents and their children. *Developmental Psychology, 31,* 105–114.

Flores, G., & Vega, L. (1998). Barriers to health care access of Latino children: A review. *Family Medicine, 30*(3), 196–203.

Florsheim, P., Tolan, P., & Gorman-Smith, D. (1998). Family relationships, parenting practices, the availability of male family members, and the behavior of inner-city boys in single-mother and two parent homes. *Child Development, 69,* 437–447.

Flynt, W. (1996). Rural poverty in America. *National Forum, 76*(3), 32–34.

Franklin, J. H. (1997). African American families: A historical note. In H. P. McAdoo (Ed.), *Black families* (pp. 5–9). Thousand Oaks, CA: Sage.

Fuller-Thomson, E., Minkler, M., & Driver, D. (1997). A profile of grandparents raising children in the United States. *Gerontologist, 37,* 406–411.

Funderburg, L. (1994). *Black, white, other: Biracial Americans talk about race and identity.* New York: William Morrow.

Garasky, S., & Meyer, D. (1996). Reconsidering the increase in father-only families. *Demography, 33*(3), 385–393.

Gay, G. (1993). Building cultural bridges: A bold proposal for teacher education. *Education and Urban Society, 25,* 285–299.

Georgiady, N., & Romano, L. (2002). *Positive parent-teacher conferences.* Bloomington, IN: Phi Delta Kappa Educational Foundation. Document Reproduction Service No. ED 478537.

Goddard, R., Tschannen-Moran, M., & Hoy, W. (2001). A multilevel examination of the distribution and effect of teacher trust in students and parents in urban elementary schools. *Elementary School Journal, 102*(1) 3–17.

Gold, S. (1999). Continuity and change among Vietnamese families in the United States. In H. P. McAdoo (Ed.), *Family ethnicity: Strength in diversity* (pp. 225–234). Thousand Oaks, CA: Sage.

Gonzales, N., Moll, L., Floyd-Tenery, M., Rivera, A., Rendon, P., Gonzales, R., et al. (1994). *Teacher research on funds of knowledge: Learning from households.* Washington, DC: Office of Educational Research and Improvement.

Gonzales, P. (1993). Historical poverty, restructuring effects, and integrative ties: Mexican American neighborhoods in a peripheral sunbelt economy. In J. Moore & R. Pinderhughes (Eds.), *In the barrios: Latinos and the underclass debate* (pp. 149–171). New York: Russel Sage Foundation.

Gorman, T. J. (1998). Paths to success: The meaning of schooling to working-class and middle-class families. *Educational Foundations, 12*(3), 35–53.

Green, R. (1982). The best interest of the child with a lesbian mother. *Bulletin of the American Academy of Psychiatry and the Law, 10,* 7–15.

Green, R., Mandel, J., Hotvedt, M., Gray, J., & Smith, L. (1986). Lesbian mothers and their children: A comparison with solo parent heterosexual mothers and their children. *Archives of Sexual Behavior, 15,* 167–184.

Greenberg, A. (2000). The church and the revitalization of politics and community. *Political Science Quarterly, 115*(3), 377–394.

Greenfield, P. (1994). Independence and interdependence as developmental scripts: Implications for theory, research, and practice. In P. Greenfield and R. Cockings (Eds.), *Cross-cultural roots of minority child development* (pp. 1–37). Mahwah, NJ: Lawrence Erlbaum Associates.

Greenfield, P., & Cocking, R. (Eds.). (1994). *Cross-cultural roots of minority, child development.* Mahwah, NJ: Lawrence Erlbaum Associates.

Grossman, S., Osterman, K., & Schmelkin, L. (1999). *Parent involvement: The relationship between beliefs and practices.* Montreal, Quebec: Annual Meeting of the American Educational Research Association. (ERIC Document Reproduction Service No. ED 433 326)

Grotto, J. (2001). Choices in census help state define self: Racial categories greatly expanded. Retrieved October 8, 2003, from http://www.projectrace.com/statefederalcensus/census/archive/census-unun 01-2.php

Hanson, C. (1997). Developing consciousness in educators II: Two stories. In J. Katz & J. Mentzos (Eds.), *Way to the river source: A community's journey to supporting diversity in schools through family and community involvement* (pp. 47–54). Saint Paul, MN: Compass.

Harjo, S. S. (1999). The American Indian experience. In H. P. McAdoo (Ed.), *Family ethnicity: Strength in diversity* (pp. 63–71). Thousand Oaks, CA: Sage.

Harris, J. (1998). Urban African American adolescent parents: Their perceptions of sex, love, intimacy, pregnancy, and parenting. *Adolescence, 33*(132), 833–844.

Hart-Shegos, E. (1999). *Homelessness and its effects on children.* Minneapolis, MN: Family Housing Fund.

Harvard Civil Rights Project. (2000). *Opportunities suspended: The devastating consequences of zero tolerance and school discipline policies.* Cambridge, MA: Harvard Civil Rights Project. ERIC Document Reproduction Service No. ED454314.

Henault, C. (2001). Zero tolerance in schools. *Journal of Law and Education, 30*(3), 547–553.

Hertz, R. (1999). Working to place family at the center of life: Dual-carner and single parent strategies. *Annals of the American Academy of Political and Social Science, 562,* 16–31.

Heymann, S., & Earle, A. (2000). How do working conditions affect their opportunity to help school-age children at risk? *American Educational Research Journal, 37*(40), 833–848.

Hines, D. C. (1989). *Black women in white: Racial conflict and cooperation in the nursing profession, 1890–1950.* Bloomington: Indiana University Press.

Hollingsworth, L. (1998). Promoting same-race adoption for children of color. *Social Work, 43,* 104–113.

Hollins, E. (1996). *Culture in school learning: Revealing the deep meaning.* Mahwah, NJ: Lawrence Erlbaum Associates.

Hoover-Dempsey, K., & Sandler, H. (1997). Why do parents become involved in the their children's education? *Review of Educational Research, 67*(1), 3–42.

Hulbert, N., Culp, A., & Jambunathan, S. (1997). Adolescent mothers' self-esteem and role identity and their relationship to parenting skill knowledge. *Adolescence, 32*(127), 639–654.

Hunt, T. (1976). The schooling of immigrants and Black Americans. Some similarities and differences. *The Journal of Negro Education, 45,* 423–431.

Hurtado, A. (1995). Variations, combinations, and evolutions. Latino families in the United States. In R. Zambrana (Ed.), *Understanding Latino families: Scholarship, policy, and practice* (pp. 40–61). Thousand Oaks, CA: Sage.

Hymes, J. (1953). *Effective home-school relations.* New York: Prentice Hall.

Hyoun, K., & McKenry, P. (1998). Social networks and support: A comparison of African Americans, Asian Americans, Whites, and Hispanics. *Journal of Comparative Family Studies, 29*(2), 313–330.

Institute for Children and Poverty. (2001). A shelter is not a home—or is it? Lessons From Family Homelessness in New York City. Retrieved April 5, 2005, from http://www.homesforthehomeless.com/index.asp?CID=3&PID=18

Irvine, J. (2002). *In search of wholeness: African American teachers and their culturally specific classroom practices.* New York: Palgrave.

Ishii-Kuntz, M. (2000). Diversity within Asian American families. In D. Demo, K. Allen, & M. Fine (Eds.), *Handbook of family diversity* (pp. 274–291). New York: Oxford Press.

Jambunathan, S., Burts, D., & Pierce, D. (2000). Comparisons of parenting attitudes among five ethnic groups in the United States. *Journal of Comparative Family Studies, 31*(4), 395–406.

Joe, J., & Malach, R. S. (1998). Families with Native American roots. In E. Lynch & M. Hanson (Eds.), *Developing cross-cultural competence* (pp. 127–164). Baltimore: Brookes.

Jones, J. (1985). *Labor of love, labor of sorrow: Black women, work and the family from slavery to the present.* New York: Vintage Books.

Jordan, C., Orozo, E., & Averett, A. (2001). Emerging issues in school, family, and community connections. Austin, TX: National Center for Family and Community Connections With Schools.

Kain, E. (1990). *The myth of family decline: Understanding families in a world of rapid social change.* Lexington, MA: Lexington Books.

Kaledin, E. (1984). *Mothers and more: American women in the 1950s.* Boston: Twayne.

Kaplan, D., Liu, X., & Kaplan, H. (2001). Influence of parents' self feelings and expectations on children's academic performance. *Journal of Educational Research, 94*(6), 360–370.

Katz, M.(1986). *In the shadow of the poorhouse: A social history of welfare in America.* New York: Praeger.

Keleher, T. (2000). *Racial disparities related to school zero tolerance policies: Testimony to the U.S. Commission on Civil Rights.* Oakland, CA: Applied Research Center. ERIC Document Reproduction No. ED454324.

Kennedy, M., & Leonard, P. (2001). *Gentrification: Practice and policies.* The LISC Center for Home Ownership/Lice Knowledge Sharing Initiative. New York.

Kernan-Schloss, A., & Plattner, A. (1998). Talking to the public about public schools. *Educational Leadership, 56*(2), 18–22.

Kissman, K. (1991). Feminist-based social work with single-parent families. *Families in Society, 72,* 23–28.

Kliebard, H. (1995). *The struggle for the American curriculum 1893–1958.* New York: Routledge.

Kozol, J. (2000). *Ordinary resurrections: Children in the years of hope.* New York: Crown.

Ladd-Taylor, M., & Umanksi, L. (1998). *"Bad" mothers: The politics of blame in twentieth century America.* New York: New York University Press.

Lamme, L., & Lamme, L. (2003). *Welcoming children from sexual-minority families into our schools.* Bloomington, IN: Phi Delta Kappa Educational Foundation. ERIC Document Reproduction Service No. ED475627.

Lareau, A. (1994). Parental involvement in schooling: A dissenting view. In C. L. Fagnano and B. Z. Werber (Eds.), *School, family and community interaction: A view from the firing lines* (pp. 61–73). Boulder, CO: Westview Press.

Lasch, C. (1977). *Haven in a heartless world.* New York: Basic Books.

Levin, B. (2001). Lives of teachers: Update on a longitudinal case study. *Teacher Education Quarterly, 28*(3), 29–47.

Lightfoot, S. L. (1978). *Worlds apart.* New York: Basic Books.

Ling, H. (2000). Family and marriage of late-nineteenth and early-twentieth century Chinese immigrant women. *Journal of Ethnic History, 19*(2), 43–63.

Livezey, L. (2001). Communities and enclaves: Where Jews, Christians, Hindus, and Muslims share the neighborhood. *Cross Currents, 51*(1), 45–70.

Lowenthal, B., & Lowenthal, R. (1997). Teenage parenting: Challenges, interventions, and programs. *Childhood Education, 74,* 29–32.

Lupi, M., & Ton, V. (2001). Reflecting on personal interaction style to promote successful cross-cultural school-home partnerships. *Preventing School Failure, 45*(4), 162–166.

Lynch, E., & Hanson, M. (1998). *Developing cross-cultural competence.* Baltimore: Brookes.

Mapp, K. (2003). Having their say: Parents describe how and why they are involved in their children's education. *School Community Journal, 13*(1), 35–64.

Marks, S. R. (2000). Teasing out the lessons of the 1960s. Family diversity and family privilege. *Journal of Marriage and the Family, 62,* 609–622.

Martinez, E. (1999). Mexican American/Chicano families: Parenting as diverse as the families themselves. In H. McAdoo (Ed.), *Family ethnicity: Strength in diversity* (121–134). Thousand Oaks, CA: Sage Publications.

Massey, D. S., Zambrana, R. E., & Bell, S. A. (1995). Contemporary issues in Latino families: Future directions for research, policy, and practice. In R. E. Zambrana (Ed.), *Understanding Latino families* (pp. 190–204). Thousand Oaks, CA: Sage Publications.

McIntosh, P. (1989). *White privilege and male privilege: A personal account of coming to see correspondence through work in women's studies.* Boston: American Educational Research Association Conference. (ERIC Document Reproduction Service No. ED335 262)

Miller, B., Xitao, F., Mathew, C., Grotevant, H., & van Dulmen, M. (2000). Comparisons of adopted and nonadopted adolescents in a large, nationally representative sample. *Child Development, 71,* 1458–1473.

Mintz, S., & Kellogg, S. (1988). *Domestic revolutions: A social history of american family life.* New York: Free Press.

Moore, J., & Pinderhughes, R. (1993). *In the barrios: Latinos and the underclass debate.* New York, Russell Sage Foundation.

Mulcare, S. L., & Aguinis, H. (1999). Effects of adoptive status on evaluations of children. *Journal of Social Psychology, 139*(2), 159–161.

Munk, D., & Bursack, W. (2001). What report card grades should and do communicate: Perceptions of parents of secondary students with and without disabilities. *Remedial and Special Education, 22*(5), 280–287.

Nakano Glenn, E. (1994). Social constructions of mothering: A thematic overview. In E. Nakano Glenn, G. Chang, & L. Renney Forcey (Eds.), *Mothering: Ideology, experience, and agency* (pp. 1–32). New York: Routledge.

National Center for Health Statistics. (2001). *Teen pregnancy rate reaches a record low in 1997.* Retrieved Sept. 5, 2000, from http://www.cdc.gov/nchs/releases/01news/trendpreg.htm

National PTA. (2005). *A brief history.* Retrieved January 29, 2005, from http://www.pta.org/aboutpta/history/history.asp

Nieto, S. (1999). *The light in their eyes: Creating multicultural learning communities.* New York: Teachers College Press.

Noble, L. S. (1997). The face of foster care. *Educational Leadership, 54,* 26–28.

Nobles, W. (1997). African American family life: An instrument of culture. In H. P. McAdoo (Ed.), *Black families* (pp. 83–93). Thousand Oaks, CA: Sage.

Nord, C., Brimhall, D., & West, D. (1998). Dad's involvement in their kids' schools. *Education Digest, 63*(7), 29–35.

Nunez, R., & Fox, C. (1999). A snap shot of family homelessness across America. *Political Science Quarterly, 114,* 289–307.

Ogbu, J. (1978). *Minority education and caste: The American system in cross-cultural perspectives.* New York: Academic Press.

Ogbu, J. (1994). From cultural differences to differences in cultural frame of references. In P. Greenfield & R. Cocking (Eds.), *Cross-cultural roots of minority child development* (pp. 365–391). Mahwah, NJ: Lawrence Erlbaum Associates.

Okpala, C., Okpala, A., & Smith, F. (2001). Parental involvement, instructional expenditures, family socioeconomic expenditures, and student achievement. *Journal of Educational Research, 95,* 110–115.

Oritz, V. (1995). The diversity of Latino families. In R. Zambrana (Ed.), *Understanding Latino families: Scholarship, policy, and practice* (pp. 18–39). Thousand Oaks, CA: Sage.

Padak, N., Sapin, C., & Baycich, D. (2002). *A decade of family literacy: Programs, outcomes, and future prospects.* Retrieved June 17, 2004, from http://www.cete.org/acve/docs/padak/famlit1.pdf

Palmer, D., McCorkle, L., Durbin, S., & O Neil, K. (2001). Preparation and experience of elementary teachers to work with community services for at-risk children. *Education, 121*(3), 554–564.

Pan, E., & Keene-Osborn, S. (1999, October 4). Culture by the campfire: Families with kids from oversees share their stories. *Newsweek, 134*(14), 75.

Pardini, P. (1995). Legislating parental involvement. *School Administrator, 52*(2), 28–30/32–33.

Parents as Teachers. (2004). *Parents as Teachers National Center.* Retrieved Sept. 2, 2004, from http://www.patnc.org/aboutus-whatispat.asp

Parke, R. (2000). Beyond white and middle class: Cultural variations in families assessments, processes and policies. *Journal of Family Psychology, 14,* 331–333.

Pasley, K., Dollahite, D., & Tallman, M. I. (1993). Clinical applications of research findings on the spouse and stepparent roles in remarriage. *Family Relations, 42,* 315–322.

Patterson, C. (2000). Family relationships of lesbians and gay men. *Journal of Marriage & the Family, 62,* 1052–1069.

Peffer, G. (1992). From under the sojourner's shadow: A historiographical study of Chinese female immigration to America, 1852–1882. *Journal of American Ethnic History, 11,* 41–67.

Pinson-Milburn, N., Fabian, E., Schlossberg, N., & Pyle, M. (1996). Grandparents raising children. *Journal of Counseling and Development, 74,* 548–554.

Polakow, V. (1993). *Lives on the edge: Single mothers and their children in the other America.* Chicago: University of Chicago Press.

Pollard, K., & O'Hare, W. (1999). America's racial and ethnic minorities. *Population Bulletin, 54*(3), 3–48.

Popenoe, D. (1993). American family decline, 1960–1990: A review and appraisal. *Journal of Marriage and the Family, 55,* 527–555.

PTO. (2005). *PTO vs PTA.* Retrieved January 29, 2005, from http://www.ptotoday.com/index.html

Purdy, J. (1999). The new culture of rural America. *American Perspective, 11*(3), 26–31.

Putnam, R. (2000). *Bowling alone: The collapse and revival of American community.* New York: Simon and Schuster.

Quiroz, B., Greenfield, P., & Altchech, M. (1999). Bridging cultures with a parent-teacher conference. *Educational Leadership, 56*(7), 68–70.

Raffaele, L., & Knoff, H. (1999). Improving home–school collaboration with disadvantaged families: Organization principles, perspectives, and approaches. *School Psychology Review, 28*(3), 448–466.

Ramsey, R. (2002). *How to say the right thing every time: Communicating with students, staff, parents, and the public.* Thousand Oaks, CA: Corwin Press.

Rank, M. (2000). Poverty and economic hardship in families. In Demo, D., Allen, K., Fine, M. (Eds.), *Handbook of family diversity* (pp. 293–315). New York: Oxford University Press.

Raver, C., & Leadbetter, B. (1999). Mothering under pressure: Environmental, child, and dyadic correlates of maternal self-efficacy among low income women. *Journal of Family Psychology, 13*(4), 223–234.

Reagan, R. (1983). Message to Congress transmitting proposed education assistance legislation. Retrieved August 5, 2002, from http://www.reagan.utexas.edu/resource/speeches/1983/31783a.htm.

Reay, D. (1995). A silent majority: Mothers in parental involvement. *Women's Studies International Forum, 18*(3), 337–348.

Ridgeway, K., & Erickson, G. (2000). Creating and spreading beliefs. *American Journal of Sociology, 106,* 579–616.

Robert, S. (1999). Socioeconomic position and health: The independent contribution of community socioeconomic context. *Annual Review of Sociology, 25,* 489–516.

Roe, K., & Minkler, M. (1998–1999). Grandparents raising grandchildren: Challenges and responses. *Generations, 22,* 25–32.

Rogers, R. (2000). The school/home communication project: A study of the effect of more frequent grade reporting on the achievement of high school mathematics students. *Humanistic Mathematics Network Journal, 23,* 26–35.

Scherer, M. (1996). On changing family values: A conversation with David Elkind. *Educational Leadership, 53*(7), 4–9.

Sealander, J. (1991). Families, World War II, and the baby boom. In J. Hawes & E. Nybakken (Eds.), *American families: A research guide and historical handbook* (pp. 157–181). New York: Greenwood Press.

Sexton, P. (1976). Women in education. Bloomington, IN: Phi Delta Kappa Educational Foundation.

Sharpe, L. (2001). The pattern and paradox of parallel worlds: The structured dis-equality in urban and rural life. Retrieved August 12, 2000, from http://www.ruralurban.org/in_depth_2.html

Shaw, S. (1986). Black women in white collars: A social history of lower professional black women workers, 1870–1954. *Dissertation Abstracts International, 47,* 06A-2292.

Sherif, B. (1999). Islamic family ideals and their relevance to American Muslim families. In H. P. McAdoo (Ed.), *Family ethnicity: Strength in diversity* (pp. 203–212). Thousand Oaks, CA: Sage.

Siddle-Walker, E. (1993). Caswell county training school, 1933–1969: Relationship between community and school. *Harvard Educational Review, 63*(2), 161–182.

Silvey, L. (1999). Firstborn American Indian daughters: Struggle to reclaim cultural and self identity. In H. P. McAdoo (Ed.), *Family ethnicity: Strength in diversity* (pp. 72–93). Thousand Oaks, CA: Sage.

Sipes, D. (1993). Cultural values and American-Indian families. In N. Chavkin (Ed.), *Families and schools in a pluralistic society* (pp. 158–173). Albany: State University of New York Press.

Smrekar, C., & Cohen-Vogel, L. (2001). The voices of parents: Rethinking the intersection of family and schools. *Peabody Journal of Education, 76*(2), 75–100.

Soltis, J. (1995). The status of Latino youth: Challenges and prospects. In R. Zambrana (Ed.), *Understanding Latino families: Scholarship, policy, and practice* (pp. 62–81). Thousand Oaks, CA: Sage.

Sommer, K., Whitman, T., & Borkowski, J. (2000). Prenatal maternal predictors of cognitive and emotional delays in children of adolescent mothers. *Adolescence, 33*(137), 87–112.

Spiers, J. (1993). Upper middle class woes. *Fortune, 128*(16), 80–86.

Spring, J. (1985). American education. An introduction to social and political aspects. New York: Longman.

Spring, J. (1989). *The sorting machine revisited: National educational policy since 1945.* New York: Longman.

Spring, J. (1994). The American school 1642–1993. New York: McGraw Hill.

Strom, P., & Strom, R. (2002/2003). Teacher–parent communication reforms. *High School Journal, 86*(2), 14–21.

Sudarkasa, N. (1997). African American families and family values. In Harriet Pipes McAdoo (Ed.), *Black families* (pp. 9–42). Thousand Oaks, CA: Sage.

Suggs, R. S. (1978). *Motherteacher: The feminization of American education.* Charlottesville: University of Virginia Press.

Swerdlik, M., Reeder, G., & Bucy, J. (1999). Full-service schools: A partnership between educators, and professional in medicine, mental health, and social services. *NASSP Bulletin, 83*(611), 72–79.

Taveras, G. (1998). *Home visits: From the teacher's perspective.* New York: Project Head Start. (ERIC Document Reproduction Service No. ED426775)

Thompson, M., & Winn Tutwiler, S. (2001). Coaching the after-school instructional staff. *Educational Leadership, 58*(7), 56–58.

Thornton Dill, B. (1988). Our mother's grief: Racial ethnic women and maintenance of families. *Journal of Family History, 13*(4), 415–431.

Ting-Tommey, S. (1999). *Communicating across cultures.* New York: Guilford Press.

Trupedo-Dworsky, M., & Cole, A. (1999). Teaching as autobiography: Connecting the personal and the professional in the academy. *Teaching Education, 10,* 131–138.

Turbiville, V., & Marquis, J. (2001). Father participation in early education programs. *Topics in Early Childhood Education, 21*(4), 223–231.

U.S. Census Bureau. (2001). *American families and living arrangements: Population characteristics.* Retrieved February 3, 2002, from http://www.census.gov/prod/2001pubs/p20-537.pdf.

U.S. Census Bureau. (2004). *Facts for features.* Retrieved August 13, 2004, from http://www.census.gov/Press-Release/www/releases/archives/facts_for_features_special_editions/001737.html

U.S. Department of Education. National Center for Education Statistics. (2001). *Efforts by public K–8 schools to involve parents in children's education: Do school and parents reports agree?* (NCES 2001-076). Washington, DC: Author.

U.S. Department of Health and Human Services. (2002). *National clearing house on child abuse and neglect information.* Retrieved May 19, 2002, from http://nccanch.acf.hhs.gov/index.cfm

U.S. Government Publications. (2001). *21st century community learning centers: Providing quality after-school learning opportunities for America's families.* Retrieved September 5, 2003, from http://www.ed.gov. pubs/Providing_Quality_Afterschool_Learning/report.html

Vega, W. (1995). The study of Latino families: A point of departure. In R. Zambrana (Ed.), *Understanding Latino families: Scholarship, policy, and practice* (pp. 3–17). Thousand Oaks, CA: Sage.

Vigil, J. (1999). Streets and schools: How educators can help Chicano marginalized gang youth. *Harvard Educational Review, 69*(3), 270–288.

Waggoner, K., & Griffith, A. (1998). Parent involvement in education: Ideology and experience. *Journal for a Just and Caring Education, 4*(1) 65–77.

Walter, S. (2001). Delinquents in suburbia. *American Enterprise, 12*(4), 20–31.

Wanat, C. (1997). Conceptualizing parental involvement from parents' perspectives. *Journal for a Just and Caring Education, 3*(4), 433–458.

Ware, F. (2002). Black teachers' perceptions of their roles and practices. In J. Irvine (Ed.), *In search of wholeness: African American teachers and their culturally specific classroom practices* (pp. 33–45). New York: Palgrave.

Wertheimer, J. (1994). Family values and the Jews. *Commentary, 97,* 30–34.

Wickens, E. (1993). Penny's Question: "I will have a child in my class with two moms—What do you know about this?" *Young Children, 48,* 25–28.

Wilkerson, D. (1970). Compensatory education. In S. Marcus & H. Rivlin (Eds.), *Conflicts in urban education.* New York: Basic Books Inc.

Williams, E., & Sadler, L. (2001). Effects of an urban high school–based childcare center on self selected adolescent parents and their children. *Journal of School Health, 71*(2), 47–52.

Willis, W. (1998). Families with African American roots (165–202). In E. Lynch and M. Hanson (Eds.), *Developing cross-cultural competence.* Baltimore: Brooks.

Wilson, W. J. (1990). *The truly disadvantaged: The inner city, the underclass, and public policy.* Chicago: University of Chicago Press.

Winn Tutwiler, S. (1992). Parental involvement in education: An analysis of perceived roles and responsibilities among low income single parents. Unpublished doctoral dissertation, University of Texas at Austin.

Wise, T. (2001). School shootings and white denial. Retrieved March 4, 2002, from http://www.alternet.org/story.html?StoryID=10560.

Zambrana, R., Dorrington, C., & Hayes-Bautista, D. (1995). Family and child health: A neglected vision. In R. Zambrana (Ed.), *Understanding Latino families: Scholarship, policy, and practice* (pp. 157–176). Thousand Oaks, CA: Sage.

Zeichner, K. (1996). Educating teachers to close the achievement gap: Issues of pedagogy, knowledge, and teacher preparation. In B. Williams (Ed.), *Closing the achievement gap: A vision for changing beliefs and practices* (pp. 56–76). Alexandria, VA: Association for Supervision and Curriculum Development.

Ziegler, W. (2000). Venturing beyond the schoolyard to bring parents in. *High School Magazine,* 7(5), 22–25.

Zuniga, C., & Alva, S. (1999). Redefining school and community relations: Teachers' perceptions of parents as participants and stakeholders. *Teacher Education Quarterly, 26*(4), 123–133.

Author Index

Page number in *italics* indicate pages with complete bibliographic information.

T

U

V

W

X

Z

Subject Index

Note: *f* indicates figure and *t* indicates table.

B

C

D

G

H

I

Q

R

CPSIA information can be obtained
at www.ICGtesting.com
Printed in the USA
LVOW11s1018160218
566866LV00018B/426/P

9 780805 839005